Unprecedented

UNPRECEDENTED

The
CONSTITUTIONAL CHALLENGE

to

OBAMACARE

Josh Blackman

PUBLICAFFAIRS
New York

PublicAffairs books are available at special discounts for bulk purchases in the
U.S. by corporations, institutions, and other organizations. For more information, please contact the Special Markets Department at the Perseus Books
Group, 2300 Chestnut Street, Suite 200, Philadelphia, PA 19103, call (800)
810-4145, ext. 5000, or e-mail special.markets@perseusbooks.com.

Book Design by Timm Bryson.

The Library of Congress has cataloged the printed edition as follows:
Library of Congress Cataloging-in-Publication Data
Blackman, Josh.
  Unprecedented : the constitutional challenge to Obamacare / Josh Blackman.
    pages cm
  ISBN 978–1-61039–328–7 (hardback)—ISBN 978–1-61039–329–4 (elec-
tronic) 1. National health insurance—Law and legislation—United States. 2.
Health care reform—United States. 3. United States. Patient Protection and
Affordable Care Act. 4. Health insurance—Law and legislation—United States.
5. Medical care—Law and legislation—United States. 6. Constitutional law—
United States. 7. Medical care—United States—Cost control. I. Title.
  KF3605.B53 2013
  344.7302'2—dc23
                                                        2013010507
First Edition
10 9 8 7 6 5 4 3 2 1

FOR GRANDPA IRVING,

who told me to always do the right thing

Contents

Foreword by Randy E. Barnett, ix
Introduction, xix
Author's Note, xxvi

PART I The Once and Future Mandate
(October 2, 1989–January 20, 2009) 1

PART II Unprecedented
(January 21, 2009–March 23, 2010) 25

PART III Regulating Inactivity
(March 24, 2010–January 31, 2011) 79

PART IV Coercing the States
(February 1–November 13, 2011) 123

PART V Strategizing for the Supreme Court
(November 14, 2011–March 25, 2012) 159

PART VI   In the Supreme Court
(March 26–28, 2012) 175

PART VII Outside the Supreme Court
(March 29–June 27, 2012) 215

PART VIII Judgment Day
(June 28, 2012) 235

vii

PART IX The Switch in Time That Saved Nine
            (June 29, 2012–January 21, 2013) 267

            Epilogue, 281
            Appendix: "Unprecedented" Top Ten List, 303
            Acknowledgments, 305
            Index, 309

Foreword

The Patient Protection and Affordable Care Act of 2010, commonly known as Obamacare, was a unique claim of congressional power. As Chief Justice John Roberts wrote, "Congress has never attempted to . . . compel individuals not engaged in commerce to purchase an unwanted product."

From November 2009 through June 2012, I dedicated myself to the constitutional challenge to Obamacare, first as a Georgetown constitutional law professor and blogger on the popular law blog The Volokh Conspiracy, and eventually as an attorney representing the National Federation of Independent Business (NFIB). Our mission was two-fold—to save our country from Obamacare and to save the Constitution for our country. Throughout the entire process, I focused on one simple idea—that the federal government cannot mandate that you purchase health insurance. Such a claim of power was not only *unprecedented,* it was also unlimited, unnecessary, and dangerous.

During that time, as a law professor, I authored dozens of law review articles, op-eds, and blog posts in which I helped develop the constitutional theory and arguments that were ultimately presented to the Supreme Court. When I first began this journey, most other academics scoffed at the very notion that this claim of power by Congress was unconstitutional. Many even deemed our objections frivolous. I and a small group of constitutional scholars and attorneys thought differently, and we continued to develop and refine our constitutional arguments as events unfolded.

To help bring this message to the general public I gave speeches, did countless interviews on television and radio, and debated the topic across the country, all of which made me the public face of the constitutional challenges to Obamacare. In addition, I worked closely behind the scenes with some superb attorneys representing various challenging parties at the district court level to hone their arguments in response to the government's evolving defense of Obamacare. Together with lawyers from the Cato Institute, I submitted amicus briefs to all the federal circuit courts of appeals considering the case. To get a sense of how these arguments played in the courts, I was the only person to be present at all of the pivotal lower court hearings in Pensacola, Richmond, Cincinnati, Atlanta, and Washington, and eventually at the U.S. Supreme Court.

After decisions by federal district court judges in Virginia, Florida, and Pennsylvania held that Obamacare was unconstitutional, the Jones Day law firm and I became the legal team for the NFIB during the appellate phase of its lawsuit as co-plaintiff with the attorneys general of twenty-six states. Through the tireless work of my co-counsel, the attorneys general and their lawyers, and those who submitted amicus briefs, we were able to secure a victory in the Eleventh Circuit Court of Appeals in Atlanta.

The Supreme Court soon granted review of our case. But the justices didn't just accept the case: they granted six hours of oral argument time, spread over the course of three days, to flesh out all the issues. As Josh Blackman details in Chapter 5, that amount of time for oral argument is exceptional in the modern era of the Court and was an indication that those who doubted the seriousness of our challenge should have reassessed their claim that it was frivolous.

After the arguments, in which a majority of the justices seemed skeptical of the government's defense of Obamacare, I became guardedly optimistic. The justices fearlessly engaged the issues head-on and placed the burden on the government to justify this *unprecedented* expansion of federal power beyond anything the Supreme Court had sanctioned before. They did not appear at all satisfied with the government's effort to identify some judicially enforceable limit on its claimed power to make all Americans purchase a product as part of a congressional scheme to regulate interstate commerce.

However, soon after the case was submitted to the Court, I became distressed by an extraordinary and *unprecedented* effort to try to influence the Court's private deliberations. When I was a criminal prosecutor in Chicago, after a case had been submitted to the jury, I could safely retire to my office to work on other cases knowing the jury would be insulated from further appeals from my adversaries. Not so here. After this case was submitted to the Supreme Court, many on the left—from President Obama to Patrick Leahy, the chairman of the Senate Judiciary Committee, to journalists such as Maureen Dowd, E. J. Dionne, and Jeffrey Rosen—vociferously waged what I called a "campaign of disdain" against the conservative justices in general, and Chief Justice Roberts in particular, in an effort to influence and even intimidate one or more of the justices to capitulate.

Their efforts were all the more troubling in light of the report that, at the very time when these attacks were at their peak, the chief justice began to pull back from his initial conference vote to invalidate the individual insurance mandate. Although we may never learn whether the chief justice changed his vote—and if so, why—these preemptive attacks on the Court's legitimacy should it invalidate the president's "signature" legislation left a stain on the entire case.

What happened on decision day in June 2012 was also *unprecedented.* Five justices (Roberts, Scalia, Kennedy, Thomas, and Alito) held that the individual mandate exceeded Congress's powers under the Constitution, just as I and others had contended since November 2009. At the same time, however, five justices upheld most of the

Affordable Care Act. Though Justices Ginsburg, Breyer, Sotomayor, and Kagan would have upheld the insurance mandate *in toto* under the commerce and tax powers of Congress, Chief Justice Roberts on his own reached the result in an *unprecedented* manner: he employed what he called a "saving construction" to revise the statute that Congress actually wrote. In other words, he chose to "save" the law by ignoring what he admitted was its most natural reading.

The statute as written by Congress included an "individual responsibility *requirement*"—better known as the "individual mandate"—that was enforced by what the statute called a monetary "penalty." In the statute as rewritten by the chief justice, the requirement and coercive penalty were replaced by an *option* either to get private insurance or pay a noncoercive *tax.*

Like the four concurring justices, some had contended that the individual mandate could be sustained under both the tax and commerce powers, notwithstanding that Congress had failed to invoke its tax power in its findings justifying the mandate. But I am unaware of any lawyer, judge, or professor who took this position ever conceding that (A) a mandate to buy insurance was unconstitutional under the Commerce and Necessary and Proper Clauses, and (B) only by construing it as an option to buy insurance could it be upheld. In adopting this reasoning, Chief Justice Roberts stood entirely alone. Although our constitutional challenge failed to stop Obamacare as we had hoped, the question of whether we ultimately won or lost the case is tougher to answer. I contend that, in at least six important respects, we were victorious in saving the Constitution for our country:

- First, we prevailed in establishing that *the federal government lacks the power to compel people to engage in economic activity.* No longer can the government claim any power to mandate that citizens buy a product or service from a private company simply because it would solve a problem, such as lowering health insurance costs.

- Second, we were vindicated in our claim that *the government's authority to solve problems that affect the "national economy" is not a blank check for the expansion of federal power.* No longer can the government contend that it can enact any law, justified by any means that do not violate an express constitutional prohibition, so long as it can be said to address a large, collective-action problem. This was a significant victory over the vision of congressional powers favored by most constitutional law professors.

- Third, we established that *Congress may not simply invoke the Necessary and Proper Clause to do an end-run around the limits of its commerce power.* Although in the past, courts have been highly deferential—indeed too deferential—to Congress's assessment of the necessity of its restrictions of liberty, this case reaffirmed that, to be constitutional, an implied power must also be proper. It must not be a great power but one that is "incidental" to an enumerated power, and the rationale that supports such a power cannot be such as to justify an unlimited police power in Congress. This was a major victory.

- Fourth, we showed that *Congress cannot avoid the limits the Constitution places on its powers to govern by simply calling something a "tax" after a law is enacted.* Although the chief justice's "saving construction" treated the "penalty" in the statute as though it was a tax—even though both Congress and the president took great pains not to call it that—he denied that a punitive tax that had the effect of mandating activity, which is beyond its commerce power, could simply be upheld by later calling the mandate a "tax." Instead, he recognized a new, but limited, power to tax inactivity. So on this front, too, we scored a partial but significant victory.

- Fifth, to be constitutional, *any such tax must be low enough to be noncoercive and preserve the choice to conform or pay the fine.* Traffic laws do not give citizens the option of speeding or paying the fine, but the chief justice's new power to tax inactivity does. This highly limited power far better preserves liberty than does the alternative on commerce power regulation that can be enforced by punitive fines and imprisonment. Imagine, for example, if all federal drug laws were solely based on the chief justice's nonpunitive tax power rather than as commerce power regulations. We would have to open the doors of federal prisons and release drug law offenders by the tens of thousands. This was a substantial victory for liberty.

- Sixth, we succeeded in showing that Congress's power to compel states to accept federal money can be coercive and unconstitutional. Now the federal government will have to find more conciliatory means to engage the states through cooperative programs. No longer can Congress put a gun to the heads of the states and tell them, "Your money or your life." This last victory was perhaps the most unexpected, but most resounding, win.

For all these reasons, with this case, we prevailed in ensuring that our government is one of limited and enumerated powers, preserving this constraint on federal authority as a means of protecting our most fundamental individual liberties. As Chief Justice Roberts wrote in his opinion, "There can be no question that it is the responsibility of this Court to enforce the limits on federal power by striking down acts of Congress that transgress those limits." On this front, our challenge was victorious both for the Constitution and for liberty.

The story of the constitutional challenge to Obamacare is *unprecedented* in every way. Never before in our nation's history has a single law received such a coordinated and concerted attack. Twenty-six states joined forces to stop Obamacare dead in its tracks. Millions of

Americans opposed the idea of the mandate, which polled—and still polls—as wildly unpopular. We saw the emergence of the Tea Party, a social movement dedicated to restoring limits on federal power and reining in the excesses of the federal leviathan, and with it the rise of a political movement for "constitutional conservatism." In the fall of 2010, Republicans gained control of the House of Representatives largely on this issue.

I first came to the challenge in November 2009, even before the Senate bill that ultimately passed had emerged from committee. At that time, though I had my doubts about the individual mandate's constitutionality, I had not deeply considered the issue. After giving a speech at the Federalist Society National Lawyers Convention at the Mayflower Hotel in Washington, D.C., I began chatting about the pending legislation with a small group of prominent conservative and libertarian attorneys and scholars in the hallway outside the ballroom. Little did I know that this casual conversation would lay the groundwork for what would become the constitutional challenge to Obamacare that rocketed through the lower courts and went all the way to the U.S. Supreme Court.

As luck would have it, joining in that initial discussion was a bright young attorney by the name of Josh Blackman. Due partly to his tenacity, and partly to fortuity, Josh was present at many of the key junctures throughout the challenge and was never far from the action. I had gotten to know Josh years earlier when he was a law student. Even then, he made a strong impression on me as someone who cares deeply about the Constitution, the Supreme Court, and our political system. As a young scholar, Josh has already distinguished himself with cutting-edge constitutional theories and an ability to address both sides of any issue fairly and dispassionately. More than any other legal observer, I believe Josh was uniquely situated to tell this story.

Over the two years we litigated this case, on his blog, JoshBlack man.com, Josh chronicled how the challenge was proceeding, documenting each step in the evolution of the case. He even made an impact on the culture surrounding the litigation, as evidenced by the title of this book, *Unprecedented.* In the early days of this debate, even before Obamacare passed in March 2010, I took to using the word "unprecedented" more often than I realized. At one event where I used "unprecedented" several times in a single paragraph, Josh live-blogged that we should have a "Randy Barnett drinking game"—take a shot whenever I said the word "unprecedented." Josh's "joshing" spurred me to make "unprecedented" the one-word centerpiece of our strategy in the courts and in the court of public opinion, much to the chagrin of the Act's defenders.

To prepare to write this book—which began almost a year before the Supreme Court ruled—Josh conducted over one hundred interviews with nearly everyone involved in the case. He spoke with almost all of the attorneys who worked on the case, from the district court level to the Supreme Court. He read every brief filed by the government and the challengers in every case. And he was able to interview dozens of members of the media, including nearly every member of the elite Supreme Court press corps, to glean their insights into how the case evolved. Josh even interviewed high-ranking current and former administration officials to learn how the government litigated the case from the inside.

From all these sources, Josh Blackman got the scoop on the constitutional case of the century, which he now shares with all of us. Combining his inside information with his constitutional expertise and the writing skills he has honed as a scholar, he is able to explain the deep constitutional doctrines involved in this litigation in language anyone can understand. In this compelling narrative, complex arguments about the Commerce Clause, the Necessary and Proper Clause, the taxing and spending powers, and standing are all presented in plain English. Even those who have been deeply involved in the case stand to learn from his exposition. I know I have.

Part political thriller and part comprehensive history, *Unprecedented* presents the definitive account of the unprecedented constitutional challenge to Obamacare. Enjoy!

Randy E. Barnett
CARMACK WATERHOUSE PROFESSOR OF LEGAL THEORY
GEORGETOWN UNIVERSITY LAW CENTER
DIRECTOR, GEORGETOWN CENTER FOR THE CONSTITUTION

Introduction

NFIB v. Sebelius is unlike any other case decided by the Supreme Court.

Three years before the case reached the Supreme Court, few took a constitutional challenge to the Patient Protection and Affordable Care Act of 2010 seriously. Speaker of the House Nancy Pelosi famously dismissed a reporter's question about the constitutionality of the law, chortling, "Are you serious? Are you serious?" Even fewer could have dreamed that the Supreme Court would come so close to invalidating the crowning legislative achievement of the Obama presidency. The Affordable Care Act (ACA) survived by the skin of its teeth, with the most unpredictable outcome imaginable.

Unprecedented is the story of the ACA's journey to the brink of oblivion and back, in the blink of an eye, and what it means for the future of our government and our Constitution.

The story of the challenge to Obamacare is the story of President Barack Obama's first term. After his historic election in 2008, Obama considered the ACA his "legacy." This law was intended to ensure that all Americans have access to affordable health care and cannot be denied coverage based on preexisting conditions. Obama was willing to stake his presidency on a law that is now popularly nicknamed after him.

The story of the challenge to Obamacare is also the story of a bitterly divided Congress. Following the president's landslide victory in 2008, Democrats won wide majorities in both houses, large enough to overcome any Republican opposition to the ACA. However, with the bill's rising unpopularity, steeped by the brewing Tea Party, the administration had to dig deep to ram the law through on a party-line vote before it was too late.

The story of the challenge to Obamacare is also the story of the courts. With the passage of the law, the president's legacy seemed to be secured, as constitutional challenges seemed futile. Yet several federal judges rebuffed the government's argument that the ACA, with its individual mandate, was justified by what the Supreme Court had sanctioned before. This law was unprecedented. Ultimately, it would be up to the Supreme Court to pass final judgment on whether Congress could compel people to purchase health insurance.

And most importantly, the story of the challenge to Obamacare is the story of our Constitution, the thread that holds together these three competing branches.

It was the Constitution that gave social movements such as the Tea Party the steam needed to oppose this law and nearly stop it in its tracks. Supported by leading libertarian constitutional theorists, the Tea Party said, no, the Constitution does not give Congress the power to regulate inactivity and make us buy broccoli.

It was the Constitution's enumerated powers and its promise of equality for all that inspired progressives to pass the ACA and build another bedrock foundation in society's pursuit of social justice. To President Obama, our fundamental charter enshrines "the core principle that everybody should have some basic security when it comes to their health care."

It was the Constitution's separation of powers that presented the Supreme Court with the opportunity to judge this monumental law.

And in the end, it was the Constitution that gave Chief Justice John Roberts the deciding vote and allowed the ACA to survive.

The challenge to the ACA bolted together our three governmental tracks into a riveting and unpredictable roller-coaster ride that spanned two decades, beginning in the White House, rocketing through Congress, careening throughout the heartland of America, and finally colliding with the Supreme Court. This wild ride created the most powerful and concerted constitutional challenge to any federal law in a generation—and its dramatic resolution provided a fitting conclusion to this chapter of our constitutional history.

With all three branches of our government uniting, and dividing, over the meaning of our Constitution, the challenge to the ACA tested our mettle and revolutionized the legal and political landscape for years to come.

This is the story of how the nine justices of the Supreme Court decided the fate of the ACA. Fittingly, this drama is told in nine parts.

Part I (October 2, 1989–January 20, 2009)

The story of the individual mandate crisscrosses two decades of inside-the-beltway politics at its finest as Democrats, Republicans, and everyone in between shifted and evolved in their positions on whether the government should force people to buy insurance, who otherwise would choose to free-ride on the system. To understand the constitutional challenge to Obamacare from 2009 to 2012, we must start with the conservative origins of the individual mandate, championed for over two decades by leading Republicans from Newt Gingrich to Mitt Romney.

Part II (January 21, 2009–March 23, 2010)

During his first term, President Obama made his primary focus the ACA. The cornerstone of the ACA was the individual mandate, which the president adopted directly from Hillary Clinton's plan—the same plan he had opposed during the Democratic primary.

At the time, most scholars laughed at the idea of any legal challenge to Obamacare. Yet a handful of constitutional scholars and attorneys, led by Georgetown law professor Randy Barnett, was undeterred. They argued that it was unconstitutional for the federal government to force people to purchase insurance. Soon, this argument would gain constitutional steam as it was adopted by the surging popularity of the Tea Party. But this opposition was not enough to "kill the bill." When, at the eleventh hour, Senate Republicans lodged constitutional objections against the ACA, it was to no avail. Shortly thereafter, the ACA cleared the Senate and House on straight party-line votes and seemed unstoppable.

Part III (March 24, 2010–January 31, 2011)

With the Congress and the president accepting the law, only one branch's approval was still needed—the courts. Before the ink of the president's signature was even dry, lawsuits were filed in courts across the country. The leading case, filed in Florida, was a coordinated constitutional challenge that eventually united twenty-six states to oppose the ACA.

Soon, judges in Florida and Virginia would find the individual mandate unconstitutional. These courts would hold that Congress's power to regulate commerce did not include the power to regulate inactivity—that is, a person's decision not to buy health insurance. With these rulings, this challenge could be considered frivolous no longer.

Part IV (February 1–November 13, 2011)

Following some victories and defeats in the federal trial courts, the case progressed to the courts of appeals, where the challengers and the government would clash in several rounds. First, the Sixth Circuit Court of Appeals in Cincinnati found that the ACA was constitutional in its entirety. Second, the Fourth Circuit Court of Appeals in Richmond rejected the challenge to the ACA; it also found that it could not even consider the suit brought by Virginia Attorney General Ken Cuccinelli because he lacked "standing" to challenge the law.

The third, and most significant, ruling was from the Eleventh Circuit Court of Appeals in Atlanta. In a blow to the administration, that court found that the individual mandate was unconstitutional—Congress could not compel individuals to purchase health insurance. With a court of appeals having invalidated the law, review by the Supreme Court was inevitable.

Part V (November 14, 2011–March 25, 2012)

On November 14, 2011, at long last, the Supreme Court accepted review of what would become known as "the Health Care Cases." The Court scheduled an unprecedented six hours of argument time, spread over three days, for this seminal case.

For the government, Donald Verrilli assumed power as the new solicitor general. With that change came a shift in strategy and a revised argument: that the Court should read the ACA as placing a tax on those who choose not to purchase health insurance, rather than as a mandate to buy health insurance. This subtle difference would ultimately save the law. After many waited in the freezing cold for up to ninety-two hours for a ticket to oral arguments, the stage was set for the main event.

Part VI (March 26–28, 2012)

The three days of oral arguments inside the Supreme Court were a wild ride. On day one, hewing closely to the administration's revised strategy, the solicitor general had the unenviable task of convincing the justices that the individual mandate was at the same time a tax and not a tax. On day two, the solicitor general choked, quite literally, and struggled to explain why the mandate was constitutional.

By the end of the third day, things were looking good for the challengers. However, the outcome of this case would remain "in flux."

Part VII (March 29–June 27, 2012)

Although the battle inside the Supreme Court concluded on March 28, 2012, this constitutional storm would soon thunder into the streets of Washington. Prominent liberals, from President Obama to Senator Patrick Leahy, urged the Supreme Court to uphold the ACA and stressed that the Court should not step into the political fray of striking it down. Prominent conservatives, from Senator Mitch McConnell to conservative columnist George Will, returned fire at what they perceived as liberal preemptive attacks and urged the chief justice to show some resolve.

We would later learn that the chief justice's vote was in play and that, at some point, he changed his mind in favor of finding that the ACA was constitutional. However, many in Washington knew this fact much earlier and acted accordingly. After two years of arguments before the courts, it would be the arguments made outside the Court that defined the legacy of *NFIB v. Sebelius*.

Part VIII (June 28, 2012)

The ACA's day of reckoning came on June 28, 2012. It was a day that will live in legal infamy, as Hollywood could not have scripted a more dramatic conclusion to this perfect constitutional storm. At 10:06 AM, Chief Justice Roberts announced that he had written the opinion in *NFIB v. Sebelius*. Years earlier, Roberts had likened the role of a judge to that of an umpire—just calling balls and strikes. In this case, the chief justice hurled a wicked constitutional curveball. Reporters outside the Court scrambled to report on the opinion. CNN and Fox News would initially report that the Court struck down the individual mandate. President Obama, watching these reports in the White House, was "crestfallen." But CNN and Fox were wrong.

In a shocking surprise, the chief justice had voted to uphold the ACA by characterizing the penalty enforcing the individual mandate as a tax. Justices Scalia, Kennedy, Thomas, and Alito jointly dissented and would have jettisoned the entire ACA. This decision stunned almost everyone who anticipated that Justice Kennedy would be the pivotal swing vote—but not the solicitor general, who had realized that "the Chief Justice could be the fifth, and not the sixth, vote." The ACA, in the words of Justice Ginsburg, survived "largely unscathed." Within minutes of the conclusion of the session, Gov. Mitt Romney and other prominent Republicans elevated the Court's decision into an issue for the 2012 election. At the White House, the president celebrated, as his "legacy" had been secured.

Part IX (June 29, 2012–January 21, 2013)

With the chief justice's stunning opinion, the battle of Obamacare entered its final phase—the 2012 presidential election. Governor Mitt Romney proved to be the worst conceivable candidate to challenge President Obama on the issue of health care reform, because Romney had imposed an individual mandate in his own state. With Obama referring to Romneycare as the "godfather" of Obamacare, the Republican had little credibility in opposing the law. President Obama was elected to a second term of office, securing his "legacy" of Obamacare. However, though this confrontation with the Supreme Court turned out to be in Obama's favor, the Roberts Court remains poised to confront Obama's administration, and those of future presidents, on the most fundamental constitutional issues of our time.

* * *

The Affordable Care Act is now the supreme law of the land. However, the battle over Obamacare, health care reform in America, and competing visions of our Constitution is far from over.

AUTHOR'S NOTE

Like most people, when I first heard about the arguments against the constitutionality of the Affordable Care Act, I was highly skeptical. Even though I was present at the birth of the challenge to the mandate in November 2009, I doubted it could work. On December 31, 2009, I predicted on my blog that the Supreme Court would not even consider this case: "The Justices are not touching this with a ten-foot pole." I could not have been more wrong.

Over the next two years, I watched in awe as this case rapidly evolved and developed in real time. I marveled at how quickly the constitutional arguments formed. I was stunned at how rapidly the Tea Party, and later the Republican Party, coalesced around this constitutional movement. I was also impressed with how the Obama administration vigorously rallied to defend this law. Though many did not initially take the challenge seriously, Justice Department lawyers dedicated themselves to the case from day one.

With each victory by the challengers in the lower courts, I reassessed my own prediction and became confident that the Supreme Court would have to take the case. Yet I remained conflicted. On the one hand, I was very sympathetic to constitutional arguments advanced by Georgetown law professor Randy Barnett and others that comported with my broader view of constitutional law and our system of government. On the other hand, I was cognizant of the political landscape in which the justices would rule on the issue. I worried about the possible repercussions during the 2012 election if the Court struck down this landmark piece of legislation. Because of the political dynamics involved, this case was unlike any before.

One episode in April 2012, days after oral arguments concluded, deepened my concern. In the span of a few days, all three branches of our government clashed. President Obama called on the Court to uphold the law, Senate Republicans criticized the president for intimidating the Court, and in response, a federal judge demanded that the attorney general state his opinion whether courts retain the power of judicial review. In my mind, this was a preview of the bitterness to come if the Court struck down the ACA. I can only speculate that Chief Justice John Roberts would have viewed the event similarly. At the time, I blogged about this internecine conflict: "I am getting really antsy about this case. Everyone—Congress, the President, and the Courts—are playing with fire. And I have little faith that any of them know what they're doing." That lingering doubt remained my sentiment until decision day. When others asked me what I wanted to happen, I was still undecided.

It is perhaps fitting that, when the case was finally decided on June 28, 2012, I was at 35,000 feet on a transatlantic flight to London. Moments before my flight took off, I received the message from a friend: "Chief Justice Roberts' vote saved the ACA." I managed to reply, "OMG," before my phone lost reception and I was in total radio silence for eight hours, with no idea of what happened. In hindsight, I realize that the time apart from the case was cathartic. The pandemonium playing out in Washington, D.C., was beneath me, quite literally. The time above it all gave me a chance to gain a new perspective on the case and reformulate how this book would conclude. (Perhaps one day I will release the alternative ending in a collector's edition of *Unprecedented.*)

In the blink of the eye, the ACA went to the brink of unconstitutionality and back. Along that rapid journey, lawyers and scholars from across the philosophical spectrum were so focused on developing, refining, and advancing constitutional arguments at breakneck speeds that they were often unable to pause and appreciate the monumental importance of what was happening.

The drama is now behind us. My aim in writing this book has been to tell the story of what occurred and provide an opportunity to reflect on what it means for our government, our laws, and our Constitution.

The legacy of the Affordable Care Act is yet to be written, but its history has already begun.

Josh Blackman
HOUSTON, TEXAS
MAY 19, 2013

PART I

The Once and Future Mandate

(October 2, 1989–January 20, 2009)

With the Patient Protection and Affordable Care Act of 2010, President Barack Obama accomplished what eluded Presidents Teddy Roosevelt, Franklin Roosevelt, Lyndon Johnson, Richard Nixon, and Bill Clinton—passing comprehensive health care reform to provide health insurance for all Americans. Yet the story of how President Obama led the movement to enact this law begins not in 2010, nor even in 2008, but in the late 1980s. This is a story of Washington politics at its finest.

Over the course of twenty years, conservatives and liberals in all three branches of government conveniently swapped positions on health care reform. The idea of the individual mandate was first advanced by conservatives as an alternative to "Hillarycare" in the 1990s. At the time, First Lady Hillary Clinton opposed the individual mandate and attempted to introduce universal health care coverage. This effort failed. Fifteen years later, during the 2008 Democratic primary, now-Senator Hillary Clinton changed her position to favor an individual mandate to guarantee universal coverage. Then-Senator Obama, who had once supported single-payer health care, at that point fiercely criticized Clinton for seeking a mandate, stating that people should not be forced to buy insurance. The candidate likened the individual mandate to "solv[ing] homelessness by mandating that everyone buy a house." Once Obama was elected president, however, he flipped the script again to endorse the mandate. After the ACA was enacted, Republicans, who had supported the mandate for nearly two decades, suddenly developed a newfound disdain for it.

The story of the battle over "Obamacare" from 2010 to 2012 begins at the beginning—with the origin of the individual mandate in 1989.

FREE-RIDING AND COST-SHIFTING

Health insurance is a difficult market to regulate because we do not know when we will become sick and need health care. Most people, who can afford to do so, purchase health insurance before they get sick as a way to pay for unexpectedly large medical services. Others, who choose to pay for health care after a medical need arises, run the risk of getting sick without coverage and not being able to afford to pay their medical bills. Prior to 1986, many people who opted for the latter choice would go to an emergency room, even for non-emergency health conditions, because they would receive some free treatment. In response to rising costs, some emergency rooms began to refuse to treat patients without health insurance.

In response to compassionate concerns about emergency rooms denying treatment to those without insurance, in 1986 President Ronald Reagan signed into law the Emergency Medical Treatment and Active Labor Act (EMTALA). The law mandated that all hospitals receiving Medicare funding—basically all of them—must offer emergency care to anyone who shows up, whether they can pay or not. Though EMTALA embodied a progressive notion of health care that ensured that no one would be denied emergency care due to lack of insurance, it was an unfunded mandate. EMTALA produced what is known as a "free-rider" problem: Those who did not have insurance could obtain free care by shifting costs to those who had purchased insurance. Specifically, increasing numbers of younger and healthier persons decided to decline to pay for health insurance. They had a relatively low risk of only needing catastrophic health care, which could now be provided without any upfront payment in an emergency room. This further exacerbated the problem of free-riding. Because the federal government did not pay for services for those admitted under EMTALA, the hospitals had to get the money from somewhere. Increased costs of health care resulted in higher insurance premiums.

Another cost-shifting problem in the health insurance market arose in response to price discrimination toward those with preexisting conditions. Unlike car or life insurance, health insurance is typically provided by employers. This policy dates back to World War II when companies provided health insurance to compensate workers without running afoul of federally imposed wage controls. However, because insurance was tied to employment, when a worker changed jobs, he or she would need a new policy. If he or she had gotten sick while previously insured, the new insurance company could deny coverage for this preexisting condition since it was no longer deemed a "possible risk"—now it was a certainty.

As a result, many people lost coverage when they changed jobs. To address this problem, many states enacted insurance reforms known as "guaranteed issue" and "community rating." These laws prevented insurers from engaging in "price discrimination" based on preexisting conditions. However, guaranteed issue allowed people to choose not to purchase health insurance until the need arose. If the price for insurance will always be the same, there is no incentive to purchase it before the need arises. In some states, insurers responded to the increased cost of treating those with preexisting conditions by leaving the market. As a result, premiums skyrocketed. This phenomenon, which sounds more like a 1980s rock band than a health care crisis, is commonly referred to as a "death spiral."

One way to prevent people from delaying their purchase of health insurance is to force them to buy it now. This simple notion produced the idea of the individual mandate, which was devised to eliminate the cost-shifting and free-rider problems created by EMTALA and guaranteed issue laws. The mandate, simply put, requires that individuals purchase a certain minimum level of health insurance. Those who do not buy insurance are forced to pay a penalty of some sort. In theory, at least, the money raised from the penalty is used to cover the health care costs of those who cannot afford to pay (though in reality it simply contributes to the general revenue of the federal government, however it is spent). The individual mandate is primarily aimed at the young and healthy, a group that poses a very low risk of incurring health care costs and would be cheap to insure. As a result, this demographic often chooses not to pay for the inflated price of insurance caused by cost-shifting. Under the individual mandate, they are forced into the system to subsidize the old and already sick. The mandate, though often characterized as a free-market reform, is a form of redistribution—from those who can afford health care but do not need it to those who need health care but cannot afford it.

As is often the case, a new government program (the individual mandate) was needed to solve problems created by old government programs (EMTALA and guaranteed issue). This death spiral never ceases.

HILLARYCARE 1.0

On January 25, 1993, shortly after his inauguration, President Bill Clinton established the Task Force on National Health Care Reform, which would be chaired by First Lady Hillary Rodham Clinton. With a nod to President Franklin Roosevelt's progressive blitz of reform, the Task Force's mission was to "prepare health care reform legislation to be submitted to Congress within one hundred days of our taking office." Hillary Clinton was assigned to develop a plan to provide universal health care for all Americans. At the time, Thomas Friedman wrote in the *New York Times,* it was "the most powerful official post ever assigned to a First Lady."

On September 29, 1993, the first lady asked Congress to join her and the president to "give the American people the health security they deserve," so that "every American will receive a health security card guaranteeing a comprehensive package of benefits that can never be taken away under any circumstance." Under the 1,300-page Health Security Act, all citizens would be required to enroll in a health plan. Those with low incomes would pay nothing to enter these plans. The crux of the plan was to force employers to provide health insurance for their employees—the so-called employer mandate. This bill would become "Hillarycare 1.0"—Clinton's first, but not last, attempt at reforming the American health care system.

The plan ran into major opposition from Republicans, epitomized by the famous "Harry and Louise" commercials. America's Health Insurance Association spent roughly $20 million on a yearlong marketing campaign that ran from September 1993 to September 1994. Television, radio, and print advertisements featured a fictional husband and wife sitting at a kitchen table worrying about the impact of Clinton's health care reform on their finances and coverage.

In one ad, Harry, a stereotypical suburban husband and father, said he was glad the president "is doing something about health care reform." But Louise, his cautious wife, was troubled. "The government caps how much the country can spend on all health care and says: 'That's it!' There's got to be a better way." The camera zoomed in ominously on Louise as the ad asks people to call Congress.

Facing massive opposition from Republicans—and rising unpopularity—the Health Security Act began to falter. In August 1994,

Senate Majority Leader George Mitchell lacked the votes to pass the bill, and he could not stop a filibuster. Ironically, Mitchell had declined President Clinton's offer to appoint him to replace the retiring Justice Harry Blackmun (no relation), in order to ensure the passage of Hillarycare. Instead, Clinton picked Stephen G. Breyer, who, in the words of White House counsel Lloyd Cutler, had "the fewest problems." By September 1994, Hillarycare 1.0 was dead.

Partly as a result of the defeat of Hillary Clinton's health reform plan, Republicans took the House for the first time in decades in the 1994 midterm elections. Evan Thomas wrote in *Newsweek,* "The 1994 mid-term election became a 'referendum on big government'—Hillary Clinton had launched a massive health-care reform plan that wound up strangled by its own red tape." The Republicans gained control of both the House and the Senate on November 8, 1994, ending the Clinton administration's hope of bringing about health care reform.

Hillary Clinton's role on the task force was subject to litigation in federal court in Washington. The D.C. Circuit Court of Appeals ruled that the first lady was considered a government official and did not have to comply with the Federal Advisory Committee Act, which requires that government meetings be open. In a future suit, the Association of American Physicians and Surgeons sued Hillary Clinton and Health and Human Services secretary Donna Shalala over their closed-door meetings. District Court Judge Royce Lamberth ruled against Clinton, criticizing her for "[a]cting dishonestly." The D.C. Circuit, however, reversed that judgment.

During the debates over Hillarycare, Republicans generated an alternative reform. In what would be seen as a red badge of hypocrisy only fifteen years later, the GOP proposed the individual mandate.

The Conservative Mandate

The idea of the individual mandate was first clearly articulated by Stuart Butler, the director of domestic policy studies at the Heritage

Foundation, a conservative think tank in Washington, D.C. In 1989, Butler published a seminal report, titled "Assuring Affordable Health Care for All Americans," in which he proposed an individual mandate as a means of reducing health care costs. "A mandate on households [to buy health insurance] certainly would force those with adequate means to obtain insurance protection, which would end the problem of middle-class 'free riders' on society's sense of obligation." Butler compared the individual mandate to state laws that "require passengers in automobiles to wear seatbelts for their own protection" and other state laws that "require anybody driving a car to have liability insurance."

The individual mandate had maintained its cachet among conservatives in the early 1990s. In 1991 libertarian icon Milton Friedman argued in the pages of the *Wall Street Journal* that Medicaid and Medicare should be replaced "with a requirement that every U.S. family unit have a major medical insurance policy." In 1991, Wharton economist Mark Pauly was part of a team that tried to persuade President George H. W. Bush to push for universal health care that included an individual mandate. This approach aimed to minimize government intervention. "Our strategy, therefore, is to design a scheme that limits governmental rules and incentives to the extent necessary to achieve the objectives." In 2011, Pauly told *Washington Post* columnist Ezra Klein that he did not remember issues about the law's constitutionality "being raised at all. The way it was viewed by the Congressional Budget Office (CBO) in 1994 was, effectively, as a tax. You either paid the tax and got insurance that way or went and got it another way." If only Congress and the president in 2009 had taken that advice.

Forbes contributor Avik Roy noted that in 1992 Republicans in Congress used Butler's ideas as a "foundation for their own health-reform proposals." In 1993, House Minority Leader Newt Gingrich supported an individual mandate—indeed, Gingrich continued to support a mandate as late as May 2011.

The Health Equity and Access Reform Today Act of 1993 (warmly dubbed HEART) was introduced in the Senate by nineteen Republicans, including two future opponents of the ACA, Senators Chuck Grassley and Orrin Hatch. That plan called for "universal coverage" and "require[d] each citizen or lawful permanent resident to be covered under a qualified health plan or equivalent health care program by January 1, 2005." Roy noted that nearly "half of the Republican Senate Caucus," including future presidential nominee Bob Dole, backed this bill that contained an individual mandate.

In August 1994, the nonpartisan CBO reviewed the Republican-sponsored HEART bill. Though the report focused on the "budgetary treatment of an individual mandate" rather than its constitutional implications, the CBO found that the "imposition of an individual mandate, or a combination of an individual and an employer mandate, would be an unprecedented form of federal action." This passage would directly inspire the litigation strategy against the individual mandate in the ACA. The report continued, "The government has never required people to buy any good or service as a condition of lawful residence in the United States." The report concluded that "because such a mandate would be unprecedented, there are no closely analogous federal actions." Ironically, it was the Republican proposal with a mandate, and not the Clinton's, that was unprecedented. Even more ironically, two decades later, Senator Hatch would routinely cite this report, which called his own individual mandate "unprecedented," as evidence that President Obama's mandate would be unconstitutional. In a December 2011 debate, Newt Gingrich stated, "In 1993, in fighting 'Hillarycare,' virtually every conservative saw the mandate as a less dangerous future than what Hillary was trying to do." John McDonough, a professor at the Harvard University School of Public Health who would help draft the ACA, later noted to the *Washington Post* "the irony of a Republican idea being the source of Republican opposition."

Not everyone in Washington who opposed Hillarycare got behind the mandate. In July 1993, Ed Crane, president of the libertarian Cato Institute, objected to the individual mandate: "Our friends at The Heritage Foundation have endorsed a mandated, compulsory, universal national health plan which flies in the face of the American heritage of individual liberty and individual responsibility." Likewise, in 1994, Tom Miller of Cato opposed a Republican proposal to implement the Heritage plan, stating that the plan "undermines the traditional principles of personal liberty and individual responsibility that provide essential bulwarks against all-intrusive governmental control of health care." Butler dismissed Crane's position as a "potshot." A 1994 article in *The New Republic* recalled that at Cato's tenth anniversary dinner, while introducing the honored guests, Crane pointed at Butler and said, "At first Stuart didn't want to come. So we decided to mandate that he appear." The joke fell flat, and Butler was "aghast."

In fairness to Heritage, the Butler report makes no mention of the Constitution or whether the states and federal government have separate powers to promote the public welfare. But Democrats would seize upon the mandate's Heritage Foundation origin to suggest that their health care reform was a bipartisan project. The Obama administration routinely cited Butler's report in its briefs supporting the constitutionality of the ACA: "The Heritage Foundation stressed these distinctions decades ago in urging that the government '[m]andate all households to obtain adequate insurance.'"

In 2012, these charges led Butler to write an editorial in *USA Today* arguing that he and "Heritage did not invent the individual mandate" and that the version he proposed was significantly different from the mandate imposed by Obamacare. Further, two decades of "health research and advances in economic analysis have convinced people like me that an insurance mandate isn't needed to achieve stable, near-universal coverage." Butler had "altered" his views and the previous year; so had Heritage. It officially revoked its support for the mandate on constitutional grounds. James Taranto, writing for the *Wall Street Journal,* responded that Heritage's changed position "overstates the extent to which the proposed Heritage mandate was 'limited.' But it is clear that Heritage has repudiated the idea of an individual mandate." Despite the retraction, many at Heritage were "pissed off" that Butler's twenty-year-old report—written without input from any constitutional scholars and before recent developments in health policy and Commerce Clause doctrine—was still seen as Heritage's definitive position. Heritage even filed a brief before the Eleventh Circuit Court of Appeals and the Supreme Court—something the think tank had never done before—explaining why it opposed the individual mandate on constitutional grounds.

Though Heritage may have been instrumental in devising the individual mandate, it was just as essential in laying the groundwork to end it two decades later.

ROMNEYCARE'S MANDATE

The most prominent conservative to implement an individual mandate was Gov. Mitt Romney. Romney's plan, enacted in 2006 with the help of Senator Edward Kennedy, imposed an individual mandate in Massachusetts and prevented insurance companies from charging higher rates to people with preexisting conditions. Romney's plan, which pejoratively became known as Romneycare, was premised on the mandates proposed by Butler and Pauly.

The fact that Mitt Romney had joined with Ted Kennedy to enact a health care plan with an individual mandate made Democrats in 2009 more hopeful about the possible bipartisan success of using a mandate for federal health care reform. Professor John McDonough said, "Democrats, based on the Massachusetts experience, became much more comfortable with the idea of an individual mandate." Romneycare begat Obamacare.

In June 2005, Romney described his plan, based on the individual mandate, as "the ultimate conservative idea, which is that people have responsibility for their own care, and they don't look to government . . . if they can afford to take care of themselves."

On July 30, 2009—five months before the ACA cleared the Senate— Mitt Romney wrote an op-ed in *USA Today* urging President Obama to learn from Massachusetts and use an individual mandate to create incentives for people to buy insurance. Romney wrote, "Our experience also demonstrates that getting every citizen insured doesn't have to break the bank. First, we established incentives for those who were uninsured to buy insurance. Using tax penalties, as we did, or tax credits, as others have proposed, encourages 'free riders' to take responsibility for themselves rather than pass their medical costs on to others. This doesn't cost the government a single dollar." Romney would be haunted by this op-ed in 2012.

But he wasn't alone. During a May 2011 *Meet the Press* appearance, Newt Gingrich recalled: "I've said consistently that we ought to have some requirement that you either have health insurance, or you post a bond, or in some way you indicate you're going to be held accountable." And Romney was happy to share the credit for the idea: as late as the October 18, 2011, debate in Las Vegas, he said, "We got the idea of an individual mandate . . . from [Newt Gingrich], and [Gingrich] got it from the Heritage Foundation."

However, on December 28, 2011, Gingrich backed away from that position. "I've said in the debates, yes, I used to be for mandates. I was wrong." Though Gingrich would shoot back at his rival for the GOP nomination, Romney, saying that Romneycare "doesn't work," he had written in a 2006 newsletter that he "agreed strongly" with Romneycare, which he described as "exciting" and as having "tremendous potential."

Democrats would not let Republicans abandon the mandate so easily. On March 28, 2012, on the steps of Capitol Hill, moments after the arguments in the Health Care Cases had concluded at the Supreme Court, Democratic Senator Chuck Schumer of New York criticized the apparent Republican change of heart: "The Republicans were the fathers of the individual mandate, and now they want to give it up for adoption."

HILLARYCARE 2.0 VS. OBAMACARE 1.0

For the first time since General Dwight D. Eisenhower defeated Governor Adlai Stevenson in 1952, in 2008 neither a sitting president nor a sitting vice president was running for the presidency. The White House seemed destined for New York senator Hillary Clinton, who had first put health care reform on the policy map for the Democrats. Barack Obama, a first-term senator from Illinois whose biggest accomplishment to date had been delivering a stirring speech at the 2004 Democratic National Convention, was seen as a long shot.

During the 2008 Democratic primary, one of these candidates proposed a health care plan requiring that all Americans purchase health insurance; the other candidate opposed such a mandate. The former candidate, of course, was Hillary Clinton, who had once opposed the mandate and favored a single-payer plan but now pivoted to endorse a mandate. The latter was Barack Obama, who had once supported single-payer, but now publicly opposed it—and also opposed the mandate. Though Obama denounced the idea of an individual mandate during his campaign, after the election he switched his position. During the nearly two-year-long battle between Clinton and Obama, their positions on health care continued to evolve, change, and even flip.

In May 2007, Senator Clinton was the first to strike when she proposed the "American Health Choices" plan, with the goal of covering all Americans. Having learned from her defeat in the 1990s—she frequently boasted that she had the "scars from that experience"—Clinton did not seek to offer a national, single-payer health care program, much to the chagrin of many progressives. Rather, her plan would offer a tax credit to assist families and small businesses in purchasing coverage. Under her plan, insurance companies would be given "an ultimatum. They have to get into the business of actually providing insurance instead of trying to avoid covering people. They cannot deny people coverage."

Clinton's proposed plans would have been portable between employers and would have stopped insurance companies from denying coverage based on preexisting conditions. "As president," she promised, "I will end the practice of insurance company cherry-picking once and for all by allowing anyone who wants to join a plan to do so and prohibiting insurance companies from carving out benefits or charging higher rates to people with health problems." To pay for this plan, Clinton's proposal would have raised taxes on those earning more than $250,000. But the linchpin of her program, and the key difference between it and Senator Obama's plan, was a mandate that *all* Americans buy health insurance. Those who did not would pay a penalty.

Obama released his health care plan in a speech at the University of Iowa on May 29, 2007—a full month after Clinton had released hers. Obama's plan had three main planks: offering all Americans access to comprehensive and portable coverage; modernizing the system to lower costs and improve care; and promoting preventative health care.

"My plan," Obama announced, "begins by covering every American. . . . If you are one of the 45 million Americans who don't have health insurance, you will have it after this plan becomes law. No one will be turned away because of a preexisting condition or illness." Obama planned to achieve universal coverage by allowing all Americans to "buy into a new health insurance plan that's similar to the one that every federal employee—from a postal worker in Iowa to a congressman in Washington—currently has for themselves." In addition to the public plan, Obama proposed a national health insurance exchange through which Americans would be able to select and purchase private insurance directly from providers. Those who could not afford it would "receive a subsidy to pay for it." Insurers would be required to issue a policy to every applicant and to charge a premium that did not depend on the applicant's health status or pre-existing conditions. Health insurance would be required for all children, and children could remain on their parents' plan up to the age of twenty-five. Obama explained that this program would be funded by "allow[ing] the temporary Bush tax cut for the wealthiest Americans to expire."

However, this had not always been Obama's approach to health care. His views "evolved" quite frequently. In June 2003, then-state senator Obama said he was "a proponent of a single-payer health care program . . . a universal health care plan. And that's what I'd like to see." Yet, as he rose to national prominence and campaigned for the presidency, he adopted a more moderate position, though he was often unclear about the details. In his 2006 memoir *The Audacity of Hope,* Obama sketches out his vision of "what a serious health-care reform plan might look like." Among his ideas was to "allow anyone to purchase . . . model healthcare plan[s] . . . through existing insurance pools." These were the exchanges that would ultimately appear in the ACA. Yet at this point he said nothing in favor of a mandate.

At one debate, Hillary Clinton summed up nicely Obama's meandering position on health insurance: "When Senator Obama ran for the Senate, he was for single-payer and said he was for single-payer if we could get a Democratic president and Democratic Congress." Now, she pointed out, his position had changed. In response, Obama conceded that, at heart, he would have preferred a single-payer system: "What I said was that if I were starting from scratch, if we didn't have a system in which employers had typically provided health care, I would probably go with a single-payer system." Clinton chided, "As time went on, the last four or so years, he said he was for single-payer in principle, then he was for universal health care. And then his policy is not, it is not universal."

Obama tried to explain his evolution, noting that though his "plan hasn't changed . . . the politics have changed a little bit." Comparing Obama's evolving position to his tendency to "vote 'present'" as a state legislator, Clinton stressed that she was "not running for president to put Band-Aids on our problems," but wanted "to get to universal health care for every single American."

The most striking difference between Obama's and Clinton's plans concerned the individual mandate. A comparison of the plans by the Kaiser Foundation highlighted that Clinton's plan mandated that all Americans obtain health insurance, while Obama's plan mandated only that children—9 million of whom lacked coverage—obtain health insurance.

Reforming health care played prominently in the 2008 Democratic presidential primary season. Over the course of twenty-six Democratic primary debates from April 2007 through April 2008, Senator Clinton and Senator Obama sparred regularly about the scope of their health care reform plans. These bouts focused on several major threads: Clinton's failed efforts to reform health care in the 1990s with a plan that would truly have provided universal coverage and, most importantly, the individual mandate.

Clinton became adept at explaining why her efforts at health care reform failed in the 1990s. Obama would counter with the claim that Clinton failed to implement health care reform in the 1990s because the proceedings were conducted "behind closed doors [and] excluded the participation even of Democratic members of Congress who had slightly different ideas than the ones that Senator Clinton had put forward." In an Obama administration, "I think we have to open up the process. Everybody has to have a seat at the table." As it happened, the 2,700-page ACA would be drafted behind closed doors and rushed through the legislative process.

Egged on by rival John Edwards, Obama and Clinton competed over whose plan would provide truly "universal coverage." During the June 3, 2007, debate at Saint Anselm College in Goffstown, New Hampshire, Senator Edwards criticized Senator Obama's plan, charging that it was not really universal health care, as it was not mandatory for everyone. Obama explained that he opposed an individual mandate, noting that the main challenge was not forcing people to have health care, but "driving down costs" so that families could "afford it" and thus "coverage for everybody else" could be provided. Though Obama insisted that his plan included "mandatory health care for children," Senator Edwards shot back that Obama's plan, lacking a mandate, would not cover 15 million Americans. "We have a threshold question about whether we're going to have truly universal care." Edwards asserted that "unless we have a law requiring that every man, woman, and child in America be covered, we're going to have millions of people who aren't covered."

The debate over the 15 million who would remain uninsured under Obama's plan continued at the July 23, 2007, debate at the Citadel in Charleston, South Carolina. Senator Clinton urged the United States to "do what most other developed countries do" and "cover everybody and provide decency and respect to every single person in this country with health care." But Obama maintained that the answer was not a mandate. "John [Edwards] thinks that the only way we get universal coverage is to mandate coverage. I think that the problem is not that people are trying to avoid getting health care coverage. It is folks like that who are desperately in desire of it, but they can't afford it."

At a campaign event in Cedar Rapids, Iowa, Clinton criticized Obama for insisting that his plan provided universal coverage when it did not. A reporter asked Clinton if Obama had a character problem for misleading people on his plan. Clinton replied, "It's beginning to look a lot like that."

Rolling the dice during the November 15, 2007, debate in Las Vegas, Senator Clinton directly challenged Senator Obama on his refusal to support true universal coverage: "Well, I hear what Senator Obama is saying, and he talks a lot about stepping up and taking responsibility and taking strong positions. But when it came time to step up and decide whether or not he would support universal health care coverage, he chose not to do that. His plan would leave 15 million Americans out." Channeling the controversial 3:00 AM phone call commercial, Clinton directly questioned Obama's ability to lead on this important issue: "We have some big issues ahead of us, and we need someone who is tested and ready to lead. I think that's what my candidacy offers."

Political reporters John Heilemann and Mark Halperin wrote in *Game Change* that at the Las Vegas debate, Obama "watched from the wings as Clinton knocked the cover off the ball." Obama was "vague and platitudinous, mouthing generalities and making excuses for not having his health care plan in order [and came] across as amateurish. The union audience was both surprised and mildly offended." After the event, Obama told his communications director, Robert Gibbs, "She was terrific. I was not."

Throughout the primaries, Obama repeatedly attacked Clinton for forcing people to purchase insurance with an individual mandate, while Clinton jabbed back that, absent a mandate, Obama's plan didn't provide universal coverage.

In a stunning moment of prescience, Senator Obama predicted the opposition to an individual mandate that would emerge at town hall meetings during the summer of 2009 amid the brewing Tea Party: "John and [Hillary] believe that, if we do not mandate care, if we don't force the government to get to—if the government does not force taxpayers to buy health care, that we will penalize them in some fashion. I disagree with that because, as I go around town hall meetings, I don't meet people who are trying to avoid getting health care. The problem is, they can't afford it. And the costs are too high. And so, as a consequence, we focus on reducing costs."

In a stark conclusion that undercut President Obama's later call for an individual mandate, candidate Obama stated quite clearly that individuals should have a choice about whether to purchase health insurance: "I have no problem, Hillary, with you pointing out areas where you think we have differences. But on health care, for example, the reason that I mandate for children is because children do not have a choice; adults do. And it's my belief that they will choose to have health care, if it is affordable."

Although Obama stressed that his and Clinton's plans were "95 percent . . . similar," he recognized a "philosophical difference" between them. Clinton, who privately called Obama's plan "an obvious rip-off of hers," denied that there was just a "philosophical difference" between their plans. She saw Obama's refusal to implement a mandate as a "significant difference." Quoting John Edwards, Clinton noted that Obama's approach would be like making Social Security or Medicare "voluntary." "If you do not have a plan that starts out attempting to achieve universal health care, you will be nibbled to death, and we will be back here with more and more people uninsured and rising costs." Clinton refused to accept a voluntary program. "We would not have a social compact with Social Security and Medicare if everyone did not have to participate. I want a universal health care plan."

The conflict over the mandate became most contentious in February 2008, when the Obama campaign sent out an alarmist mailer to homes in the battleground state of Ohio. The mailer depicted a husband and wife sitting together at a kitchen table, channeling the famous "Harry and Louise" ads that were targeted against Hillarycare in the 1990s. In big letters, the mailing cautioned, "Hillary's health care plan forces everyone to buy insurance, even if you can't afford it." The back of the mailer warned, " . . . and you pay a penalty if you don't."

The mailer quoted *The Daily Iowan*, noting that Clinton's plan would "force those who cannot afford health insurance to buy it through mandates . . . [and] punish those who don't fall in line with fines." Echoing the mailer, Obama said at an event in an Ohio hospital that Clinton's individual mandate would "have the government force you to buy health insurance, and she said that she'd consider 'going after your wages' if you don't."

Paul Starr wrote in *The New Republic* that "Obama's stance on the mandate had clear political advantages in the fight for the nomination." It made him "more of a centrist than Clinton" and allowed him to come off as "cool, relaxed, and easy-going," in contrast with Clinton, who was seen as "controlling and coercive." And indeed, Clinton reacted fiercely, saying that Obama's mailing was "right out of Karl Rove's playbook." Neera Tanden, a Clinton adviser, called the mailer "politically dangerous." Politifact rated the mailer as "half true." While Clinton's plan did "'force' people to buy insurance . . . her plan's intention clearly is that everyone will be able to afford it."

Days later, Obama and Clinton clashed at a debate in Cleveland, Ohio. Obama disputed Clinton's claim that the "mailing that we put out was inaccurate." Obama argued that it "accurately indicates that the main difference between Senator Clinton's plan and mine is the fact that she would force in some fashion individuals to purchase health care." Clinton found the mailer "regrettable" and said that "it is almost as though the health insurance companies and the Republicans wrote it."

In response, Obama pressed a point Clinton had continually elided—"Senator Clinton has not indicated how she would enforce this mandate." This very question would vex the Supreme Court less than three years later.

Perhaps most ironically, candidate Obama repeatedly faulted Romneycare—the very plan he praised during the 2012 presidential campaign against Romney. In order to respond to Senator Clinton's preference for the mandate, Senator Obama criticized Romney's individual mandate in Massachusetts as an example of a failed policy. "Now, what is happening in Massachusetts right now—there are articles being written about it—which is that folks are having to pay fines and they don't have health care. They'd rather go ahead and take the fine because they can't afford the coverage." Obama was right. In 2014, when Obamacare's individual mandate goes into effect, this is precisely what will happen, but on a national scale.

Emphasizing the vagueness of Clinton's plan, Obama pointed out that the penalty for not complying with the mandate would be severe. In Massachusetts, uninsured people, he asserted, were "paying a fine. In order for you to force people to get health insurance, you've got to have a very harsh penalty." Those subject to the Romneycare mandate, he observed, were "worse off than they were" without it. By contrast, Obamacare's weak penalty would not only save its constitutionality, but also render it largely ineffective. Barely four years later, in debates with Governor Romney, President Obama routinely praised Romney's mandate in Massachusetts. Karl Rove couldn't have scripted it any better.

OBAMACARE 2.0 VS. McCAINCARE

The 2008 Democratic primary was the main event with respect to health care policy debates; the general election was a mere sideshow. Health care was not an important aspect of Senator John McCain's dismal 2008 campaign. Former Senator Tom Daschle wrote in *Getting It Done: How Obama and Congress Finally Broke the Stalemate to Make Way for Health Care Reform* that McCain "put together a health care plan because he needed one, but you could tell his heart was not in it." Only one reference to health care was made during the entire Republican National Convention in St. Paul, Minnesota, when business executive Meg Whitman mentioned, in passing, that "the cost of everything from gasoline to groceries to health care has gone up." That was it.

The GOP's 2008 platform offered only two general proposals to improve access to health care. First, "Republicans support tax credits for health care and medical expenses." Second, "our plan to return control of health care to patients and providers will benefit small business employers and employees alike." The platform offered only a vague reference to the Democratic plan as it harkened back to Hillarycare in the early 1990s. "The American people rejected Democrats' attempted government takeover of health care in 1993, and they remain skeptical of politicians who would send us down that road."

In the first presidential debate at the University of Mississippi on September 26, 2008, Obama claimed that the American health care system "is broken" and that he would "make sure that we have a health care system that allows for everyone to have basic coverage." McCain's plan focused on providing families with a "$5,000 refundable tax credit so they can go out and purchase their own health care." Obama countered that the $5,000 tax credit was inadequate because, "if you end up losing your health care from your employer, you've got to go out on the open market and try to buy it. It is not a good deal for the American people." In other words, because all health insurance is tied to working at a particular job, those who lose their jobs would not keep their benefits. That was the only reference to health care in the first presidential debate.

The theme of health care was also discussed briefly during the only vice presidential debate, held on October 2, 2008, at Washington University in St. Louis between Governor Sarah Palin and Senator Joe Biden. Governor Palin contrasted Senator McCain's "budget-neutral" $5,000 tax credit plan with "Barack Obama's plan to mandate health care coverage and have [a] universal government-run program." Palin cautioned that Obama wanted "health care [to be] taken over by the feds," and she doubted that Americans were "pleased with the way the federal government has been running anything lately." The comment was premature at the time. Obama still opposed a mandate, though ultimately Palin's comments would prove largely accurate. Her more famous claim that Obamacare would create so-called "death panels," made in August 2009, would also resonate among the Tea Party opposition to the ACA.

The next presidential debate, a town hall forum held on October 7, 2008, at Belmont University in Nashville, Tennessee, offered a deeper glimpse into the mechanics of Obamacare. When asked to rank his priorities among health care, energy, and entitlement reform, Senator McCain said, "I think you can work on all three at once." With respect to health care, McCain said that "everyone is struggling to make sure that they can afford their premiums and that they can have affordable and available health care." Obama, by contrast, called health care "priority number two, because that broken health care system is bad not only for families, but it's making our businesses less competitive."

The candidates were then asked if they saw health care as a "privilege, a right, or a responsibility." McCain characterized health care as a "responsibility" because "we should have available and affordable health care to every American citizen, to every family member." Though McCain was "always a little nervous about . . . government mandates," he noted that Americans "certainly are a little nervous when Senator Obama says, if you don't get the health care policy that I think you should have, then you're going to get fined." Continuing an attack that Obama himself had launched repeatedly against Clinton, McCain noted that "Senator Obama has never mentioned how much that fine might be. Perhaps we might find that out tonight."

Obama had frequently asked Clinton how she planned to enforce the mandate, and she never provided an answer. Now it was Obama's turn to dodge this question. He stressed clearly and unequivocally that, in his plan, "there's no mandate involved" other than a mandate to "make sure that your child has health care." Four years later, President Obama's solicitor general would dodge the same question again before the Supreme Court.

During the final presidential debate on October 15, 2008, at Hofstra University in Hempstead, New York, McCain repeated the refrain that Obama's plan imposed a "mandate" and that failure to purchase coverage would result in a "fine." Referring to Joe Wurzelbacher, who had recently gained his fifteen minutes of fame as "Joe the Plumber," McCain asked, "Now, Senator Obama, I'd like—still like to know what that fine is going to be, and I don't think that Joe right now wants to pay a fine when he is seeing such difficult times in America's economy." Continuing a point that Governor Palin had made in the vice presidential debate, McCain charged that "Senator Obama wants to set up health care bureaucracies, take over the health care of America through—as he said, his object is a single-payer system. If you like that, you'll love Canada and England."

Obama answered that the fine would be "zero" because there was no mandate for small businesses. This proved not to be the case. Notably, the constitutionality of the individual mandate was never addressed—not at any point during any debate.

Hope and "Change"

On November 4, 2008, Barack Obama soundly defeated John McCain by 365 electoral votes to 173. An election-day poll showed that voters supporting Obama listed health care as their second-highest priority. Now the president had the platform to change the American health care system.

But to reach that goal, Obama himself would have to "change," literally. Soon enough, he would renege on his opposition to Clinton's individual mandate and make it his own. Republicans who had long supported the mandate, from Newt Gingrich to Mitt Romney, would soon vehemently oppose this conservative solution to cost-shifting. Over the next two years, politicians across the spectrum would throw consistency to the wind in their pursuit of partisan gains. The battle over Obamacare was about to begin.

PART II

Unprecedented

(January 21, 2009–March 23, 2010)

The story of the constitutional challenge to the Affordable Care Act continued through the first year of President Obama's first term, when, together with managing the economy, health care reform became his top priority. After opposing the individual mandate on the campaign trail, the president reversed course and adopted Senator Hillary Clinton's approach to guaranteeing universal coverage.

Seizing on the growing influence of the Tea Party and the rising unpopularity of what would soon be called Obamacare, Republicans directed all of their efforts at killing the bill. However, with sixty votes in the Senate and an overwhelming majority in the House, the Democrats were able to enact their proposal without having to attract a single Republican vote. With all legislative means exhausted, Republicans turned to their last refuge—the Constitution.

THE MANDATE FLIP-FLOP

Prodded by congressional Democrats, Obama changed his mind barely eight months after his inauguration and after a grueling two-year campaign in which he had repeatedly attacked Clinton for proposing a health insurance mandate. Now he sought an individual mandate in the plan that would soon be nicknamed after him. Politifact awarded Obama's change of course with the ignominious "Full Flop!" award, writing that "Obama was vigorous in his attacks on Clinton for including an individual mandate in her plan. Now that the Democrats in the House have included a mandate in health reform legislation, he's fine with it."

Obama explained his second thoughts during a CBS interview on July 17, 2009. "I have come to [the] conclusion" that Americans should be required to buy health insurance, the president said. "During the campaign I was opposed to this idea because my general attitude was, the reason people don't have health insurance is not because they don't want it, it's because they can't afford it. And if you make it affordable, then they'll come. I am now in favor of some sort of individual mandate as long as there's a hardship exemption."

Yet Obama's change of heart wasn't quite that simple. His views had shifted during the summer of 2008, after he had locked up the nomination but before the general election, according to Princeton University professor Paul Starr, a Clinton administration health policy adviser. Shortly after Obama secured the nomination for president, Karen Ignagni, the president of America's Health Insurance Plans (formerly America's Health Insurance Association), the insurance industry's primary lobbyist, traveled to Obama's Chicago campaign headquarters. There, she told Senator Obama that the "industry would accept a reform plan that included the guaranteed issue of policies with no preexisting-condition exclusions if the legislation also included a mandate that everyone be covered. In other words, the mandate was the price for the insurance industry's cooperation." (Ultimately, however, America's Health Insurance Plans refused to endorse the ACA.)

Tom Daschle wrote: "To the health insurers, it was the only way to make sure people wouldn't take advantage of the new rules by waiting to buy insurance until they were already sick." Daschle recognized the economic motivations behind this position: "If millions of uninsured Americans gained health insurance, the health industry groups stood to gain millions of new customers." As Senator Orrin Hatch charged in December 2009, "The insurance companies are the most direct winners under this insurance mandate." Daschle recalled that this backroom dealing represented a recognition that "the stars were lining up for health care reform for the first time since the defeat of the Clinton plan, and the smartest interest-group leaders wanted to make sure they had seats at the table."

Obama was faced with a stark choice. Unlike the Clinton task force, which had tried to develop a health care reform law in secrecy, Obama knew he needed buy-in from the insurance industry. Rahm Emanuel, Obama's chief of staff, had learned that lesson well from his time in the Clinton White House. To obtain the support of the health care lobby, Obama would need to add a mandate to his plan.

In another ironic twist, candidate Obama had attacked Hillary Clinton at a February debate in Cleveland for proposing a mandate to curry favor with the industry: "Insurance companies actually are happy to have a mandate. The insurance companies don't mind making sure that everybody has to purchase their product. That's not something they're objecting to." Yet now, with the nomination in hand, Obama turned and adopted the mandate in an effort to secure the insurance industry's political support.

Though the mandate was not a big deal during the race against Senator McCain, inside the campaign Obama was already coming around before the election. Paul Starr reported that "behind the scenes, the thinking inside Obama's orbit was clearly shifting." Obama "dropped or marginalized his health policy advisers from the

campaign and brought in advisers with old Clinton connections."
Neera Tanden, who had been Clinton's adviser—and who attacked
Obama repeatedly on his failure to articulate a viable health care
plan—joined Obama's policy staff. She recalled that when she asked
Obama what he thought of a mandate, Obama replied, "I kind of
think Hillary was right."

Ultimately, Obama determined that the mandate was the best way
to get as close to universal coverage as possible. In December 2008,
President-Elect Obama met with Tom Daschle, who was then his
nominee for secretary of Health and Human Services. "To my pleas-
ant surprise," wrote Daschle later, "the president-elect told us, for the
first time, that he might be willing to reconsider his thinking." Starr
reported that later, in the Obama White House, the mandate became
"the assumed policy," though Obama was able to lay low "and did
not have to reverse himself publicly on the issue because Congress
took the lead on legislation. All the bills that came out of Senate and
House committees included a mandate."

OBAMACARE 3.0

There was general uneasiness among those in the new administration about the president-elect's decision to tackle health care right
away. Daschle recalled that "Larry Summers, the director of the National Economic Council, [was] concerned that the president would
have his hands full with the biggest economic crisis since the Great
Depression." Summers "asked whether this was really the best time
to take on health care, too." Peter Orszag, the Office of Management
and Budget director, "tried to mediate . . . this debate within the
president's inner circle." In January 2009, Vice President-Elect Biden
"spoke at length about why it would be too much to attempt health
care reform in the middle of the [financial] crisis."

In fact, "there were times when it was not clear that the president himself was fully committed to taking on the problem early on," Daschle remembered. Ultimately, however, in spite of the doubts of Obama's advisers, it became apparent to Daschle that "the president himself was sure—and that meant health care reform just might succeed after so many years." After the inauguration, Obama told Daschle, "Tom, health care is the most important thing we will ever do. It will be my legacy. And it is more important to me now than ever before. Don't ever doubt that."

During his February 2009 address to a joint session of Congress, Obama put everyone on notice that he was prepared for battle. "I suffer no illusions that this will be an easy process. Once again, it will be hard," Obama told Congress. "But I also know that nearly a century after Teddy Roosevelt first called for reform, the cost of our health care has weighed down our economy and our conscience long enough. So let there be no doubt: health care reform cannot wait, it must not wait, and it will not wait another year." The battle of Obamacare had begun.

The Affordable Care Act

President Obama's signature health care reform law would become known as the Patient Protection and Affordable Care Act of 2010, or ACA for short. Many critics labeled it "Obamacare," though ultimately the president and his supporters embraced this term. As one Obamacare acolyte explained it to me, "'Obamacare' shows that Obama cares."

Three key provisions of the ACA were controversial. The first was the individual mandate, which compelled people who earned a certain income to purchase health insurance. If they failed to do so, they would pay a penalty. Second, the Act required that states cover more of their residents under Medicaid. The extra cost to cover the new Medicaid enrollees would initially be paid for by the federal government, though eventually the costs would burden the budgets of states. We will return to these two provisions later.

Third, in an earlier version of the bill, the ACA included a public health care option. The public option was a Medicare-like alternative to private insurance that people could purchase through the ACA's so-called exchange. Rather than establishing a single-payer system similar to that of Canada, the government would create a health care plan to "compete" with private insurance options, with the intent of keeping rates low. Private insurers would need to keep their rates in line with those of the government plan or risk losing customers.

No one was really happy with the public option. To Democrats, it did not go far enough—many of the more progressive members of the caucus sought single-payer health care. But in February 2009, Democratic Senator Max Baucus, chairman of the Senate Finance Committee, said, "There may come a time when we can push for single-payer. At this time, it's not going to get to first base in Congress." House Speaker Nancy Pelosi agreed: "For thirty years I have supported a single-payer plan, but our next best choice is to support an exchange and a public option."

The public option provoked serious opposition from Republicans. Daschle noted that the public option, for Republicans, "was Exhibit A in their charge that the Democrats were trying to impose 'government-run health care.'" Republican senators on the Finance Committee sent Obama a letter in March 2009 opposing the public option and calling it a deal-breaker. "Forcing free market plans to compete with these government-run programs would create an unlevel playing field and inevitably doom true competition," the senators said. "Ultimately, we would be left with a single government-run program controlling all of the market. This would take health care decisions out of [the hands of] doctors and patients and place them in the hands of another Washington bureaucracy."

Shortly after this letter, the online magazine *Slate* questioned whether Obama might be going "soft" on the public option. At a March 11, 2009, health care forum, Republican Senator Chuck Grassley from Iowa told the president, "There's a lot of us that feel that the public option [makes] the government . . . an unfair competitor and that we're going to get an awful lot of crowd-out, and we have to keep what we have now strong, and make it stronger." Obama responded, quite strategically, "So I recognize that there's that concern [about the public option]. I think it's a serious one and a real one. And we'll make sure that it gets addressed, partly because I assume it will be very . . . hard to come out of committee unless we're thinking about it a little bit."

Ultimately, the public option was killed in the Senate Finance Committee. By July 2009, Chairman Baucus, the Senate's main champion of the public option, had largely backed away, realizing that it was unlikely to get through committee. In classic Washington-ese, Baucus said, "I'll fight tooth and nail for a version [of a public option] that works, if we can get it passed." In other words, he had already conceded defeat. By July 28, Baucus had dropped the public option from the bill.

With this setback, the ACA had to be adjusted. Because the public option could no longer be relied on to keep insurance companies from increasing their rates, the law had to shift all of its weight onto the individual mandate.

However, the tenor of the debates in the Senate changed in June 2009, when Al Franken won a disputed recount following his Senate race in Minnesota. This victory gave the Democrats a filibuster-proof vote majority in the Senate. President Obama seized the opportunity. He gave Senate Democrats a new lightning-paced timetable: they should pass the bill before Congress recessed in August and send the bill to the White House for his signature in October. Obama said, "This is going to be a heavy lift. I think everybody understands that. But I'm also confident that people want to get this done this year."

OBAMA'S CHICAGO TEA PARTY

Not everyone was happy with the president's plan. Since his inauguration, there had been a growing sense of dissatisfaction among conservatives and libertarians over federal bailouts and stimulus laws, which they viewed as fiscally reckless and harmful to individual freedom.

This proverbial teapot boiled over on February 19, 2009, when CNBC financial analyst Rick Santelli took to the air from the floor of the Chicago Mercantile Exchange to condemn proposed bailouts in what has been dubbed the "rant heard round the world." Santelli's speech became a call to arms to those opposed to what was seen as the overreaching leviathan in Washington: "We're thinking of having a Chicago Tea Party in July. All you capitalists that want to show up to Lake Michigan, I'm gonna start organizing." Santelli's clarion call stirred up the movement that became the Tea Party: a grassroots group of diffuse origins, all loosely united around the goal of opposing an expanding federal government—and President Obama. If Santelli's rant against the federal bailouts was the spark, it was Obamacare that provided the Tea Party with the fuel to become a powerful opposition to President Obama's agenda.

On April 15, 2009, Tax Day, Tea Party protests sprang up in over two hundred cities, drawing as many as half a million people. The Tea Party had emerged as a powerful political foe. Throughout the summer of 2009, various Tea Party groups organized local rallies from sea to shining sea, aimed in part at blocking Obamacare.

The Tea Party Patriots dubbed July 17 "National Health Care Rally Day." In Nashville, four thousand protesters "took aim at universal health care" as they waved Gadsden flags (the iconic Revolutionary-era flag that depicts a coiled snake above the words "DON'T TREAD ON ME") as well as signs that read REVOLT AGAINST SOCIALISM and OVERTHROW CONGRESS. In Great Falls, Montana, protesters camped out in front of the offices of senators Jon Tester and Max Baucus. One anti-Obamacare protester proclaimed, "My message is, let's get our foot off the accelerator. Put the brakes on. Let's stop. And let's park it for now." Several thousand Tea Partiers rallied at Centennial Park in Atlanta bearing signs that read OBAMACARE MAKES ME SICK! and SOCIALIZED MEDICINE HOTLINE: 1–800-YOU-DEAD. Dick Armey, former House majority leader and chairman of the popular Tea Party group FreedomWorks, told the crowd, "What we've got today is an assault on liberty that is larger than anything we have ever seen." A protester at a rally in Mobile, Alabama, said, "The goal is to get them to be aware we're looking for our senators and our legislators to make a stand for us and vote no." At a Tea Party rally in Austin, Texas, one protester sent a message to the White House: "This is letting the people know that Obama and his cronies aren't going to push this down our throats. We will fight it."

Even early protests over the law focused on its alleged unconstitutionality. The Tea Party Healthcare Freedom Rally in Oklahoma City drew hundreds of protesters trying to send a message to Washington. One proclaimed, "Nowhere in the entire Constitution does it say government has the right or power to mess with health care." At one of the many rallies scheduled for September 12, the coordinator of the Tulsa, Oklahoma, Tea Party regaled the "9/12 Tea Party" crowd: "We want to get back to honoring the Constitution." In Houston, Texas, hundreds packed Sam Houston Race Park and wore T-shirts that said I AM A TEA PARTY PATRIOT—I WILL DEFEND OUR CONSTITUTION.

Many Tea Party groups organized such protests. However, detractors derided these supposedly grassroots organizations for being more akin to AstroTurf. In July 2009, Americans for Prosperity organized a "Hands Off My Health Care" bus tour to meet President Obama in Bristol, Virginia, where he was speaking about his health care reform plan. Dick Armey's Tea Party group FreedomWorks offered organizers an "August Recess Action Kit" to use when challenging politicians at town hall meetings during the summer congressional recess. Liberty Central, a group founded by Justice Clarence Thomas's wife, Ginni Thomas, provided social media support and organization for these rallies. (Her role with this group would later cause many to request Justice Clarence Thomas's recusal.)

In August 2009, Sarah Palin spoke alarmingly of "death panels" that would decide who receives medical care based on cost-saving procedures and rationing. "The America I know and love is not one in which my parents or my baby with Down's syndrome will have to stand in front of Obama's 'death panel' so his bureaucrats can decide, based on a subjective judgment of their 'level of productivity in society,' whether they are worthy of health care. Such a system is downright evil." This message would resonate deeply in Tea Party circles. Eventually, the end-of-life "consultation payments" were removed from the ACA, and the president deleted all references to "end-of-life" planning from his agenda. *Time* magazine reported that "a single phrase—'death panels'—nearly derailed health care reform." However, the Independent Payment Advisory Board (IPAB), which did become law, has authority that could evolve to make similar types of decisions.

The rallies gained strength, and Tea Partiers began attending the town hall meetings of members of Congress during the summer recess. Senator Arlen Specter of Pennsylvania, who had recently switched from the Republican to the Democratic Party, was booed at a town hall meeting as he tried to explain the bill. Seniors turned their backs on longtime Democratic representative John Dingell of Michigan when he promised at a town hall meeting that "Medicare will be here to take care of you." At a public meet-and-greet in Austin,

Texas, Democratic representative Lloyd Doggett faced a barrage of fiery questions. One attendee shouted, "How in the world can you sign and pass bills without ever reading them?" Tea Party protesters followed Doggett to his car, chanting, "Just say no!"

The opposition became loud and clear: vote for the Affordable Care Act, and the Tea Party will oppose you.

Just as the Tea Party was gaining steam, the health care reform movement suffered a monumental loss. On August 25, 2009, Senator Edward Kennedy of Massachusetts, who had spent decades championing the cause of universal coverage, passed away. On September 9, President Obama returned to address a joint session of Congress. He read from a letter that Kennedy had written before his death, saying that health care reform was "the great unfinished business of our society."

Drawing inspiration from Kennedy, Obama issued a call for action: "I understand that the politically safe move would be to kick the can further down the road, to defer reform one more year, or one more election, or one more term. But that is not what this moment calls for. I still believe we can act, even when it's hard." Obama's address is perhaps most remembered for South Carolina representative Joe Wilson yelling at the president, "You lie!" in response to Obama's claim that the health care reform would not provide coverage for undocumented immigrants.

Beyond being the liberal lion of the Senate, Kennedy was also, more importantly, the Democrats' sixtieth vote in the Senate. His death meant the filibuster—the Republicans' last line of defense to prevent the enactment of the bill—would soon be back in play.

"ARE YOU SERIOUS?"

During the summer of 2009, beyond the fields of the Tea Party, the constitutionality of the ACA went largely unquestioned. In April

2009, the House Committee on Ways and Means had held a hearing on the Act that focused entirely on the number of uninsured Americans and how to increase access to coverage. Only one constitutional reference was made in the hearing, when Representative John Lewis of Georgia asked Princeton health economics professor Uwe Reinhardt: "Do you accept the idea, the concept, that health care is a right . . . that should be guaranteed by our government?" Reinhardt, who grew up in postwar-Germany and later lived in Canada, said that health care was "a constitutional right."

In April 2009, Professor Mark Hall, one of the first law professors to analyze the constitutionality of forcing a person to buy health insurance, wrote a report for the O'Neill Institute that was submitted to Congress. Hall had contacted a number of leading constitutional scholars to ask their opinion about the law's constitutionality. Few had given it any thought. Hall concluded that the mandate was constitutional.

One of the few doubts about the law's constitutionality was raised by a July 2009 Congressional Research Service (CRS) report that questioned whether the mandate "would be constitutional under the Commerce Clause." This "is perhaps the most challenging question posed by such a proposal, as it is a novel issue whether Congress may use this clause to require an individual to purchase a good or service." Also in July 2009, former Bush administration officials Peter Urbanowicz and Dennis G. Smith wrote a paper for the Federalist Society arguing that the mandate was unconstitutional. Yet these criticisms were mere blips in the national dialogue at the time. Discussion of the constitutionality of the ACA was heard at hardly more than a whisper.

However, two former Reagan Justice Department attorneys, David B. Rivkin Jr. and Lee A. Casey, would soon challenge that apathy. The pair, who had been working together since 1987, "lived and breathed the Constitution." Rivkin and Casey had been battling the individual mandate for over two decades, having opposed the Republican individual mandate proposal in a September 29, 1993, *Wall Street Journal* editorial: "If the legality of a health care package featuring federally mandated universal participation is litigated (and we can bet it will be), and the system is upheld, it will mark the final extension of this originally modest grant of federal authority. Thereafter, Congress will be able to regulate you not because of who you are, what you do for a living, or whether you use the interstate highways, but merely because you exist."

Now, they took to the papers again, writing two of the earliest critiques of the ACA's constitutionality in an August 22, 2009, editorial in the *Washington Post* and a September 18, 2009, piece in the *Wall Street Journal:* "Federal legislation requiring that every American have health insurance is part of all the major health-care reform plans now being considered in Washington. Such a mandate, however, would expand the federal government's authority over individual Americans to an unprecedented degree. It is also profoundly unconstitutional." Rivkin and Casey were among the first to articulate why the Act's mandate was unconstitutional.

Rivkin and Casey's early arguments were raw and unrefined, but they laid a foundation for the constitutional challenge. At first "no one on the right came out to support" them, Rivkin later told me. His "colleagues were privately skeptical." But he and Casey firmly believed that "the Supreme Court had never accepted such a proposition, and it [was] unlikely to accept it now, even in an area as important as health care." Rivkin thought "from day one this was eminently winnable."

At the time, many ridiculed constitutional arguments against the mandate. Speaker of the House Nancy Pelosi famously dismissed a question about the constitutionality of the law by chortling, "Are you serious? Are you serious?" At a town hall meeting, Representative Pete Stark boldly stated that "the federal government can do most anything in this country." Senator Patrick Leahy said that "there's no question there's authority for Congress to enact the mandate. Nobody questions that."

Few senators expressed doubts about the individual mandate's constitutionality at this early juncture. On September 22, 2009, before the Senate Committee on Finance, Senator Orrin Hatch asked Tom Barthold, chief of staff of the Joint Committee on Taxation, whether the mandate complied with the Constitution. Barthold's response was telling. "Well, I cannot really comment about the Constitution." Hatch asked him again: "Do you believe this individual mandate raises possible constitutional issues?" Barthold replied, "Senator, it is just not something that I am qualified to answer. . . . I am not the right person to engage in a constitutional discussion." Hatch opened the question up to anyone testifying that day. "I mean, can anyone on the panel say whether the mandate or excise tax would be constitutional? Anyone?" In a scene right out of *Ferris Bueller's Day Off,* Hatch's question was met with dead silence. Anyone? Constitutional? Anyone?

The only person willing to answer was Chairman Baucus. "I think it is a stretch to say this is unconstitutional. I will take that argument any day that it is not constitutional. It is constitutional."

Hatch was not so sanguine. "Well, again, we are passing this bill without answering questions that are really important, like the constitutionality of some of the provisions. These are important issues. They are not just itty-bitty issues."

David Rivkin recalled that, with the exception of Senator Hatch, there was "very little interest in the constitutional issues on the right and the left." Everything was "completely dominated" by policy compromises.

On October 1, 2009, before the Senate Finance Committee, Senator Hatch addressed the constitutional defects of the individual mandate, echoing many of the points that Rivkin and Casey had made in their op-eds. "The only conceivable constitutional basis for Congress requiring that Americans purchase a particular good or service is the power to regulate interstate commerce." Though the Supreme Court has "expanded the commerce power, there has been one constant: Congress was always regulating activities." To stress his point, Hatch said it again. "Let me repeat that: Congress was always regulating activities in which people chose to engage. They might be noncommercial activities or intrastate activities, but they were activities."

This bill, Hatch cautioned, would "do something entirely different" from Congress's past actions to regulate activities. "Rather than regulate what people have chosen to do, it would require them to do something they have *not* chosen to do at all." Hatch later concluded: "These problems are real, and as the [CRS] report concluded, they are 'novel' and 'unprecedented.'" Hatch proclaimed that this law "would have Congress boldly go where we have never gone before, at least as far as I can see, in the history of our country."

Except that the GOP had already been there. What Hatch did not mention was that the individual mandate, the provision deemed "unprecedented" by the CRS in 2009, had already appeared in 1993 in the Republican-sponsored HEART Act, which he, along with Chuck Grassley, had supported.

Despite Hatch's objections, on October 13, the Senate Finance Committee passed a version of the bill by a vote of 14–9 that included the mandate. Moderate senator Olympia Snowe of Maine was the only Republican who voted in favor of the ACA. The bill would now proceed to the full Senate.

THE MAYFLOWER COMPACT

The historic Mayflower Hotel in Washington, D.C., opened in 1925. Located blocks from the White House, it served as the home of some of the most important political meetings of the twentieth century and has sponsored an inaugural ball for every president since Calvin Coolidge. President Franklin D. Roosevelt prepared his first inaugural address—in which he proclaimed "the only thing we have to fear is fear itself"—in suite 776. While the White House was under renovation, President Truman lived in the Mayflower for three months and later announced at the hotel his intention to run for reelection. J. Edgar Hoover, the longtime director of the FBI, dined at the Mayflower daily.

The hotel has also served as the site of some recent scandals. The iconic photograph of intern Monica Lewinsky embracing President Bill Clinton was taken at an event at the Mayflower Hotel. On Valentine's Day Eve 2008, New York Governor Eliot Spitzer checked into suite 871, registered as "George Brown," and entertained Ashley Alexandra Dupré, a call girl who labeled him as "Client 9." The scandal, conceived in the Mayflower, led to Spitzer's resignation on March 12, 2008.

Each November, the Federalist Society for Law and Public Policy Studies (known mainly as the Federalist Society) hosts its biggest event of the year, the National Lawyers Convention, at the Mayflower Hotel. The society, the nation's most influential conservative and libertarian legal organization, takes its name from the *Federalist Papers*. These treasures of political theory were authored by James Madison, Alexander Hamilton, and John Jay from 1787 to 1788 to gin up support for the ratification of the Constitution. Founded in 1982 by several law students who were frustrated with liberal homogeny on law school campuses, the Federalist Society was created with "the principles that the state exists to preserve freedom, that the separation of governmental powers is central to our Constitution, and that it is emphatically the province and duty of the judiciary to say what the law is, not what it should be."

The Federalist Society boasts a membership roll that includes several Supreme Court justices (though Chief Justice Roberts controversially had "no recollection of ever being a member"), countless politicians and influential policymakers, prominent academics, and over 40,000 members nationwide. The *Washington Post* dubbed this influential group "the pinstriped tribe of conservative minds called the Federalist Society." I have been involved with the Federalist Society since I was a law student.

The 2008 convention, held only days after the election of President Obama, was a dour affair. At the annual dinner, Attorney General Michael Mukasey, the guest of honor, dramatically collapsed in the middle of his address. But a year later, the 2009 convention would open up with a sense of resolve. Indeed, the challenge to the ACA would begin that day at the Mayflower Hotel.

The convention draws prominent academics, politicians, and judges from across the ideological spectrum to discuss and debate the key legal issues of the day. As is often the case at such conventions, some panels are more interesting than others. During lulls, attendants frequently recess to the grand hallway in the Mayflower to catch up with old friends, argue about the most recent Supreme Court case, or brainstorm and strategize. November 12, 2009, was just such a day. At 10:15 AM, a panel began on "Bailouts and Government as Insurer of Last Resort." Though certainly an interesting topic, a number of already-fatigued Federalists made their way out into the cavernous hallway. I joined them.

Todd Gaziano, director of the Center for Legal and Judicial Studies at the Heritage Foundation—the same Heritage Foundation that had first advanced the individual mandate two decades earlier—was talking about the pending health care bill along with Nelson Lund, my former professor at George Mason University School of Law; Andrew Grossman, a former classmate; and a few others. At this point the law still had not cleared the Senate, but conservatives were already getting worried.

Gaziano, brainstorming ways to challenge the law, asked the group if there were any possible constitutional infirmities in the law. I chimed in that all mandates in the past had been imposed by the states—such as automobile insurance—rather than the federal government. However, I recognized, under the Court's existing Commerce Clause doctrine, regulating health insurance was certainly permissible. One professor was dismissive and suggested that the Court would never go along with striking down the mandate. When someone said he didn't know if Justice Kennedy would vote to strike down the law, Gaziano presciently predicted that he was most worried about Chief Justice Roberts, who had shown a streak of judicial restraint in his opinions.

Gaziano threw out a slew of extreme hypotheticals that, at the time, seemed crazy. The bespectacled think-tanker asked if the government could compel someone to purchase a General Motors vehicle in order to help out Detroit. Then he asked if the government could compel a person to purchase a gym membership to stay healthy. (This was perhaps the first precursor to the broccoli horrible.)

Gaziano kept repeating one thought over and over again: that the Supreme Court's opinions all dealt with regulating activities, such as growing wheat or marijuana. This case, Gaziano argued, involved the regulation of the choice *not* to buy insurance—that is, the regulation of inactivity. With the bill coming up for a vote in the Senate in a month, Gaziano said that he wanted to write a report for Congress that would give constitutional arguments as to why the law was invalid.

He approached me and said something to the effect of, "Josh, I would love for a young and bright lawyer such as yourself to help write this report with me." I knew what that flattery meant in D.C.-speak: prominent lawyers frequently ask young lawyers to ghostwrite articles for them. In truth, I was not opposed to that idea—and in fact I had done it before—but I recognized that for someone who was clerking, writing a white paper about a pending piece of litigation that would soon be litigated in the federal courts was inappropriate. I respectfully declined.

A few moments later, Georgetown University Law Center professor Randy Barnett joined the conversation. At a Federalist Society convention, Barnett is a rock star. He had just finished a debate. Tall and lean, with a piercing glance and sly grin, Barnett radiates confidence and warmth. Making his way through a throng of admirers, he always takes time to talk to inquisitive students.

In addition to writing some of the most influential books and articles on originalism, constitutional theory, and the structures of liberty, Barnett had argued *Gonzales v. Raich* before the Supreme Court in 2005. That case, which Barnett lost, held that Congress had the power to regulate marijuana that never leaves a farm. More importantly, Barnett was a leading expert on the scope of federal power and constitutional law.

In hindsight, Barnett's entry into our conversation was providential. Gaziano later told me that he was "looking for someone with real knowledge in the area," someone who had "gravitas," to help make the case against Obamacare. Barnett was perhaps the ideal candidate. This conversation, though it started out innocently enough, would change the fate of constitutional law.

Gaziano asked Barnett, "Hey, Randy, do you have any thoughts about the constitutionality of the health care law?" Randy replied, "You know, I really haven't give it much thought."

At the time, Barnett had written a few blog posts on the bill, but otherwise had given it scant attention. He was focused primarily on *McDonald v. Chicago,* a key gun rights case before the Supreme Court that would decide whether Chicago's handgun ban was unconstitutional.

Gaziano told Barnett that he had a "guy" who could help them formulate a paper, though he stressed that they had to act quickly. "Whatever we do," he said, "we need to do it right away." Barnett seemed skeptical and said that he was very busy at the time. Following his defeat in *Gonzales v. Raich,* Barnett was "very pessimistic" about the prospects of a challenge to the ACA, but he was open to persuasion. Barnett would later tell me that he was not persuaded by Rivkin and Casey's editorials. After reading their pieces in the *Wall Street Journal* and *Washington Post*, he concluded that, "If those were the best arguments that the law is unconstitutional, then I figured it must be constitutional."

Gaziano, tenacious as ever, kept at it and asked if Barnett wanted to write a report and "do something about the law." Barnett agreed, but said, "You will have to get someone to do the first draft." Gaziano coaxed Barnett further. "Stop by my office this week. We can talk more about this case. And I have a young associate who can help write this." Reading between the lines, I got the impression that Heritage would write the report and Barnett would put his imprimatur on it. Intrigued, Barnett flashed his trademark smirk and agreed.

Exactly three years later, at the 2012 convention, Gaziano told me that he had been much further along on his theory than he had let on: He had already concluded that the case was a "step beyond" what the Supreme Court had sanctioned before. His goal was to "convince people to write" something to lay the foundation for future constitutional challenges and to "get it in the legislative record." His plan was to write something and "distribute it widely on Capitol Hill." Gaziano, with only a few weeks to get it done, recognized that Barnett had ample clout and gravitas, and that he needed the professor's constitutional reputation to make this challenge work.

The associate Gaziano was considering was Nathaniel Stewart, an attorney who at the time worked for the D.C. law firm of White & Case LLP. Told that they needed to get "something out in less than two weeks," Stewart was essential in preparing the first draft of Heritage's report.

Over the next two years, all of the players involved in this "Mayflower Compact" proved instrumental in the lawsuits that would follow. The *New York Times* would label Barnett the "intellectual godfather" of the ACA challenge. Gaziano would continue to orchestrate the litigation strategy behind the scenes. Andrew Grossman, perhaps fittingly, served as counsel along with Rivkin and Casey in the challenge to the ACA in Florida. And, fortuitously, I was present to document the genesis of this unprecedented ride.

OF GRAIN AND GANJA

The two landmark Supreme Court cases that many said supported Congress's power to compel people to purchase health insurance dealt, oddly enough, with wheat and weed.

The Constitution gives Congress power to regulate commerce between the states, and to pass all laws that are "necessary and proper" to pass those regulations. But what about commercial activities that occur entirely within one state and never cross state lines, such as growing wheat or marijuana on your own property? In the 1942 decision of *Wickard v. Filburn,* the Supreme Court held that Congress could regulate the production of wheat on Roscoe Filburn's farm, even if the wheat was only used to feed himself, his family, and his livestock. In the 2005 case of *Gonzales v. Raich,* the Supreme Court held that Congress could prohibit Angel Raich, who had an invasive tumor, from using medicinal marijuana grown wholly within the state. This was the case that Barnett had argued unsuccessfully.

Thanks to these and other decisions, when the ACA was being debated in 2009, few doubted that Congress could require people to purchase health insurance, even if the decision not to purchase health insurance was wholly within one state.

From early on, anyone who challenged this conclusion was ridiculed by what was deemed to be an "expert consensus" of law professors. Jack Balkin, a constitutional law professor at Yale, claimed that this was "not even a close question." Akhil Amar, another professor at Yale, asserted that none of these arguments could "hold water."

The arguments didn't "have the slightest merit from a constitutional perspective," quipped Erwin Chemerinsky, dean of the University of California–Irvine Law School. Senator Max Baucus quoted Chemerinsky on the Senate floor on December 22, 2009, two days before the Senate passed the Act: "Most legal scholars who have considered the question of a requirement for individuals to purchase health coverage argue forcefully that the requirement is within Congress's power to regulate interstate commerce." Baucus was right about that.

However, this "expert consensus" would soon give way to a rising popular constitutionalist movement against the ACA.

The small cadre of attorneys devising constitutional arguments against the individual mandate—Rivkin, Barnett, Gaziano, Stewart, and several other law professors who write on the Volokh Conspiracy blog, including Jonathan Adler, David Kopel, and Ilya Somin—recognized a small sliver of hope. In *Wickard v. Filburn,* Congress was regulating Farmer Filburn's decision to grow wheat—an *activity.* In *Gonzales v. Raich,* Congress was regulating the growing of marijuana on Raich's farm—this too was an *activity.* With the individual mandate, however, Congress was regulating a person's decision *not* to purchase health insurance—this was *inactivity.* In this way, the challengers attempted to thread the constitutional needle by "distinguishing" (as lawyers say) the seemingly broad Supreme Court precedents. They provided a colorable claim that the individual mandate went beyond any previous act of Congress that the Supreme Court had upheld in the past and was therefore unprecedented. The constitutional argument against Obamacare was born.

AN UNPRECEDENTED HERITAGE

Less than three weeks after the meeting at the Mayflower—over a very busy Thanksgiving break—Gaziano, Stewart, and Barnett wrote what would become the seminal report asserting that the ACA was unconstitutional.

Stewart, working from an article he had authored as a law student, fashioned and developed the Commerce Clause argument that explored the distinction between activity and inactivity. Gaziano had originally planned on simply coordinating the project, but in the end his contribution was significant enough, specifically with respect to the taxing power, that he felt "justified putting [his] name on the report." Barnett's role was limited to editing and improving the drafts. The fourth, unnamed, contributor was Heritage associate Robert Alt.

The report was titled: "Why the Personal Mandate to Buy Health Insurance Is Unprecedented and Unconstitutional." It is unclear exactly who first added the word "Unprecedented," though Gaziano stressed the importance of a catchy title ("That's the kind of thing I care about"). The word "unprecedented" would soon come to define the challenge. After some more substantial edits from Barnett, including the addition of a section on how the ACA was, in fact, "unprecedented" and inconsistent with existing Supreme Court precedents, the paper was complete.

Gaziano knew that in order for this report to make an impact, it would have to be accepted by Republicans in Congress. The perfect candidate was Senator Hatch, who for months had been one of the few voices questioning the ACA's constitutionality. Gaziano said that in Washington the best way to get a politician to read a report is to invite him to speak about it. This was "what we are supposed to do at Heritage. Encourage people to take issues seriously."

At the senator's request, Gaziano invited Hatch to speak at a December 9, 2012, public event at Heritage's Capitol Hill auditorium. At the time, Gaziano noted that Hatch would "laud the paper in a floor speech he is set to make" later that day. The report would be released on that date, and Barnett would debate prominent UCLA law professor Eugene Volokh. Volokh, who holds mostly conservative and libertarian views, had been critical of the challenges to the ACA. Gaziano wanted Volokh because "he was a skeptic" and debating him would "get academic play." During the event, Volokh would disagree with Barnett's positions and argue that the mandate was constitutional under existing law.

Before the event began, Senator Hatch met Barnett, Gaziano, and Stewart in the green room. Stewart was introduced as the "original coauthor who had worked on the draft." Hatch thanked him and stressed how important the report was. Then Barnett, meeting Stewart in person for the first time, thanked him for his work. Barnett told Stewart: "I wouldn't have thought to draft the report that way. Once you framed it that way, it became very clear, and that was a great way to tackle it." Barnett told me that Stewart deserved "a ton of credit" for the Heritage paper, especially in its focus on the "class of activities" that Congress had been permitted to regulate in the past.

Before a packed auditorium, Senator Hatch praised the report and promised to continue the battle against Obamacare in the Senate. One beltway veteran who attended the event told me that Hatch was "looking to turn himself into a Tea Partier."

Of even greater importance than the public forum, after the event was finished, as is tradition at Heritage, a few dozen staffers from Capitol Hill were invited to a lunch where they would receive a private briefing. At that meeting, having heard that the staffers could not think of a constitutional argument against the ACA, Barnett was tasked with explaining the legal theory of the paper and fielding questions. It was stressed how important it was to get this report into the *Congressional Record* and to persuade senators who opposed the Act on policy grounds to also oppose it on constitutional grounds. More important, Gaziano urged them to make a "constitutional point of order," a parliamentary proceeding that would force a vote on the constitutionality of the law. The staffers were also told that this issue was going to the Supreme Court and that the justices would want to know whether the issue had been argued in Congress.

The report proved to be of the utmost importance. Later that day, Senator Hatch took to the Senate floor to note that "the Heritage

Foundation has just published an important paper arguing that this health insurance mandate is both unprecedented and unconstitutional," and mentioned Barnett, Gaziano, and Stewart by name. Hatch asked for consent to have the conclusion of the report printed in the *Congressional Record,* which was granted. This report would be cited, and read from, over and over again during the next two weeks of Senate debate.

During the pivotal constitutional point of order weeks later, Senator John Ensign of Nevada quoted directly from the report, stressing the fact that the authors had stuck their necks out to argue quite an unpopular position at the time. "There are constitutional experts out there telling us this bill is doing something the federal government has never done in its history." Thanks to Gaziano's foresight, the report that emerged from the Mayflower Compact set the stage for the ultimate constitutional battle before the Supreme Court.

Constitutional Findings

Before the Senate bill emerged from committee, the Democrats were so confident of the law's constitutionality that they made few efforts to prove it. No hearings were held about the law's constitutional implications until *after* it was enacted. However, a number of progressives were already wary of the Supreme Court. In the fall of 2009, Michael Myers, staff director and chief counsel to the Senate Health Committee, contacted Caroline Fredrickson, the executive director of the American Constitution Society. ACS, created as a liberal counterweight to the Federalist Society, promotes the values of "individual rights and liberties, genuine equality, access to justice, democracy and the rule of law." Myers asked Fredrickson to put together a series of "constitutional findings" to insert into the bill to explain why the ACA was constitutional. This could prove vital, as in recent years the Supreme Court had struck down laws as unconstitutional due to inadequate Congressional findings.

Fredrickson quickly contacted several leading scholars and policy experts, including Simon Lazarus of the National Senior Citizens Law Center (now at the Constitutional Accountability Center),
David Lyle, who at the time was the deputy director of the ACS (and
now works at Media Matters), and others. Over the course of two
frenzied days, declarations to fend off charges of unconstitutionality
were compiled. The Senate incorporated the ACS's points, as well as
reports from Professor Mark Hall, into the law.

Ultimately, the 2,700-page Affordable Care Act contained three pages
of constitutional findings to show that the "requirement to maintain
minimum essential coverage" was constitutional. First, "the individual
responsibility requirement provided for in this section . . . is commercial and economic in nature, and substantially affects interstate commerce." Second, the findings listed a number of "effects on the national
and interstate commerce" that resulted from uninsured people shifting
costs. Third, the "findings" stated that "the requirement regulates *activity* that is commercial and economic in nature: economic and financial
decisions about how and when health care is paid for, and when health
insurance is purchased [emphasis added]." The word "activity" would
prove decisive. Fourth, "in *United States v. South-Eastern Underwriters
Association,* the Supreme Court of the United States ruled that insurance is interstate commerce subject to Federal regulation."

That was all the bill said on the topic of constitutionality. Tellingly,
none of these official findings alluded to the tax power of Congress.
All concerned the effects of the uninsured—and (somewhat inco-
herently) the effects of the mandate itself—on interstate commerce.
Though brief, these essential points served as the focus of much of
the litigation and formed the core of the government's arguments as
to why the law should survive. Their limited focus on interstate commerce helps explain why the tax power argument was slow to gain
traction as the litigation progressed.

Rising to address the constitutional findings of the ACA on December 11, 2009, Senator Baucus added a second constitutional justification for the mandate: "We thoroughly studied this issue. I believe there is ample authority for Congress to enact such a provision under the Commerce Clause, and also under the congressional authority to tax and spend for the general welfare provided for in the Constitution." The taxing power argument had not been included in the official findings.

Senator Hatch rose to respond to Baucus's constitutional claims. He ignored the new arguments about the taxing power and confined his response to the official findings, insisting that they failed "in at least four ways." First, although Hatch agreed that it was "self-evident" that "requiring more people to purchase health insurance will result in more people having health insurance, [the] question is not the effect of the mandate but the authority for the mandate. Liberty requires that the ends cannot justify the means." Of course, under the Supreme Court's reading of the Necessary and Proper Clause, broadly speaking, if the ends are legitimate, the Supreme Court is hesitant to question the means Congress employs.

Second, the findings failed "to offer . . . a single case in which Congress has required individuals to purchase a particular good or service or the courts have upheld such a requirement." Indeed, no such case existed. "Rather, all of the Court's precedents involve the regulation of activity in which individuals choose to engage. Requiring that the individual engage in such activity is a difference not in degree but in kind." It was unprecedented. Here Hatch was directly paraphrasing the Heritage report, which found that "an individual mandate to enter into a contract with or buy a particular product from a private party is literally unprecedented, not just in scope but in kind, and unconstitutional either as a matter of first principles or under any reasonable reading of judicial precedents."

Third, Hatch argued that the findings obscured the fact that federalism "allows states to do many things that the federal government may not." For example, Massachusetts under Romneycare could require "that individuals purchase health insurance," but Congress lacked such authority. This was a point candidate Romney would repeatedly fail to make in 2012.

Fourth, Congress's power to "regulate the sale of insurance" did not "mean that the Congress may require it." Here, Hatch emphasized the key distinction between activity and inactivity. "This legislation requires you to believe that *nonactivity* is the same as *activity;* that choosing not to do something is the same as choosing to do it; that regulating what individuals do is the same as requiring them to do it. That notion makes no common sense, and it certainly makes no constitutional sense." With such a broad scope of power, there "will be no limits to the federal government's power over each and every one of our lives."

Hatch concluded that the "power to regulate activities that substantially affect interstate commerce . . . [doesn't] go that far." Then, with an eye toward the imminent litigation, Hatch dropped the gauntlet: "Any of these [constitutional issues], and others I have not mentioned, could well be the basis for future litigation challenging this legislation should it become law."

As the Senate debates were concluding, one hundred miles south of Washington, D.C., in Richmond, Virginia, Republican leaders were preparing to strike the first blow in the legal battle. In December, the Virginia Health Care Freedom Act (VHCFA) was first submitted for consideration in the General Assembly. The bill was aimed at preventing citizens of the Commonwealth from being forced to purchase health insurance under the federal mandate. In theory, the act would give Virginia—and its Tea Party–supported attorney general, Ken Cuccinelli—the authority to sue the federal government to enforce the VHCFA and ask a court to strike down Obamacare.

As originally drafted, the act provided that "no law shall restrict a person's natural right and power of contract to secure the blessings of liberty to choose private health care systems or private plans." The bill was introduced by Tea Party representative Robert Marshall of Manassas, Virginia, who put out a press release stating that "Obamacare is not a battle over health insurance. It is a struggle over whether America will remain a nation of self-directing citizens or docile, powerless serfs." Marshall found support for this bill in the Declaration of Independence, as "America's Founders held that it was both the right and duty of citizens to resist Government which usurps rights given to us by our Creator."

This bill, which would linger for some time, would serve as the basis for one of the two leading lawsuits brought against the ACA's constitutionality.

SIXTY VOTES

With a sixty-vote, filibuster-proof majority, Senate Majority Leader Harry Reid proceeded to push the ACA for a vote, with minimal time for debate. Texas Senator Kay Bailey Hutchison stressed how strong the opposition was. "This bill was drafted behind closed doors without Republican input. The votes are 60–40. Sixty Democrats and forty Republicans make up the Senate, and that is what is providing cloture on this bill." By December, it became clear that Reid would be able to hold together his caucus and hold a vote before the recess, probably on Christmas Eve.

Senator Jim DeMint of South Carolina predicted that the "majority wants to force this major piece of legislation through before Christmas while people aren't paying attention." DeMint stressed that nothing in the Constitution empowered Congress to legislate in this area. "As we have wandered off the path of liberty, there are few crumbs left of the Constitution in the Halls of Congress to lead us out of the woods." (In 2013, DeMint would resign from the Senate to serve as the president of the Heritage Foundation.) Likewise Senator Judd Gregg of New Hampshire expressed disappointment that, "unfortunately, we received this [2,000-plus-page] health care bill about eight days ago, after it had been worked on for eight weeks in camera, behind closed doors by the Democratic leadership. We have only had eight days to look at it."

President Obama would have been well served to listen to the advice of Senator Obama from February 2008: "The only way we're going to be able to overcome the insurance companies, and the drug companies, and the HMOs who are profiting from the current system is if we are having all these negotiations in a public setting." Likewise, during the September 27, 2007, Democratic primary debate at Dartmouth College in Hanover, New Hampshire, Delaware Senator Joe Biden presaged the strong political opposition to the ACA. Biden focused on the fact that without bipartisan buy-in, this contentious law would be argued until the very end. "In order to get health care, you're going to have to be able to persuade at least 15 percent of the Republicans to vote for it." President Obama did not get 15 percent of Republicans to vote for his law. In fact, he got 0 percent, and thirty-nine Democrats in the House defected to vote against the ACA.

Though Senate Majority Leader Reid had sixty votes in the Senate, it was a fragile caucus that included independent senator Joe Lieberman, who called the public option "radical," as well as moderate senators Mary Landrieu of Louisiana and Ben Nelson of Nebraska. Apparently intending to get Nelson's support, Reid included in the bill the so-called "Cornhusker Kickback," which gave Nebraska—and Nebraska alone—additional money to pay for its Medicaid program. Likewise, similar provisions were made for additional funding for Louisiana's Medicaid costs—this was the aptly named "Louisiana Purchase." No one was proud of this legislative graft. Democratic Senator Jay Rockefeller of West Virginia said of the deals, "We all walked around with our heads bowed down." But the deals secured the fifty-ninth and sixtieth votes.

Senator Hutchison attacked the special carve-outs for Louisiana and Nebraska as unconstitutional, citing the Constitution's guarantee of equal protection of the laws: "The deals that have been made to get votes from specific senators cannot be considered equal protection under the law." Many states became leery at the prospect of Louisiana and Nebraska receiving sweetheart deals while they were forced to pay a lot of money for the Medicaid expansion. In addition, several Republican attorneys general, perceptive of the rising tide of the Tea Party, saw political gain from filing suit against this unpopular law— even if the law would benefit Medicaid coverage in their own states.

Republicans, realizing that they had failed to kill the bill through the political process, turned to their last refuge—the Constitution.

A Point of Constitutional Order

The constitutional point of order, aimed at raising constitutional objections to a law, is a parliamentary procedure that is seldom invoked. Unlike most points of orders, which the presiding officer can rule out of order, "the presiding officer may not rule on a constitutional point of order and instead must submit the point of order to the full Senate for a vote." In other words, Senate Majority Leader Harry Reid could not stop the constitutional point of order and the ensuing debate. The purpose of this constitutional point of order was not really to defeat the bill. As Todd Gaziano later told me, the sole goal was to place this evidence into the *Congressional Record* in order to give a court some ground on which it could strike down the mandate. Lacking the forty-one votes needed to sustain a filibuster, Republicans could only raise constitutional objections in the hope that they would influence the public debate that would follow. It also put additional pressure on senators from Reid's fragile caucus. With the analysis of the Heritage report, and the editorials by Rivkin and Casey, the Senate Republicans made their point of constitutional order on December 21, 2009. A televised floor debate was then held on the day before the bill's ultimate passage on Christmas Eve.

Senator Ensign began by posing the all-important question, and the ever-more-important follow-up. "Is it really constitutional for this body to tell all Americans they must buy health insurance coverage? If so, what is next?" Ensign asked about "legislation in the future requiring every American to buy a car, to buy a house."

He continued: "Although the Supreme Court has upheld some far-reaching regulations of economic activity—most notably in *Wickard v. Filburn* and *Gonzales v. Raich*—neither case supports enacting the independent health insurance mandate based on the Commerce Clause." The individual mandate "purports to regulate *inactivity* by converting the *inactivity* of not buying insurance into commercial *activity* [emphasis added]."

Ensign cited and quoted from the *Wall Street Journal* editorial by Rivkin and Casey, which was duly entered into the *Congressional Record*. Next, he read from the executive summary of the Heritage paper and asked to have it reprinted in the *Congressional Record*.

Senator Hatch spoke next, noting that the ACA was a "terrible piece of legislation" from a policy perspective and should not be passed on that ground. "Perhaps more importantly, from the standpoint of the Constitution, we may not pass it." Hatch repeated his constitutional objections that Congress's power to regulate interstate commerce "has never crossed the line between regulating what people choose to do and ordering them to do it." Getting to the nub of the issue, Hatch concluded that, "[s]hould this legislation become law, there would be nothing that the federal government could not do."

Hatch continued: "We cannot ignore this question by simply punting it to the courts. . . . Speculating about how courts may decide a hypothetical case in the future, however, is no substitute for senators making a decision about an actual piece of legislation today." Regardless, "litigation is likely, to be sure, which means that the courts will be asked to decide certain legal questions, including whether this legislation is constitutional."

Senator Hutchison was next to speak. She raised an alternate constitutional point of order. She warned that her state would not take this law sitting down. Texas rarely does. "I have asked the attorney general of Texas to use every resource at his disposal to investigate the provisions in this legislation and to challenge any unconstitutional attempt to limit the authority of Texas." Indeed, plans were already under way to file suits in other states. As Senator Hutchison noted, "The attorney general of Texas is on it, just like the attorney general of South Carolina and probably many more by the time we will end this day."

As required by the rules, the chair submitted the question to the Senate for a vote. Senator Baucus rose to defend the ACA. The Finance Committee, he said, "gave a lot of thought to the constitutionality of the provisions . . . particularly under the Commerce Clause and the tax-and-spending powers of the Constitution." Baucus said that "it is very strongly our considered judgment, and that of many constitutional scholars who have looked at these provisions—and many articles have been put in the *Record* that clearly [show] these provisions are constitutional." Baucus found support for the law in both the commerce power and the taxing power.

The point of order was put to a vote: sixty nays, and thirty-nine yeas, on a straight party-line vote, with one Republican senator not present. The constitutional point of order was "not well-taken" and defeated. Although the point of constitutional order was defeated, it put every Republican senator on record objecting to the mandate's constitutionality. Most importantly, because the debates were broadcasted on C-SPAN and covered by the press, the issue of the mandate's constitutionality was then picked up by conservative talk radio and cable news and given wide play. What is sometimes called "popular constitutionalism" would now assert itself even before the Senate bill was approved by the House. And, between the Senate debate in December and House approval in March, lawsuits were prepared to be filed the moment Obamacare became law. For now, with the final vote on the bill imminent, Hatch and Ensign gazed longingly across First Street at the Supreme Court as their best and last hope.

THE SENATE VOTES

After months of debate in the Senate, the final vote was slated for December 24, 2009. The last time the Senate had met on Christmas Eve was in 1895. District Court Judge Roger Vinson, who would soon be asked to rule on the ACA, faulted the "haste with which the final version of the 2,700-page bill was rushed to the floor for a Christmas Eve vote."

To ensure that the senators would have time to get home for the holidays, the session began shortly after the break of dawn. As the sun was creeping above the horizon, Senate Minority Leader Mitch McConnell rose to address Vice President Biden, who was sitting as president of the Senate. "It is early and I will be brief. This debate was supposed to produce a bill that reformed health care in America. Instead, we are left with party-line votes in the middle of the night, a couple of sweetheart deals to get it over the finish line, and a truly outraged public. A problem they were told would be fixed wasn't. I guarantee you that the people who voted for this bill are going to get an earful when they finally get home for the first time since Thanksgiving. They know there is widespread opposition to this monstrosity. I want to assure you, Mr. President, this fight isn't over. In fact, this fight is long from over. My colleagues and I will work to stop this bill from becoming law. That is the clear will of the American people, and we are going to continue to fight on their behalf." Yet all of the Republicans' opposition tactics in the Senate had been exhausted.

On December 24, 2009, at 7:00 AM, the Senate would finally vote on the Affordable Care Act.

Senator Dick Durbin of Illinois said, "Mr. President, I ask for the yeas and nays." Vice President Biden replied, "Is there a sufficient second?" There was. Biden, an expert at parliamentary proceedings from his three decades in the Senate, grinned beatifically. "Shall the bill pass? The clerk will call the roll."

"The result was announced—yeas sixty, nays thirty-nine."

All Republicans voted "no." All Democrats and independents who caucused with the Democrats voted "aye." Delirious after round-the-clock debates, Senator Reid inadvertently voted "no" and, after some laughter, quickly changed his vote. At 7:15, Vice President Biden announced that the Affordable Care Act had passed the Senate.

President Obama had a very merry Christmas as he celebrated victory from his vacation home in Oahu, Hawaii. The ACA was on its way to becoming his primary legacy.

At this point, the finality of the Act seemed like manifest destiny. The House had secured the requisite 218 votes in an earlier vote. The Senate had secured 60 votes.

One of the sixty "aye" votes was that of Massachusetts Senator Paul Kirk, the former Democratic National Committee chairman who had been selected by Massachusetts governor Deval Patrick to fill the seat left vacant by Senator Kennedy's death. However, Kirk would not be the sixtieth vote for much longer. A special election was set to be held in the Bay State, the site of the original Tea Party in 1773.

SHUCKING THE CORNHUSKER KICKBACK

Before the bill had cleared the Senate, South Carolina Attorney General Henry McMaster, who was vying for the GOP gubernatorial nomination against Representative Nikki Haley, started to contact other states that might be interested in challenging the constitutionality of these kickbacks. Florida Attorney General Bill McCollum, who was also eyeing a gubernatorial run, agreed to join the effort. McCollum asked his deputy, Joe Jacquot, and Tim Osterhaus, Florida's deputy solicitor general, to begin researching whether the states could challenge not only the Medicaid funding but also the individual mandate.

On December 30, 2009, South Carolina Attorney General Henry McMaster wrote a letter to Speaker Pelosi and Majority Leader Reid on behalf of the attorneys general of thirteen states: Washington, Michigan, Texas, Colorado, Alabama, North Dakota, Virginia, Pennsylvania, Utah, Idaho, South Dakota, and Florida. The letter expressed "our grave concern" over a "provision that affords special treatment to the state of Nebraska under the federal Medicaid program. We believe this provision is constitutionally flawed. As chief legal officers of our states we are contemplating a legal challenge to this provision and we ask you to take action to render this challenge unnecessary by striking that provision." However, the letter only addressed the Cornhusker Kickback and did not mention the constitutionality of the individual mandate.

The letter was ghostwritten by David Rivkin, who was recommended to McMaster by his friend, South Carolina senator Lindsey Graham. Florida Attorney General Bill McCollum had also worked at the same firm as Rivkin. The day before, McCollum had sent McMaster a separate letter, based on Joe Jacquot's research. Instead of focusing solely on the Cornhusker Kickback, the letter asked McMaster to "join me in launching a full review of the constitutionality of the individual mandate and potential legal options for States to pursue on behalf of their citizens should this mandate become law." This letter focused more broadly on whether the mandate exceeded Congress's powers under the taxing and commerce powers. Indeed, at this point, only Florida had seen constitutional flaws beyond the Medicaid expansion provisions of the ACA. The purpose of McCollum's letter was to "stake Florida's claim" on this case. He closed it by stating his commitment "to pursuing any legal action necessary" to defend the constitutional rights of the "individuals who call Florida home." Shortly thereafter, twelve states would join Florida's effort.

Florida was beginning to dominate the litigation. Because it was the first state to take a position publicly on the constitutionality of the mandate rather than just the Medicaid function, it would soon take the lead as the challenge developed.

THE FORTY-FIRST VOTE

The special election to fill Senator Kennedy's seat was scheduled for January 19, 2010. The Democratic candidate, Martha Coakley, was Massachusetts' attorney general. Her challenger was a relatively un-known Republican state senator, Scott Brown. Seizing the Tea Party zeitgeist, Brown based his campaign on being the "forty-first vote" to kill the ACA.

However, to add another level of irony, Scott Brown had voted for Romneycare in 2006 as a state senator. Now he claimed, as Romney would, that he opposed the individual mandate being imposed na-tionwide by the federal government. Brown explained to conserva-tive talk radio host Sean Hannity, "Everyone is entitled to some form of insurance, but why do we need a one-size-fits-all?"

With Brown's impending election, Tom Daschle recalled, "the talks suddenly took on a greater sense of urgency." "It seemed that the Democrats were running out of time, sooner than they had ever expected." Reid had not intended the Christmas Eve vote to be the final vote on the bill. The Senate version of the ACA was merely in-tended to get sixty votes. The ultimate bill would then be written in a conference in the House. If Reid was to lose his sixtieth vote, how-ever, the Republicans could sustain a filibuster to whatever emerged from Conference. Daschle related that at a meeting with top Demo-crats from the Senate and the House, Obama said, "I'm looking at the possibility of losing my sixtieth vote next Tuesday. Can't you work this out?" In the Senate, the only option would be for the House to approve the Senate bill as-is, with its individual mandate supported only by Commerce Clause findings.

Backed by strong Tea Party support—and massive funding from conservatives who realized that a victory in Massachusetts could derail Obamacare—Brown beat Coakley by a margin of 52–47. Let's put this in perspective. In Massachusetts, one of the most liberal states in the Union, a state where a Republican governor had imposed an individual mandate five years earlier, a Republican opposing health care reform beat a Democrat to fill the Senate seat held by Ted Kennedy! This staggering feat was truly a sign of the times and a testament to the growing national opposition to Obamacare. In tracking polls from 2009 until 2012, and beyond, the popularity of the ACA never increased above 50 percent. The law was, and remains, very unpopular.

Daschle wrote that on election night "the health care reform effort seemed to collapse. Obama and the Democrats in Congress had been on the verge of making history, and they were closing in on the finish line. Now, the finish line had vanished." Massachusetts, the home of the original Tea Party in 1773, had propelled the modern Tea Party to the forty-first Senate vote. With Brown's victory, one Capitol Hill insider predicted confidently that Obamacare's demise was a "done deal."

On the same day as the special election, Florida Attorney General McCollum sent a letter to Harry Reid, Nancy Pelosi, Mitch McConnell, and John Boehner, explaining in detail why the ACA was unconstitutional, and how the states could challenge it. "Please find my analysis of the constitutionality of the individual mandate provision being considered in the federal health legislation attached. I call your attention to these legal concerns so that constitutional issues may be remedied before a final bill is negotiated." McCollum closed ominously. "I will continue to work with my Attorney General colleagues in order to pursue appropriate legal action should these provisions be in a bill that becomes law."

The race to the courthouses was on, and the leaders of Congress had been put on notice. McCollum stated in a press release, "If the individual mandate is in the final bill signed by the President, the States and citizens should pursue legal action to challenge it."

As the political and constitutional opposition to the law became stronger, the administration finally woke up to the need to defend it. On Friday, January 8, Brian Hauck (a senior counsel at the Justice Department) emailed Neal Katyal (the deputy solicitor general in the Department of Justice who was on leave from his position as a constitutional law professor at Georgetown). In a message titled "Health Care Defense," Attorney General Eric Holder, Hauck wrote, "wants to put together a group to get thinking about how to defend against inevitable challenges to the health care proposals that are pending, and hope[s] that the [Office of the Solicitor General] could participate. Could you figure out the right person or people for that? More the merrier. He is hoping to meet next week if we can."

Katyal replied, "Absolutely right on. Let's crush them. I'll speak with Elena [Kagan] and designate someone." Katyal forwarded that message to his boss, Solicitor General Elena Kagan, and wrote, "I am happy to do this if you are ok with it . . . or both of us." Three minutes later, Kagan replied, "You should do it." The future justice, a frontrunner for the next vacancy on the Supreme Court, was already sectioning herself off from what would become the most important case of the Roberts Court.

Two hours later, no doubt after some reflection to formulate the right response, Katyal replied to Hauck, "Elena would definitely like OSG [Office of the Solicitor General] to be involved in this set of issues. I will handle this myself, along with an Assistant from my office, and we will bring Elena in as needed."

The Justice Department held a meeting on January 13, 2010. It was attended by representatives from the Civil Division, the Office of Legal Counsel, and the Antitrust Department. Kagan was not present. The purpose of the meeting was to do some "anticipatory thinking about claims that will be asserted and how we will defend against them." Even at this early stage, the Civil Division had "already started" this process and was working on "produc[ing] some model briefs or memos."

The plan was for Ian Gershengorn—a deputy assistant attorney general in the Civil Division who would ultimately argue all of the cases in the district court—and Assistant Attorney General Tony West to "make a recommendation . . . on how to structure the process going forward." Katyal was included in this process and wrote in an email that "I want to make sure our office is heavily involved, even in the [district court litigation]." The government was already shoring up its defense.

Lawsuits Brewing

The same day, a mile away, at the National Press Club, South Carolina Attorney General Henry McMaster spoke with reporters about the constitutionality of the ACA. McMaster stated that he and twelve other state attorneys general were considering bringing a lawsuit to challenge the Cornhusker Kickback. Many of those present had an eye on higher office. Bill McCollum was running for governor of Florida. John Bruning of Nebraska was running for the Senate. Texas Attorney General Greg Abbott had his sights on the governor's mansion in Austin or perhaps the Senate. Unsurprisingly, they were all Republicans. During oral argument at the Supreme Court, Justice Antonin Scalia would quip, "I didn't take the time to figure this out, but maybe you did. Is there any chance that all twenty-six states opposing it have Republican governors, and all of the states supporting it have Democratic governors? Is that possible?" Attorney Paul Clement replied to his former boss, "There's a correlation, Justice Scalia."

When it became clear that the Senate bill would go back to the House, Florida began preparing its own lawsuit. In February, attorneys from Florida's Solicitor General's office, including Timothy Osterhaus, Charles B. Upton II, and Blaine Winship, began to draft what would become the first complaint challenging the constitutionality of the law.

At this point, Department of Justice emails reveal the government had the "expectation . . . that a bill could pass and be signed by mid-February." DOJ "could be in litigation soon after." Noting that the challengers were formidable, an internal email described "the possibility of both well-financed, sophisticated challenges, as well as numerous pro se and frivolous claims."

The main suit was to be filed by Florida on behalf of eleven other states: South Carolina, Nebraska, Texas, Utah, Louisiana, Michigan, Colorado, Pennsylvania, Washington, Idaho, and South Dakota. The Heritage Foundation had already been involved as the state attorneys general contacted Heritage for support and to "get their ducks in order." Todd Gaziano told me that it was "unusual that attorneys general were getting ready to file a constitutional case before [the legislation] is even passed."

However, Virginia, led by its aggressive attorney general, Ken Cuccinelli, broke off from the other states, determined to file its own suit. In his Tea Party–themed manifesto *The Last Line of Defense*, Cuccinelli wrote, "Once passage of the federal bill began to appear imminent in mid-March, Duncan Getchell, Wes Russell, my senior appellate counsel Steve McCullough, and I began to draft Virginia's formal complaint and to finalize our constitutional reasoning for challenging the new law."

The race to the courthouse was already under way.

THE STATE OF THE UNION

One week later, on January 21, 2010, in a 5–4 opinion by Justice Kennedy, the Supreme Court decided *Citizens United v. FEC*. The Court held that provisions of a campaign finance reform law could not be used to block a corporation from spending money within thirty days of an election to promote a documentary attacking Hillary Clinton. Perhaps fittingly, *Citizens United* was the first case that Elena Kagan argued before the Supreme Court as solicitor general. She lost. It was also the first case in which Justice Sonia Sotomayor voted on the Court. She also lost.

The *Citizens United* majority opinion rejected any narrow approach to the issue. Justice Kennedy wrote, "It is not judicial restraint to accept an unsound, narrow argument just so the Court can avoid another argument with broader implications. Indeed, a court would be remiss in performing its duties were it to accept an unsound principle merely to avoid the necessity of making a broader ruling."

Chief Justice Roberts, who had promised during his confirmation hearings to be a neutral umpire and who aimed to strengthen the institutional reputation of the Court, wrote to moderate the majority's approach. "I write separately to address the important principles of judicial restraint." Though Roberts agreed that the law was unconstitutional, he sought to identify factors with which to limit the power of judicial review. "There is a difference between judicial restraint and judicial abdication." Continuing, Roberts cited his judicial icon, the legendary Chief Justice John Marshall: when constitutional questions are "indispensably necessary" to resolving the case at hand, "the Court must meet and decide them." But when the constitutional question is not "indispensably necessary," he urged his fellow justices to avoid answering it. Twenty months later, Roberts's fidelity to this principle would be tested.

Citizens United proved to be a lightning rod of controversy. MSNBC pundit Keith Olbermann said that *Citizens United* "might actually have more dire implications than *Dred Scott*," the infamous 1857 opinion in which Chief Justice Roger Taney stated that African Americans had "no rights which the white man was bound to respect."

Six days later, on January 27, the president delivered his State of the Union Address to an audience that included Chief Justice Roberts and Justices Kennedy, Ginsburg, Breyer, Sotomayor, and Alito. Justices Scalia and Thomas stayed home, as is their custom. Justice Scalia labeled the address a "juvenile spectacle." Justice Thomas said he could not tolerate "the catcalls, the whooping and hollering and under-the-breath comments." (All nine of the justices had been absent from the 2000 State of the Union—there is speculation that they did not attend owing to President Clinton's impeachment, though Justice Breyer, who has near-perfect attendance, was reportedly sick.) Chief Justice Roberts also had concerns about the separation-of-powers implications of the justices attending. "I'm not sure why we are there," he said. "The image of having the members of one branch of government standing up, literally surrounding the Supreme Court, cheering and hollering while the Court, according to the requirements of protocol, has to sit there expressionless, I think, is very troubling."

During the address, Obama tried to gin up support for his health care law, which at the time was drifting. "I didn't choose to tackle this issue to get some legislative victory under my belt. And by now it should be fairly obvious that I didn't take on health care because it was good politics. I took on health care because of the stories I've heard from Americans . . . who've been denied coverage." Later, Obama chose to address the Supreme Court in response to the *Citizens United* ruling. With the justices sitting right in front of him, Obama began, "With all due deference to separation of powers. . . . " He continued: "Last week the Supreme Court reversed a century of law." The camera shot of the audience zoomed in to focus on the justices. Obama said that the decision in *Citizens United* would "open the floodgates for special interests." Decorum dictates that the justices show no reaction to what is said, but for one justice, the president had gone too far.

In response to the president's comments, Justice Alito cringed, shook his head no, and seemed to mouth, *Not true*. The other justices sat stoically stone-faced. Later, Justice Alito would comment that the State of the Union Address is a "very political event" and "very awkward." "We have to sit there like the proverbial potted plant most of the time."

Alito would join Scalia and Thomas by watching subsequent addresses at home—or not at all. Though Chief Justice Roberts has referred to the event as a "political pep rally," he has not missed a State of the Union during his tenure.

Still focused on the Supreme Court, Obama said that the *Citizens United* decision would allow "foreign corporations to spend without limit in our elections." The chamber boomed in applause, and there was a standing ovation. The camera panned back to Alito, who had continued to shake his head. Attorney General Holder, standing paces away, clapped loudly. "I don't think American elections should be bankrolled by America's most powerful interests, or worse, by foreign entities." Another standing ovation for the president. "They should be decided by the American people." By implication, Obama was saying that the issue should not have been decided by the Supreme Court. In other words, the justices should have deferred to the democratic process and Congress's judgments. Obama concluded, "I'd urge Democrats and Republicans to pass a bill that helps to correct some of these problems."

Of course, an act of Congress could not reverse the effects of a constitutional decision like *Citizens United*—the former constitutional-law-lecturer-in-chief knew that. Only a constitutional amendment would suffice. But Obama shrewdly tapped into his base. This speech was the beginning of a campaign to influence the public. Perhaps the president, whose administration was already planning to defend the ACA—they had held a strategic meeting days earlier—was putting the justices on notice that he would not tolerate an activist court thwarting his agenda.

Professor and legal affairs commentator Jeffrey Rosen made a prescient comment at the time. "It's a relief to see former Professor Obama having the nerve to stand up for judicial restraint and to criticize the conservative justices to their faces. If the justices don't take the criticism to heart, they're headed toward a full-blown confrontation with the White House and Congress that won't end well for the Court." Less than two years later, the Court would have to confront this issue head-on. Chief Justice Roberts, who showed no emotion at the time, no doubt understood the significance of this clash.

MASTER OF THE HOUSE

Once Senate Democrats lost their sixtieth vote, Senate Majority Leader Harry Reid could not pass any new versions of the reform bill—especially after he chose to bypass debate and to rely on the sixty-vote caucus to block any filibusters. Many Democrats considered scaling back and trying for more modest reform. But the president was not ready to call it quits on his "legacy." The easiest solution was for the House to simply pass the Senate bill. However, the House did not have the votes because members did not like many of its provisions.

At one juncture, the Democrats considered using a procedure known as "deem and pass" (pejoratively pronounced as *demon pass*) to get the law through. In effect, members of the House would be voting on a rule that would pass the Senate bill automatically, without actually voting on that bill. After encountering massive opposition, however, Speaker Pelosi abandoned this idea.

Rather than "deem and pass," House Democrats devised a different parliamentary maneuver. They would vote on the bill that had already passed the Senate, with amendments, in such a way to avoid sending it back to the Senate for another full vote. First, the House would pass the Senate bill, along with a separate act containing a number of "fixes" that remedied the problems that House Democrats had with the Senate bill. Among the fixes were eliminating the Cornhusker Kickback and Louisiana Purchase. Second, the president would be able to sign that bill, as it had cleared both the House and the Senate. Third, *after* the president had signed it into law, the Senate would pass a reconciliation bill accepting the changes in the House's other bill. Critically, under Senate rules, a "reconciliation" would require only fifty-one votes rather than sixty. Then the president would sign the bill, which had separately passed both houses, into law. In this way a House–Senate conference would be avoided, and the Senate would not need to revisit the ACA. The strategy was set.

Now Pelosi, the master of the House, had to once again find 218 votes. As the March 21 vote approached, "Blue Dog" Democrats and other centrists began to fall in line. Yet many pro-life Democrats were balking. On the suggestion of Chief of Staff Rahm Emanuel, the president offered pro-life representative Bart Stupak and his colleagues an executive order clarifying that ACA funding could not be used for abortions. Stupak and other pro-life Representatives originally rejected Obama's draft order, calling it "flowery and meaningless." At the time, columnist Tim Carney called Stupak "perhaps the single most important rank-and-file House member in passing the bill." Stupak sent back a revised version, which White House lawyers incorporated into the final version. Yet, Stupak's vote remained up in the air until the very end.

Deputy Solicitor General Neal Katyal wrote to the assistant attorney general about the "inevitable challenges to this litigation." "Now that this may be coming back with the votes in place, I wanted to circle back and see if you are still developing such a litigation group." The government was ready for the imminent challenge.

ONE DAY MORE

On Saturday, May 20, 2010, the day before the decisive vote in the House, the Tea Party arrived again in Washington, D.C. On very short notice, more than sixty Tea Party groups had rounded up over sixty thousand protesters who marched on Capitol Hill.

By chance, I was in Washington that weekend and went to Capitol Hill to take in the sights. Thousands of Tea Partiers lined the streets around the Capitol and near the House office buildings, alternating between chanting, "Kill the bill," and taunting Speaker Pelosi by slowly repeating, "Nancy" (similar to Bart Simpson's taunts of Mets legend Darryl Strawberry). One protester, who saw me taking pictures of the protest while wearing a suit, was convinced I worked for a Democratic member of Congress. Unbeknownst to me, Randy Barnett and his wife were also there.

With the final vote still up in the air, President Obama flew from the White House to Capitol Hill aboard Marine One—no doubt looking down, figuratively and literally, on the massive protests below—to make one final push to pass the bill.

After I finished taking some pictures of the Tea Party rally, I walked past the Supreme Court and ventured into the Capitol Visitor Center. The center—a museum, theater, and meeting space built underneath the Capitol—is a classic Washington boondoggle. Ground was broken in 2000, with an estimated budget of $71 million and a completion time of 2004. It would not actually be finished until 2008, at a cost of over $600 million—and not without even more controversy. The Visitor Center had erroneously chiseled into stone that the national motto is "E. Pluribus Unum," Latin for "from many, one." In fact, the national motto is "In God We Trust." Many conservative politicians, led by Senator Jim DeMint, objected to the Visitor Center's failure to "appropriately honor our religious heritage that has been critical to America's success." Since DeMint's criticism, the motto had been changed.

Shortly after I arrived, I was hastily asked to leave. I was not told why. But, as I was walking out, I saw a huge commotion and many people in suits quickly blocking all points of entry. I would later learn that President Obama had touched down on Marine One and was making his way to the Visitor Center to make one final push for Congress to enact the ACA. The entire Democratic caucus was assembling in the Visitor Center right as I was leaving.

Obama had given the pep talk many times before and did not need notes. He appealed directly to those still on the fence. "Now, I still know this is a tough vote, though. I know this is a tough vote. I've talked to many of you individually. And I have to say that if you honestly believe in your heart of hearts, in your conscience, that this is not an improvement over the status quo . . . then you should vote no on this bill." Yet he implored the legislators to do the right thing for America. "But if you agree that the system is not working for ordinary families, if you've heard the same stories that I've heard everywhere, all across the country, then help us fix this system. Don't do it for me. Don't do it for Nancy Pelosi or Harry Reid. Do it for all those people out there who are struggling."

The president also told his fellow Democrats that he thought their vote for the ACA would be pragmatic as well as principled. "I am actually confident—I've talked to some of you individually—that it will end up being the smart thing to do politically because I believe that good policy is good politics." Obama's forecast that this vote would be good politics proved inaccurate—many Democrats would lose their seats in 2010, largely owing to their ACA vote, and Nancy Pelosi would become the leader of the Democratic minority.

Obama closed with an impassioned plea. "It is in your hands. It is time to pass health care reform for America, and I am confident that you are going to do it tomorrow." The president left the podium to a rousing round of applause.

Pelosi emerged from the Visitor Center, choosing to wade through the crowd rather than take the underground passage reserved for members of Congress. Undeterred, and likely emboldened, by the raucous Tea Party protesters, Pelosi linked arms with John Lewis and Steny Hoyer to march across the street to the Capitol, proudly bearing a large gavel that was used during the debates over the creation of Medicare in 1965. It was a staged photo-op meant to evoke memories of a civil rights march of the 1960s. Lewis claimed he heard a protester hurl a racial slur at him, and Representative Emanuel Cleaver claimed he was spit on by a protester. (There is no known video of such events.)

The House had the votes for the Senate version of the ACA, and the Senate had the votes for the House's reconciliation bill. It was full steam ahead for the ACA. The vote was set for Sunday, March 21, 2010. One day more, another day, another destiny for the president.

At 11:39 AM, about a mile down Pennsylvania Avenue at the Department of Justice, Solicitor General Elena Kagan, the former dean at Harvard Law School, watched the developments with rapt attention and replied to an email to her former colleague, Harvard law professor Laurence Tribe.

Tribe was a huge fan of Kagan. In May 2009, he had written a letter to President Obama, another one of his former students (as was Chief Justice Roberts), urging him to select Kagan as a replacement for the retiring Justice David H. Souter. Tribe lavished praise on Kagan. "I can't think of anyone nearly as strong as Elena Kagan, whose combination of intellectual brilliance and political skill would make her a 10-strike, if you'll forgive my reference to bowling. . . . A scholar of the first rank and a star as a teacher . . . [Kagan combines] personal modesty with an appealing public persona and would project a well-grounded image of justice as fairness and of law as codified common sense." Tribe noted that Kagan's skills as dean of the

Harvard Law School would translate well to the Supreme Court. "Her techniques . . . for gently but firmly persuading" others "with a light touch and with an open mind" are "precisely the techniques I can readily envision her employing" with all the justices.

The subject of Tribe's message to Kagan was "fingers and toes crossed today!" Kagan replied, with gusto, "I hear they have the votes, Larry!!" Two exclamation points, for extra emphasis. She continued, "Simply Amazing." At 5:06 PM, as the vote was about to proceed in the house, Tribe replied, "So health care is basically done! Remarkable."

An hour later, Associate Attorney General Tom Perrelli sent an email to a number of Justice Department attorneys, including Ian Gershengorn, who would argue all of the Health Care Cases in the district courts, and Deputy Solicitor General Neal Katyal, who would argue the cases in the courts of appeals. Perrelli called for a meeting "with some of the health care policy team tomorrow at 4 to help us prepare for litigation." He asked for everyone's information quickly, as the White House "wants it tonight, if possible."

In the Department of Justice, the Civil Division is responsible for litigating cases at the trial level and has "final sign-off unless the attorney general overrules it," one DOJ lawyer told me. The Appellate Division and the solicitor general are involved, but at first they take a back seat. The solicitor general has a "voice, but not a vote." At 6:19 PM, Katyal forwarded the invitation to Kagan and wrote, "This is the first I've heard of this. I think you should go, no? I will, regardless, but feel like this is litigation of singular importance."

One minute later, at 6:20 PM, without hesitation, Kagan replied: "What's your phone number?" At 6:22 PM, Katyal replied with his phone number and no other text. Kagan would not discuss this matter of "singular importance" over email, where a future Freedom of Information Act request could reveal it. Kagan, who was on many short lists for the next Supreme Court vacancy, made the conscious decision not to be involved with what would be the most important case of the Roberts Court—a case she knew she could likely hear as a justice. Kagan would never publicly offer any rationale for why she walled herself off from this case.

Later that night, at 11:04 PM, moments before the final vote, Kagan responded to Tribe's request for dinner. She could "do April 12."

Two months later, President Obama would appoint Kagan to replace the retiring Justice John Paul Stevens. During her confirmation hearings, Kagan made clear that she was not involved in the health care litigation. However, these email threads would soon become the basis for calls for Kagan to recuse herself.

Meanwhile, on March 21 at 3:00 PM, mere hours before the final vote, Obama called Bart Stupak, the pivotal pro-life vote, and agreed to his terms. The president told him, "We have a deal." Obama had accepted the executive order that Stupak wanted (and had largely drafted). The votes were secured.

At a press conference later that day with other pro-life representatives, Stupak, who claimed he "stood on principle," told reporters: "With the help of the president [we can] respect the sanctity of life." To Stupak, providing access to health care "was a principle that meant more to us."

But Tea Party representative Jean Schmidt said that the executive order from the president "is not worth the paper it is printed on . . . it is not the law of the land." It "can be rescinded in the blink of an eye by that jot of the president's pen." Hours after Stupak reached this compromise, Tribe emailed Kagan, expressing incredulity that the ACA was about to be passed "with the Stupak group accepting the magic of what amounts to a signing statement on steroids!" Tribe stated the obvious, and what any first-year constitutional law student would know—that Schmidt was right. The president's signing statement with respect to abortion was legally impotent.

As a result, the Susan B. Anthony List, a prominent pro-life organization, revoked its "Defender of Life" award for Stupak. A few months later, Stupak would announce his retirement from Congress. He left in January 2011. But Stupak had played his role in history.

The Final Countdown

The day of the final vote arrived. House Minority Leader John Boehner, who would soon become Speaker of the House—largely because of the voter backlash against the ACA—rose to speak.

"Today this body, this institution, enshrined in the first article of the Constitution by our Founding Fathers as a sign of the importance they placed on this House, should be looking with pride on this legislation and our work. But it is not so. My colleagues, this is the People's House. When we came here, we each swore an oath to uphold and abide by the Constitution as representatives of the people. But the process here is broken. . . . And as a result, this bill is not what the American people need nor what our constituents want."

The Republicans failed to stop the ACA in the executive branch when they lost the 2008 presidential election. They failed to stop the ACA in the legislative branch when they won neither house in the 2008 election. There was only one branch left. Representative Tom McClintock from California looked across the street at the U.S. Supreme Court, where Tea Party protesters were still rallying outside. Chants of "Kill the bill" continued to rain down on Independence Avenue. On the House floor, McClintock said, "Fortunately, the Constitution still protects our freedom from such usurpations. It will fall to the Supreme Court to hold this act accountable to the Constitution, and it will fall to 'We the People' to hold those responsible for it accountable at the polls."

Two years later, Justice Kagan would look back across the other side of First Street, recognizing the difficult process by which the law had been passed. "I mean, we have never suggested that we're going to say, look, this legislation was a brokered compromise, and we're going to try to figure out exactly what would have happened in the complex parliamentary shenanigans that go on across the street and figure out whether they would have made a difference." Soon enough, this congressionally brokered compromise, guided behind the scenes by President Obama, would rest before the highest court in the land.

As the vote began in the House at 9:45 PM, a tired Pelosi urged everyone "to complete the great unfinished business of our society and pass health insurance reform for all Americans that is a right and not a privilege." Outside, Boehner gave a rousing speech to the Tea Party protesters. But at that point it was too late.

The pivotal 216th vote was cast at 10:45 PM. The bill passed with 220 votes by 11:30 PM. Thirty-nine Democrats crossed the aisle to vote against the law. Not a single Republican voted for it. With the same gavel used during the passage of Medicaid, Speaker Pelosi closed the session and declared victory.

Tom Daschle recalled that the president and vice president watched the final vote from the Roosevelt Room in the West Wing. "As the 216th vote registered on the screen, Obama, with a look of immense satisfaction and relief, turned to Biden and applauded." As the loquacious vice president would say the next day when the president was introduced at the White House to sign the ACA, this was "a big fucking deal."

At midnight the president gave a victory proclamation:

> Tonight, after nearly 100 years of talk and frustration, after decades of trying, and a year of sustained effort and debate, the United States Congress finally declared that America's workers and America's families and America's small businesses deserve the security of knowing that here, in this country, neither illness nor accident should endanger the dreams they've worked a lifetime to achieve. . . . In the end, what this day represents is another stone firmly laid in the foundation of the American Dream. Tonight, we answered the call of history as so many generations of Americans have before us. When faced with crisis, we did not shrink from our challenge—we overcame it. We

did not avoid our responsibility—we embraced it. We did not
fear our future—we shaped it.

Minutes after the president signed the Affordable Care Act into
law early the next morning, the opening salvo of the legal battle
commenced.

PART III

Regulating Inactivity

(March 24, 2010–January 31, 2011)

The first round in the challenge to Obamacare would be waged in federal district courts in Virginia and Florida. Moments after President Obama signed the Affordable Care Act into law on March 23, 2010, lawsuits were filed across the country. Over the course of the next year, twenty-eight states confronted the federal government over whether the individual mandate could compel people to purchase health insurance—or broccoli.

THE BATTLE HAD ALREADY BEGUN

President Obama's signing ceremony for the ACA was scheduled for March 23, 2010. But by then, the campaign to repeal it had already started. On March 22, at 9:24 AM—roughly nine hours after the ACA passed the House and before the president signed the law—presidential candidate Mitt Romney published an article in the *National Review Online* titled "The Campaign Begins Today," in which he charged Congress with "an unconscionable abuse of power." He faulted Obama's bill, which he called "unhealthy for America. It raises taxes . . . [and] the act should be repealed." Of course, Romney's inability to challenge Obama's health insurance mandate due to his advocacy of a similar mandate in Massachusetts ultimately weakened his ability to run for president. Romney was the worst conceivable candidate to challenge Obama on one of the most significant domestic issues of 2012.

The day before, the House and Senate of the Virginia General Assembly passed the Virginia Health Care Freedom Act, which had first been introduced in December 2009. This law stated that citizens of Virginia could not be forced to purchase health insurance. Virginia's attorney general could sue the federal government to ensure that the state statute was enforced. Meanwhile, lawyers in the Florida Attorney General's office were putting the finishing touches on the complaint that would be filed on behalf of thirteen states.

Back in Washington, the administration was bracing for the storm and shoring up its defenses. On March 18, 2010, Neal Katyal, Elena Kagan's deputy, emailed the associate to Attorney General Eric Holder, Tom Perrelli, and commented on a pending complaint by Landmark Legal Foundation, a group operated by popular talk radio host Mark Levin. The complaint was "clearly written to be filed" right away. Katyal wrote, "We could be in court very soon. In light of this, for what it is worth, my advice (I haven't discussed this with Elena, but am cc'ing her here) would be that we start assembling a response, so that we have it ready to go. They obviously have their piece ready to go, and I think it'd be great if we are ahead of the ball game here." Kagan, although copied on this message, did not reply.

Everyone was simply waiting for the ink to dry from the president's pen.

At the White House on the morning of March 23, President Obama emerged to thundering applause and chants of "Fired up, ready to go." Reveling in the moment and glowing with pride, he told everyone, "Today, after almost a century of trying; today, after over a year of debate; today, after all the votes have been tallied—health insurance reform becomes law in the United States of America. . . . And we have now enshrined, as soon as I sign this bill, the core principle that everybody should have some basic security when it comes to their health care. And it is an extraordinary achievement that has happened because of all of you and all the advocates all across the country." He had secured his "legacy." Or so he thought.

The southpaw president sat down to sign the bill, using twenty-two different commemorative pens. Standing in front of a throng of admirers and supporters, Obama joked, "This is going to take a little while. I've got to use every pen, so it's going to take a really long time. I didn't practice." He paused to reflect and then said, "When I sign this bill, all of the overheated rhetoric over reform will finally confront the reality of reform."

The president could not have been more wrong. Minutes after the Affordable Care Act was signed into law, in Richmond, Virginia, and Pensacola, Florida, another two-year front in the battle over Obamacare would erupt. On March 24, 2010, at an event in Iowa City, Iowa, the day after he signed the ACA into law, the president mocked attacks on the law. "If they want to have that fight, I welcome that fight." This was President Obama's version of President George W. Bush's "bring 'em on" comment. Obama continued: "I don't believe the American people are going to put the insurance industry back in the driver's seat. We've been there already and we're not going back," he said.

The Department of Justice was ready to wage that fight. That day Tom Perrelli, Ian Gershengorn, and Beth Brinkmann hosted a "nationwide conference call" with all of the chiefs in the Civil Division. The battle had begun.

THE SUNSHINE CASE

Florida, representing twelve other states, was the first to file. Initially, the Sunshine State had trouble uploading the complaint to the federal courts' notoriously unreliable electronic filing system. Florida Attorney General Bill McCollum had to wait "seven agonizing minutes" before the documents were properly filed. But they were first—and beat Virginia by eleven minutes.

The complaint, which had been drafted in February before the law even cleared the House, boldly stated that the ACA "represents an unprecedented encroachment on the liberty of individuals living in the Plaintiffs' respective states, by mandating that all citizens and legal residents of the United States have qualifying healthcare coverage or pay a tax penalty." The complaint also challenged the expansion of Medicaid, arguing that it "represents an unprecedented encroachment on the sovereignty of the states." David B. Rivkin Jr. and Lee A. Casey were listed as "of counsel" on the complaint. They had been formally retained on March 19, 2010, right before the complaint was filed, for a fee not to exceed $50,000.

Florida Attorney General Bill McCollum made the decision to file in federal court in Pensacola rather than in Tallahassee, the court closest to his office. Robert Weiner, who at the time served as the associate deputy attorney general at the Department of Justice, later criticized this politicized forum shopping. "Bypassing the federal courthouse only six blocks from his office in Tallahassee, the Florida attorney general sued more than two hundred miles away in Pensacola, a jurisdiction that had no connection to any party or any issue in the case. What it had was a bench of three federal district court judges, all conservatives appointed by Republican presidents."

The choice of forum was actually more complicated and was "one of the last decisions" made. Initially, Greg Abbott, the attorney general of Texas, wanted to file in Texas, reasoning that the Fifth Circuit Court of Appeals, which includes Texas, would be more favorable to the challenge. At the time, Texas was the second state in the suit. Indeed, during the hiatus between passage of the bill in the Senate and the House, and before joining with Florida and the other states,

Abbott and his solicitor general, James Ho, had privately reached out to discuss their legal options with Randy Barnett. Florida quickly asserted control. An attorney from Florida told me that they had to "tussle with Texas," which was trying to "move on this issue before us." Texas grew "very frustrated by how Florida was commandeering the entire project," but "ultimately yielded to Florida. Some lawyers were convinced that filing in federal court in the District of Columbia would be ideal, as the D.C. Circuit was best suited for this challenge." The Florida attorney general, who had taken the lead in the case, decided that Florida would be ideal, as it didn't make sense for them to litigate in another state. The question of where to file in Florida proved more difficult.

The Attorney General's office is located in Tallahassee, which is situated in the Northern District of Florida. This court had divisions in Pensacola, Gainesville, and Tallahassee. Attorney General McCollum decided against filing in Tallahassee because he and his staff had grown "very frustrated" with that court's chief judge, Robert Lewis Hinkle, who was appointed by President Clinton in 1996.

If the action was filed in Tallahassee, McCollum thought that Hinkle could assign the case to whomever he wanted. Under the local practice, a case filed in Gainesville could be pulled to Tallahassee. A senior attorney in the office told me that McCollum, concerned with how this big and political case "might be handled before Hinkle," decided that filing in Pensacola would be ideal.

One attorney said that McCollum "knows his benches," but said it was "horseshit" that the attorney general picked Pensacola based on the political affiliation of the judges. But in response to a question about the affiliations of the judges, another lawyer from Florida told me, coyly, "We knew where judges come from." Be that as it may, the three judges in Pensacola had been appointed by Republican presidents. Judge Margaret Rodgers was appointed by President George W. Bush in 2003. Judge Lacey Collier was appointed by President

George H. W. Bush in 1991. And most importantly, Judge Roger Vinson was appointed by President Ronald Reagan in 1983. The case was assigned to Judge Vinson.

However, there was one serious defect with Florida's initial complaint. It was brought only on behalf of the states, not on behalf of any individual people. The individual mandate did not operate on the states—it operated on individuals. That Florida later remedied this problem and Virginia did not would distinguish the fates of these two cases.

Virginia Is for Lawyers

Virginia's complaint was filed eleven minutes after Florida's. Two years later, at a Tea Party rally on the eve of the Supreme Court's hearing of the ACA case, Virginia Attorney General Ken Cuccinelli reminisced about the historic timing of the lawsuit. Speaking in front of a Gadsden flag that proclaimed, DON'T TREAD ON ME, Cuccinelli spoke to the crowd on a rainy day across the street from the Supreme Court. "Yesterday was the second anniversary of the president signing the bill." There was a smattering of boos. "That's the bad news. The good news is, yesterday was the 237th anniversary of Patrick Henry's, 'Give me liberty or give me death' speech. And he gave that speech at St. John's Church in Richmond on Broad Street. Two years ago in the same city, seventeen blocks west of the same street, is where we filed the first lawsuit filed by any state that got the individual mandate declared unconstitutional."

Though Cuccinelli would be the first to score a legal victory, his decision to break off from the other states was controversial. An attorney with the Florida Attorney General's office described Virginia's interests as "very insular" and suggested that Cuccinelli, who had his eyes set on the 2013 gubernatorial race, was guided by his own "ambition." David Rivkin said there was "anger towards Cuccinelli for going his own way." Cuccinelli would later write in *The Last Line of Defense*, "While we fully supported the Florida lawsuit, the venue to defend a Virginia law was rightly a federal court in Virginia, not in Florida." However, it was his insistence on defending the Virginia law that led to a decisive loss in court.

Moments after the Virginia suit was filed on March 23, 2010, it was assigned to Senior Judge Robert E. Payne, who had been appointed to the court by President George H. W. Bush on May 12, 1992, and who took senior status (a form of semi-retirement for judges with lifetime tenure) on May 7, 2007. Payne promptly disqualified himself from hearing Virginia's case. "The undersigned recuses himself from presiding over this action. It is hereby ORDERED that the clerk reassign this action to another judge in accord with the standard assignment system. It is so ordered." Judge Payne offered no reason why he decided not to hear the case.

Shortly thereafter, the case was "reassigned by [the] standard assignment system." Fate took its cue, and the historical role of presiding over this landmark case fell to District Judge Henry E. Hudson. Hudson, most famous for sentencing NFL quarterback Michael Vick for his involvement in dogfighting, would become the first judge to find the ACA unconstitutional.

On March 24, 2010, Virginia governor Bob McDonnell, then viewed as a potential 2012 presidential candidate, signed the Virginia Health Care Freedom Act into law. The ACA, he said, was "an unprecedented federal mandate on individuals that we believe violates the U.S. Constitution. The Virginia Health Care Freedom Act sets as the policy of the Commonwealth that no individual, with several specific exceptions, can be required to purchase health insurance coverage."

Flanking McDonnell at the press conference was Cuccinelli, whose next comment spelled the ultimate fate of his lawsuit. "The traditional role of the attorney general is to defend Virginia's laws. It is now my job to vigorously defend this law from the federal government's overreach of the Constitution and its attempted encroachment on the rights of Virginians." With perhaps the slightest bit of irony concerning a suit over the individual mandate, Cuccinelli closed, "That is my *mandate,* and that is my promise to our citizens [emphasis added]." The case in court was styled, *Commonwealth of Virginia Ex Rel. Kenneth T. Cuccinelli, II, in his official capacity as Attorney General of Virginia, v. Kathleen Sebelius.*

Under our Constitution, federal laws are the supreme law of the land and trump, or preempt, any conflicting state law. In effect, the Virginia Health Care Freedom Act aimed to create a conflict with the federal law that would give it standing to assert in federal court that Congress had exceeded its powers under the Constitution. Only an act of Congress consistent with the Constitution is "supreme." During the press conference, Virginia lieutenant governor Bill Bolling, who at the time was presumed to be the next Republican candidate for governor (but in 2013 he would step aside and acquiesce to Cuccinelli's candidacy) put it succinctly: the VHCFA "sent a strong message that [Virginia wants] no part of this national fiasco."

Virginia has a long, but mixed, history of resisting the imposition of federal laws. On one hand, in 1798 the Virginia Resolution, authored secretly by James Madison, along with the Kentucky Resolution, penned secretly by Thomas Jefferson, stated that the Alien and Sedition Acts were unconstitutional because they exceeded the enumerated powers of Congress and violated the first amendment's protection of the freedom of speech. The resolutions stressed that the Alien and Sedition Acts applied to citizens, but not the states. Virginia and Kentucky were "interposing" their opinion that the law was unconstitutional, and urging other states to join them in expressing this view (but none did). On the other hand, during the period leading up to the Civil War, many Southerners who supported slavery, most prominently South Carolina senator John C. Calhoun, built on these resolutions to develop the Doctrine of Nullification: "the right

of a State to interpose, in the last resort, in order to arrest an unconstitutional act of the General Government, within its limits." Here,
however, rather than purport to "nullify" the ACA, Virginia went to
federal court to assert its constitutional claim.

Nevertheless, the Democratic Party of Virginia compared the
state resistance to the ACA to the "massive resistance" to civil rights
legislation during the 1960s. Linda Greenhouse would write in the
Opinionator blog of the *New York Times* that "a few weeks shy of the
[151st] anniversary of Virginia's 'ordinance of secession' [on April 17,
1861], the Commonwealth of Virginia seceded from the reach of the
federal health care law's individual mandate."

However, hanging all hope on the Virginia Health Care Freedom
Act inflicted on Virginia's case one incurable defect. No private parties joined the suit. Members from a conservative beltway think tank
met with Attorney General Cuccinelli in March 2010, after the complaint was filed, and urged him strongly to add private plaintiffs. At
Cuccinelli's request, the Cato Institute provided him with a fifteen-
page memo to the same effect. He "stubbornly refused." With his eyes
set on getting to the Supreme Court, Cuccinelli would not accept
any delays. An attorney from the Florida Attorney General's office
told me that it soon became a "competition of who would get the
case to the Supreme Court first. It didn't take long to realize where
it was going." This was Cuccinelli's goal. Indeed, at a hearing on June
3, 2010, Judge Hudson asked Duncan Getchell, one of Cuccinelli's
deputies, if he "intend[ed] to file an amended complaint" and add
individual plaintiffs. Getchell reaffirmed Cuccinelli's strategy: "We do
not intend to file an amended complaint." The think-tankers saw an
"unfortunate train wreck" coming with this "more pedestrian" case.

Regardless of its ultimate legal merit, Cuccinelli's suit played a
pivotal role in advancing the challenge when Judge Henry Hudson
ruled that the ACA exceeded the commerce power of Congress. That
ruling, by a single district court judge, changed the entire discourse

surrounding the case. Immediately after the ruling, Yale law professor Jack Balkin fired off an email to his adversary and longtime friend, Randy Barnett. It read, "Your argument is officially not frivolous." For the first time, Obamacare supporters started to worry. And Judge Hudson's ruling made it that much easier for any other judge to rule the same way—as one soon would. Perhaps fittingly, Judge Hudson's opinion accepting the Commonwealth's argument came one week shy of the 212th anniversary of James Madison's Virginia Resolution of 1798.

Without an individual plaintiff, however, Cuccinelli's suit would ultimately be dismissed by the court of appeals for its fatal defect. The Fourth Circuit Court of Appeals took critical note of "the timing of the VHCFA, along with the statements accompanying its passage" at the press conference. Those statements "make clear that Virginia officials enacted the statute for precisely [the purpose of declaring] Virginia's opposition to a federal insurance mandate." As the court noted, "In doing so, the VHCFA reflects no exercise of 'sovereign power,' for Virginia lacks the sovereign authority to *nullify federal law* [emphasis added]." Of course, this had not been Virginia's theory. By this route, the Fourth Circuit was able to avoid the constitutional issue that Judge Hudson had reached, a strategy of avoidance that would tempt other lower court judges as well.

THE LIMITING PRINCIPLE

On November 8, 1994, the Supreme Court heard oral argument in *United States v. Lopez*. This case considered whether Congress had the power to ban possession of firearms within a school zone. For nearly six decades, since *Wickard v. Filburn* held that Congress could regulate wheat grown on a farm that never leaves the farm (let alone the state), most academics had assumed the Commerce Clause gave Congress essentially complete power to accomplish whatever legitimate ends the government desired. *Lopez* would radically challenge that dogma.

During argument in the case, President Clinton's solicitor general, Drew Days, was repeatedly pressed by the justices' questions about what limitations existed on Congress's commerce power. Chief Justice William Rehnquist said that the commerce power "is not limitless." Justice Sandra Day O'Connor stated, "Well, but there ought to be limits within the Commerce Clause itself." Yet Days refused to answer their questions. Ever the skilled advocate, he tap-danced around the questions and would not say what limits the government conceded that existed on their own power. Trying to throw Days a lifeline, Justice Ruth Bader Ginsburg asked him clearly, "What are the limits, then?" Days still would not latch on. "Well, I'm perhaps left to repeat myself in some respects. This Court has never said that there are absolute limits to the exercise of the commerce power." In 1994, that was the wrong answer.

The Supreme Court rejected his expansive view of the Commerce Clause. In a 5–4 opinion by Chief Justice Rehnquist, the Court found that because the act of possessing a gun in a school zone was not economic activity, it was beyond the reach of Congress, even if it did have a "substantial effect on interstate commerce." Rehnquist wrote, "Under the theories that the Government presents . . . it is difficult to perceive *any limitation* on federal power [emphasis added]." Without offering a limiting principle, the government could not prevail. This case represented the first time in six decades that the Court found that Congress lacked power to enact a law under its powers to regulate interstate commerce. By drawing a line between "economic" and "noneconomic" intrastate activity—with the latter outside the power of Congress—the Rehnquist Court sent shock waves through the legal system.

Sitting in the Court that fateful November morning, watching Solicitor General Days unsuccessfully bob and weave away from the justices' questions about the Commerce Clause, was an attentive and bright Yale law student named Neal Katyal.

Katyal never forgot the moment. As his briefs and arguments confirm, Katyal believed that the only way to win a Commerce Clause challenge to the ACA was to affirm that *Lopez* and a related case, *United States v. Morrison,* set ironclad limits on the scope of the government's power. (Katyal's successor, Solicitor General Donald Verrilli, would take a different approach.)

The National Federation of Independent Business

Twice a year, the Heritage Foundation hosts a conference for fifty of the leading conservative legal thinkers, pundits, and policymakers to discuss the pressing legal issues of the day. Perhaps fortuitously, the spring 2010 meeting convened in Miami, Florida, not far from the locus of the ACA litigation. Many echoed the concern that both Florida and Virginia had brought the suits only on behalf of the states and did not include private plaintiffs—that is, individuals who did not want to be bound by the insurance mandate. Many worried that the states would lack "standing" to sue. Virginia attempted to remedy this defect by enacting the Virginia Health Care Freedom Act, but most scholars, even those who opposed the ACA, believed that this would not work. Florida, however, did not even have a statute to hang its hat on. The states needed to add new parties to their suits.

Heritage's Gaziano invited Florida Deputy Attorney General Joe Jacquot to speak. Jacquot had supervised the drafting of Florida's initial briefings in court. Jacquot was scheduled to speak on a panel with Karen Harned, the executive director of the National Federation of Independent Business (NFIB) Legal Center. The NFIB represents hundreds of thousands of small businesses, most of which opposed Obamacare. Harned's view was that Obamacare would increase the costs to NFIB members and make it difficult for them to be profit-able. It would "kill our guys."

The pairing of the two on the panel proved fortuitous. At first, the NFIB wanted to file a friend-of-the-court brief, known as an "amicus" brief, in the Florida litigation. But several people at the conference, I was told, "nudged" Harned to join the Florida suit. Realizing that she "would add value on standing," she agreed. Soon, Florida amended its complaint to include the NFIB and two small-business owners who opposed Obamacare, Mary Brown and Kaj Ahlburg.

Harned found Brown on "short notice" by searching for "members through the grass roots [who] didn't have insurance" and did not want to purchase it. Ahlburg, a small business owner located by Rivkin, "has not had health care insurance for more than six years, does not have health care insurance now, and has no intention or desire to have health care insurance in the future." Likewise, Brown had "not had health care insurance for the last four years, and devotes her resources to maintaining her business and paying her employees." Ironically, Mary Brown would ultimately file for bankruptcy, owing, in small part, to "thousands of dollars in unpaid medical bills." The solicitor general, with the slightest bit of self-satisfaction, would tell the Supreme Court, "Mary Brown thought she had made a rational choice to forgo insurance. . . . That belief proved incorrect."

The NFIB was brought on as an "accommodation plaintiff" and did not contribute a "single sentence" to the district court briefing. Rivkin recalled that the organization just "came along for the ride." Yet this move proved decisive. While Virginia's suit was ultimately dismissed because it lacked standing, Florida's suit would reach the Supreme Court because the NFIB was there. Ultimately, the decision would even bear its name, since NFIB was the first to file its appeal to the Supreme Court and had the earlier docket number.

More new faces were soon added. In April 2010, seven more states joined the lawsuit, bringing the total to twenty: Indiana, North

Dakota, Mississippi, Arizona (with Tea Party–backed governor Jan Brewer), Nevada, Georgia, and Alaska. In addition, separate suits were filed in Virginia and Oklahoma. Eventually, twenty-six states would be party to the suit—over half the states in the Union. As the *New York Times* reported, "It became possible for the first time in American history to count a clear majority of states in litigation with the federal government, each claiming that the federal government has exceeded its enumerated powers." Such stunning opposition was a testament to the unpopularity of the law.

Broccoli and Government Motors

Perhaps the most enduring image of the ACA saga was a stalk of broccoli. The earliest known invocation of this leafy green was in an article by Terence Jeffrey, a reporter for CNS News, on October 21, 2009. He asked rhetorically, "Can President Barack Obama and Congress enact legislation that orders Americans to buy broccoli?" Jeffrey reasoned that all America "wants from the government is to be left alone." This philosophy resonated well with the burgeoning Tea Party. Indeed, several weeks later at the Mayflower Hotel, Todd Gaziano mentioned the broccoli horrible as a reason why the health care law was invalid.

Why broccoli? Perhaps it evoked the famous moment in 1990 when President George H. W. Bush banned broccoli from Air Force One, expressing disgust at it: "I do not like broccoli. And I haven't liked it since I was a little kid and my mother made me eat it. And I'm president of the United States, and I'm not going to eat any more broccoli!" Or, as Professor Jared Goldstein notes, broccoli "calls to mind an overbearing mother who thinks she knows what's best for us and can tell us what to do," and thus evokes a "nanny state" in which "Mommy is in power." Professor Andrew Koppelman observes, "The fear of being thus infantilized and emasculated elicits an instinctive revulsion."

But the first judicial question concerning a green vegetable was in fact about asparagus. On November 18, 2010, Judge Hudson asked the government lawyer, "I don't want to go back and rehash things we discussed during the prior hearing, but [your limiting principle] could apply to one's decision to buy an automobile, to join a gym, to eat asparagus. I mean, it's boundless under your theory."

Judge Vinson asked a similar question on December 16, 2010, though he switched vegetables: if Congress "decided that everybody needs to eat broccoli because broccoli is healthy, [can] they . . . mandate that everybody has to buy a certain quantity of broccoli each week?" In his opinion, Vinson continued the theme: "Congress could require that people buy and consume broccoli at regular intervals, not only because the required purchases will positively impact interstate commerce, but also because people who eat healthier tend to be healthier, and are thus more productive and put less of a strain on the health care system."

In addition to broccoli, the second most potent image of unbridled federal power was compelling people to purchase a car from General Motors, at the time partially owned by the U.S. taxpayer. Judge Vinson asked, "If we had testimony in Congress that GM's only hope of salvation and survival is to require people to buy their cars otherwise the government is going to lose its investment," would that "authorize Congress to do that?"

Vinson was particularly troubled by a ReasonTV interview with the dean of the University of California–Irvine School of Law, Erwin Chemerinsky, who had opined that although "what people choose to eat well might be regarded as a personal liberty [and thus cannot be regulated], Congress could use its commerce power to require people to buy cars." When Vinson mentioned this possibility to the government's attorney at oral argument, the lawyer conceded that "maybe Dean Chemerinsky is right." In his opinion, Vinson concluded, "because virtually no one can be divorced from the transportation

market, Congress could require that everyone above a certain income threshold buy a General Motors automobile because those who
do not buy GM cars (or those who buy foreign cars) are adversely
impacting commerce and a taxpayer-subsidized business."

The broccoli and GM arguments continued at the courts of appeals. In his opinion upholding the ACA's constitutionality, Sixth Circuit Court of Appeals Judge Jeffrey Sutton wrote, "That brings me
to the lingering intuition—shared by most Americans, I suspect—
that Congress should not be able to compel citizens to buy products
they do not want. If Congress can require Americans to buy medical
insurance today, what of tomorrow? Could it compel individuals to
buy . . . insurance, vegetables, cars, and so on?"

Judge Laurence Silberman also asked a DOJ lawyer, during a hearing in the D.C. Circuit Court of Appeals, "You mean if Congress
passed a law requiring people above a certain income to buy broccoli,
well, that would be unconstitutional?" She replied, evasively, "No. It
depends, Your Honor." Silberman followed up with the General Motors example. "Let's suppose General Motors was close to bankruptcy
again—please, God, [I hope] that doesn't happen—and Congress
passed a law requiring everybody with an income over $500,000
to buy a General Motors product, let's say, annually or every three
years. . . . Would that be constitutional?" The DOJ attorney again
tried to dodge the question: "The right analogy would be. . . ." Silberman shot back, "Counsel, answer my question. Would that be constitutional?" But the lawyer would not answer, saying only, "I would
have to know much more about the empirical findings because. . . ."
She wasn't going to answer the question, because no answer would, or
could, completely resolve the question.

Broccoli finally made it to the Supreme Court when Justice Scalia
asked the same question: "Everybody has to buy food sooner or later,
so you define the market as food, therefore, everybody is in the market; therefore, you can make people buy broccoli." Likewise, Chief

Justice Roberts told the solicitor general, "You say health insurance is not purchased for its own sake, like a car or broccoli; it is a means of financing health care consumption and covering universal risks. Well, a car or broccoli aren't purchased for their own sake, either. They are purchased for the sake of transportation or in broccoli, covering the need for food." Broccoli became the defining constitutional vegetable.

The typical government response to the broccoli challenge was that health care is "unique," so that a precedent allowing Congress to force people to buy insurance would not open the door to other kinds of mandates. The administration advanced three different theories to support drawing the line here. First, the health care market is unique because it is unlike all other markets, including broccoli and GM car markets. Eventually, everyone needs health care. No one can "opt out" of the health care market.

Judge Vinson rejected these arguments:

> Uniqueness is not an adequate limiting principle, as every market problem is, at some level and in some respects, unique. If Congress asserts power that exceeds its enumerated powers, then it is unconstitutional, regardless of the purported uniqueness of the context in which it is being asserted. In short, the government's argument that people without health insurance are actively engaged in interstate commerce based on the purported "unique" features of the much broader health care market is neither factually convincing nor legally supportable.

Second, hospitals are required by law to provide care to those who cannot pay. The government asserted that this is the only market where private providers are forced to give a service to a person with no means to pay for it. Before the Sixth Circuit Court of Appeals in Cincinnati, Acting Solicitor General Neal Katyal distinguished

health insurance from broccoli. "The difference is health care providers can't opt out. . . . I can't show up at [a] broccoli store and ask for
broccoli without money. . . . I can't show up at a GM dealer and say,
give me a car." But EMTALA and other federal laws prohibit hospitals
from turning away poor patients. This is a problem, and solution, of
the government's own making. In Washington, a problem often be-
gets a solution that causes another problem.

Third, if a health care cost is not paid by the consumer, that cost
is shifted to third parties, raising rates for everyone. Again, this issue
is hardly unique, as many federal programs result in cost-shifting to
others who can afford to pay.

Perhaps most importantly, as Vinson stated, "it is not at all clear
whether or why the three allegedly unique factors of the health care
market are constitutionally significant." They were policy rationales,
not constitutional arguments. If these were the government's only
limiting principles, as Judge Vinson found, then in fact there was no
judicially administrable limit on the government's vision of its own
power.

Though easily stated, persuading Judges Vinson and Hudson that
these limiting principles were valid constraints on the federal government's power proved unsuccessful. These faults would lead the
government to wisely change course before the Supreme Court.

"Not a Tax"

Seven decades earlier, another Democratic president tried to pass a
piece of transformational progressive legislation—President Franklin
Delano Roosevelt was trying to enact the Social Security Act. At the
time, Roosevelt and his secretary of labor, Frances Perkins, were worried about "very severe constitutional problems" that could lead the
Supreme Court to declare the Social Security Act unconstitutional.

Specifically, the administration doubted whether Congress's power to regulate interstate commerce could support the law.

In a 1962 speech to Social Security Administration employees, Perkins recounted a stunning tale about how the president came up with the right way to structure the law. Secretary Perkins received some rock-solid constitutional advice from Justice Harlan Stone during a weekly tea party hosted by the justice's wife. Perkins told Justice Stone that she was unsure about what constitutional basis would support the Social Security Act: "You know, we are having big troubles, Mr. Justice, because we don't know in this draft of the Economic Security Act, which we are working on—we are not quite sure, you know, what will be a wise method of establishing this law. It is a very difficult constitutional problem, you know. We are guided by this, that, and the other case."

Stone looked around to ensure that no one else was listening, then leaned over to Perkins, covered his mouth with his hand, and whispered: "The taxing power of the federal government, my dear. The taxing power is sufficient for everything you want and need."

Eureka! As Perkins retold it, she quickly told her staff to base the Social Security Act on the government's taxing power—though for years she kept to herself the source of this revelation. "As far as they knew, I went out into the wilderness and had a vision," Perkins recounted.

The Social Security Act was duly enacted as a payroll tax. In 1937 the Supreme Court in *Helvering v. Davis* upheld the Social Security Act as a valid tax by a vote of 7–2. Justice Stone, to no one's surprise, voted with the majority. After the decision, Perkins recalled telling her staff that "'[under] the taxing power of the United States—you can do anything under it,' said I. And so it proved, did it not?" Perkins quipped. "The opinion was written in elaborate, fine social language by Mr. Justice Benjamin Cardozo—not by Mr. Justice Stone—but he voted 'Aye' on the matter and we were safe." Under the circumstances, Stone should have recused.

The taxing power was indeed "everything [Roosevelt would] want and need." So, seventy years later, was the health insurance mandate a tax? President Obama said clearly that it was *not*. In contrast, and perhaps more importantly, Chief Justice Roberts would revise the statute so he could find that it was.

In a September 20, 2009, interview on ABC's *This Week,* host George Stephanopoulos asked Obama, "Under this mandate, the government is forcing people to spend money, fining you if you don't. How is that not a tax?" The president tried to talk, instead, about how the mandate would reduce premiums, but Stephanopoulos doubled back: "That may be, but it's still a tax increase." "No," answered Obama, "That's not true, George. . . . Nobody considers that a tax increase." After some more back-and-forth in which Obama faulted the host for reading the definition of "tax" from the dictionary, Stephanopoulos asked, "But you reject that it's a tax increase?" Obama replied, "I absolutely reject that notion."

Indeed, Congressional Democrats went out of their way not to label the law a tax, calling the mandate a "penalty" instead to avoid the political repercussions of imposing a new tax. At the time, Senator John Ensign called it what it was: "Let's call this penalty what it really is—a tax." After all, "this penalty is assessed through the Internal Revenue Code." Later, Politifact rated as true Sarah Palin's statement that Obama lied when he said the mandate wasn't a tax.

Before the government filed its opening briefs in the district court, one of the first internal battles between the White House and the Department of Justice was waged over the political implications of their litigation strategy. The White House felt committed to the president's statement that the mandate was not a tax and did not want to raise the taxing power argument in court. The Solicitor General's office, then under the leadership of Neal Katyal (thanks to Kagan's unexplained decision to section herself off), disagreed with this strategy vehemently. Katyal urged the government to argue in court that the mandate was authorized by the taxing power. But the White House disagreed. The president's attorneys were concerned that there would be "political repercussions to calling it a tax" in court, especially in light of the president's public statement.

Katyal wrote a letter to the White House Counsel's office, explaining why the government needed to use the taxing power argument. One DOJ lawyer told me that the office was worried that the "politicos would create a problem," and Katyal needed to be the "muscle." Attorney General Holder was "supportive" of Katyal's decision.

Ultimately, the White House accepted, perhaps begrudgingly, the taxing power argument, well aware of the political hit that was imminent. The Solicitor General's office was "never bothered again" after this letter. As this vignette highlights, internal debates would often rage over the political ramifications of taking unpopular positions in courts. These conflicts would prove to be a recurring theme as the government's litigation strategy evolved over the next two years.

DOJ lawyers tried at every juncture to justify the change of positions publicly. During oral argument in Florida, Judge Vinson specifically mentioned the president's statements: "The Senate went to great extreme measures to make sure that this was not characterized as a tax. . . . Even the president himself said, 'Absolutely not, this is not a tax,' shortly before it was enacted." Ian Gershengorn tried to respond, "Your Honor, there's a lot packed into that, and if I could, and I'd like to respond to a lot." But Judge Vinson wasn't interested in double-talk. "Well, I'm just saying that it's—you've got to be intellectually honest with me. And what we have here is a situation where, in the adoption of this, they went to great measures to say it's not a tax, and now you're coming in this morning and telling me, oh, yes, it is a tax."

Vinson's opinion was brutal on this point:

By far the most publicized and controversial part of the act was the individual mandate and penalty, it would no doubt have been even more difficult to pass the penalty as a tax. Not only are taxes always unpopular, but to do so at that time would have arguably violated pledges by politicians (including the president) to not raise taxes, which could have made it that much more difficult to secure the necessary votes for passage.

Vinson concluded with a powerful jab at the federal government:

Congress should not be permitted to secure and cast politically difficult votes on controversial legislation by deliberately calling something one thing, after which the defenders of that legislation take an "Alice-in-Wonderland" tack and argue in court that Congress really meant something else entirely.

In *Through the Looking Glass,* Humpty Dumpty tells Alice that, "When I use a word, it means just what I choose it to mean—neither more or less." Alice replies, "The question is whether you can make words mean so many different things." A political cartoon at the time showed Humpty Dumpty arguing in front of the Supreme Court: "The Health Care mandate is not a tax." In a second speech bubble, the egg-shaped advocate adds, "Except when we say it is." Humpty Dumpty was a fitting image, as the president's taxing chickens had come home to roost.

The unpopularity of the taxes imposed by the ACA permeated all corners of society—even the beaches of Seaside Heights, New Jersey. On the season premiere of the hit reality show *Jersey Shore,* the Garden State's pint-sized provocateur Nicole "Snooki" Polizzi opined on Obamacare: "I don't go tanning anymore because Obama put a 10 percent tax on tanning." What would become known as Obamacare's "Snooki tax" placed a 10 percent surcharge on all UV-tanning salons.

Snooki knew why that tax was in there. "He did that because of us," referring to the cast of *Jersey Shore,* who were known to take tanning very seriously. Snooki showered praise on Obama's 2008 Republican opponent: "McCain would never put a 10 percent tax on tanning. Because he's pale and he'd probably want to be tan." This remark would have been an insignificant event—but McCain responded! Senator McCain responded on Twitter, punning on the nickname of her housemate, Michael "The Situation" Sorrentino: "I would never tax your tanning bed! Pres Obama's tax/spend policy is quite The Situation. but I do rec wearing sunscreen!" Then the president got into the fray. At a White House Correspondents' Dinner, he joked that he would exclude members of *Jersey Shore* and a special guest from the Snooki tax: "The following individuals shall be excluded from the indoor tanning tax within this bill: Snooki, JWOWW, The Situation, and House Minority Leader John Boehner."

The administration's new embrace of the once-spurned tax theory continued to trouble the public. The *New York Times* concluded in a June 2010 article, "When Congress required most Americans to obtain health insurance or pay a penalty, Democrats denied that they were creating a new tax. But in court, the Obama administration and its allies now defend the requirement as an exercise of the government's 'power to lay and collect taxes.'" These statements would come back to haunt Obama throughout the litigation.

During a hearing in his Virginia courtroom, Judge Hudson asked if the president was attempting to fool the public. "They denied it was a tax. The president denied it. Was he trying to deceive the people in doing that?" Gershengorn tried to play word games in his reply, distinguishing between "not a tax" and "not a tax increase." "He definitely was not, Your Honor. What the president said was that it was not a tax *increase.*"

Judge Hudson was not persuaded. "Before the act was passed into law," he wrote, "one of its chief proponents, President Barack Obama, strongly and emphatically denied that the penalty was a tax. When confronted with the dictionary definition of a 'tax' during a much-publicized interview widely disseminated by all of the news media, and asked how the penalty did not meet that definition, the president said it was 'absolutely not a tax' and, in fact, 'Nobody considers [it] a tax increase.'" Hudson would ultimately reject the government's argument that the mandate should be upheld under the taxing power. "At bottom, the defendants are asking that I divine hidden and unstated intentions, and despite considerable evidence to the contrary, conclude that Congress really meant to say one thing when it expressly said something else." To do so, "I would have to ignore [what] Congress [did]."

Yet, ignoring what Congress wrote and rewriting the statute is precisely how Chief Justice Roberts would save the ACA two years later.

Justice Elena Kagan

Solicitor General Elena Kagan was nominated to replace the retiring Justice John Paul Stevens on May 10, 2010. Though she had taken steps to separate herself from the health insurance litigation during her brief stint in the Solicitor General's office, her role would soon be the focus of Republican opposition to her nomination and their calls for her to recuse herself from hearing the monumental case. Her confirmation hearings provide insight into the curious and somewhat unexpected vote of Justice Kagan.

On May 17, Tracy Schmaler, the chief spokeswoman for the DOJ, asked Neal Katyal if "Elena [has] been involved in any of [the health care case litigation] to the extent SG office was consulted? Know you've been point but expect I'll get this q[uestion]." Katyal replied, one minute later, "No, she never has been involved in any of it. I've run it for the Office, and have never discussed the issues with her one bit." No doubt, Katyal understood Kagan's position on this matter.

Fifteen minutes later, perhaps after some reflection, Katyal forwarded that message to Kagan, adding, "This is what I told [her] about health care." One minute later, Kagan replied, somewhat irritated, and copied Schmaler. "This needs to be coordinated . . . you should not say anything about this before talking to me." A few minutes later, Katyal replied, "I have received a plethora of inquiries . . . about a whole variety of things like the below for several days now"—no doubt since Kagan's nomination a week earlier. "Most of them aren't that sensitive so I don't pass them on to you. I am very happy to just stay out of this and have you field these inquiries if you'd like. Just let me know."

That same day, in a letter sent to the U.S. Supreme Court, Kagan informed clerk William K. Suter that she would be resigning as solicitor general during the confirmation process. Kagan wrote that Deputy Solicitor General Neal K. Katyal would serve as acting solicitor general. "I ask that you please address future correspondence from the Court to him, and that the Court's docket sheets reflect his designation as Counsel of Record."

On Kagan's resignation, there was much speculation that the president would nominate Katyal as the new solicitor general. However, the administration passed over him. Instead, on January 26, 2011, after letting the office sit without a Senate-confirmed solicitor general for over six months, President Obama nominated Donald Verrilli, his White House deputy counsel, to be the solicitor general. Verrilli was not confirmed until June 6, another six months later. During that time Katyal was in charge.

On June 15, 2010, Katyal emailed Kagan, whose confirmation hearing was still a month away. Attorney General Holder, he told her, "just told me that he expects a big story coming out shortly about whether you are recused in health care litigation. I went over the timing and that you have been walled off from Day One." No doubt, the walling off took place after Kagan asked for Katyal's telephone number a year earlier. Minutes later, Kagan forwarded that message to several undisclosed recipients not working for the government, probably friends helping her prepare for her hearings.

During these hearings, held from June 28-30, 2010, several references were made to the pending challenges to the ACA. In his opening statement, Senator Jeff Sessions referred directly to the litigation in Florida: "Ms. Kagan, at this very moment, sits as a solicitor general of the United States—in title, if not fully acting—and was, I think, before this lawsuit was filed, fully acting, and it impacts the federal government. The question we have asked that I think must be answered by her is exactly what kind of relationship and discussion she may have had concerning this legislation."

Senator John Cornyn of Texas asked Kagan about the pending health care litigation. It "would represent an unprecedented reach of Congress's authority to . . . force people who are sitting on their couch at home to purchase a product and penalize them if they don't purchase the government-approved product." With this power, "it seems to me there is no limit to the federal government's authority and we've come a long, long way from what our founders intended."

"Well," answered Kagan, "I think the current state of the law is to grant broad deference to Congress in this area, to assume that Congress knows what's necessary in terms of the regulation of the country's economy, but to have some limits."

Senator Tom Coburn of Oklahoma was not satisfied: "What if I said that if eating three fruits and three vegetables a day would cut health care costs 20 percent, now we're into commerce. And since the government pays 65 percent of all the health care costs, why isn't that constitutional?" Kagan stammered back, "Well, Senator Coburn, I—I—I feel as though the—the—the principles that I've given you are the principles that the court should apply."

Coburn interrupted her. "So the fact is, is that we have this expansive [Commerce] Clause, and we have to have some limit on it." Kagan struggled to get a word in. "Well, Senator Coburn, I—I—I guess a few points. The first is—is, I think that there are limits on the Commerce Clause." Yet she also stressed that for over two centuries courts had read the Commerce Clause power with "real deference to Congress about the scope of that clause." To Kagan, rampant spending under the powers of the Commerce Clause was not "a problem for courts to solve; I think it's a problem for the political process to solve."

Coburn continued to press the issue. "You missed my whole point. We're here because the courts didn't do their job in limiting our ability to go outside of original intent on what the Commerce Clause was supposed to be." After a day's recess, he continued this questioning. "Do you recall I asked you about the vegetable question yesterday? That's on the front of a lot of people's minds, not vegetables, health care. You know where I was going. The very fact that the government is going to have the ability to take away, mandate what I must buy or must not buy [is] a very large loss of freedom." Coburn's statement focused not so much on the Constitution as on the public's confidence in the Court. "Should Americans be concerned," he asked, "about the fact that confidence in all government institutions is at an all-time low?" Kagan answered in much the same way as her colleague John G. Roberts had six years earlier. "I believe that confidence in our institutions is terribly important. The confidence in the Supreme Court is terribly important."

In a 2007 interview with Jeffrey Rosen in *The Atlantic,* Roberts, too, had emphasized the importance of the Court as an institution and discussed the steps he would take as chief justice to maintain its legitimacy. "I think the Court is also ripe for a similar refocus on functioning as an institution, because if it doesn't, it's going to lose its credibility and legitimacy as an institution." Rosen reported that

Roberts would "make it his priority, as [Chief Justice John] Marshall did, to discourage his colleagues from issuing separate opinions." Roberts reasoned, "I think that every justice should be worried about the Court acting as a Court and functioning as a Court, and they should all be worried, when they're writing separately, about the effect on the Court as an institution." This desire of the chief justice to protect the Court "as an institution" would guide the ACA toward its survival.

Coincidentally, then-Senator Obama voted against Roberts's confirmation. Presciently, Obama expressed concerns about how Roberts would judge "whether the Commerce Clause empowers Congress to speak on those issues of broad national concern that may be only tangentially related to what is easily defined as interstate commerce."

Now Coburn asked Kagan directly whether there was ever a time when she was asked in her position as solicitor general "to express an opinion on the merits of the health care bill." Kagan replied, "There was not." The hearing concluded. On July 20, 2010, the Committee voted 13–6 to confirm Kagan. After she cleared the Senate by a vote of 63–37, she began her tenure on the first Monday in October 2010—roughly one year before the justices would agree to hear the challenge to the ACA.

In the past, new justices who had arrived as federal attorneys recused themselves in most pending cases involving the United States. Thurgood Marshall, who had also served as solicitor general, recused himself in almost 60 percent of the cases decided by the Court during his first year on the bench. Many expected Kagan to recuse herself in a case of such monumental importance.

But in a letter Kagan wrote in response to last-minute questions from Senate Republicans, the future justice explained that she had no reason to do so: "In *Florida v. U.S. Department of Health and Human Services,* I neither served as counsel of record nor played any substantial role," she wrote. "I would consider recusal on a case-by-case basis, carefully considering any arguments made for recusal and consulting with my colleagues and, if appropriate, with experts on judicial ethics." In other words, she wouldn't recuse herself—but that wouldn't stop Republicans from calling for her recusal one year later.

FIRST TO RULE

In civil litigation, the first step in which the defendant can challenge the strength of a case is by filing a brief called a "motion to dismiss." The government filed nearly identical motions to dismiss in the Virginia and Florida cases, asserting that the challengers' arguments lacked legal merit.

The motion-to-dismiss hearings would also be the first opportunities for judges Hudson and Vinson to show their cards. Hudson began his hearing in Richmond by noting that it was "an extremely important case," and that he would be as "generous as I can with the time." In Pensacola, Vinson set the appropriate tone of this important constitutional case by noting that the following day would "mark the 223rd anniversary of the completion of all the work by the Constitutional Convention." The motion-to-dismiss hearing was held in a packed courtroom, and members of the press watched a closed-circuit TV monitor in an overflow room.

On August 2, barely a month after he heard arguments in Richmond, Judge Henry Hudson issued an opinion denying the government's motion to dismiss the case. This had the effect of allowing Virginia to continue its challenge of the law. Hudson was the first to rule, and more importantly, the first federal judge to allow the case to proceed so that a state could challenge the law's constitutionality.

Judge Hudson began, "Although this case is laden with public policy implications and has a distinctive political undercurrent, at this stage the sole issues before the court are narrow, and limited to whether Virginia's case should be able to proceed." His opinion—which postponed the important question of whether Virginia had standing—though thinly reasoned, was premised on the government's failure to identify any limits on the government "extending its tentacles to an individual's decision not to engage in economic activity."

Judge Hudson allowed the suit to proceed, accepting Virginia's claim that its Health Care Freedom Act gave standing to Attorney General Cuccinelli to file suit. No other judge would ever accept this position. Hudson concluded, "The congressional enactment under review—the Minimum Essential Coverage Provision—literally forges new ground and extends Commerce Clause powers beyond its current high watermark." This decision buoyed Virginia's case, which to that point had been thought by many as doomed from the start.

The next day, Missouri voters enacted Proposition C, a referendum that purported to block the federal government from enforcing the individual mandate in the Show-Me State. The referendum passed by a huge margin, with over 71 percent of voters casting their lot to "deny the government authority to penalize citizens for refusing to purchase private health insurance." Of the referendum, Representative Todd Akin (who later became infamous for statements he made as a Senate candidate) said, "It is unconstitutional to require people to buy health insurance, [to] be part of this big government bailout, socialized medicine boondoggle. They didn't want it." Driven by broad Tea Party support, Missouri voters were the first to express their disapproval about the ACA.

On October 14, 2010, the other shoe dropped in Florida. Judge Vinson denied the government's motion to dismiss less than a month after oral arguments were held, with a comprehensive sixty-seven-page opinion—in contrast to Hudson's much shorter decision. Vinson's lucid opening paragraphs were aimed at a larger audience than the lawyers in his courtroom.

> The Act is a controversial and polarizing law about which reasonable and intelligent people can disagree in good faith. There are some who believe it will expand access to medical treatment,

reduce costs, lead to improved care, have a positive effect on the national economy, and reduce the annual federal budgetary deficit, while others expect that it will do exactly the opposite. Some say it was the product of an open and honest process between lawmakers sufficiently acquainted with its myriad provisions, while others contend that it was drafted behind closed doors and pushed through Congress by parliamentary tricks, late night [and] weekend votes, and last minute deals among members of Congress who did not read or otherwise know what was in it. There are some who believe the Act is designed to strengthen the private insurance market and build upon free market principles, and others who believe it will greatly expand the size and reach of the federal government and is intended to create a socialized government healthcare system.

While these competing arguments would make for an interesting debate and discussion, it is not my task or duty to wade into the thicket of conflicting opinion on any of these points of disagreement. For purposes of this case, it matters not whether the Act is wise or unwise, or whether it will positively or negatively impact healthcare and the economy. Nor am I concerned with the manner in which it was passed into law. My review of the statute is not to question or second guess the wisdom, motives, or methods of Congress. I am only charged with deciding if the Act is Constitutional. If it is, the legislation must be upheld—even if it is a bad law. At this stage in the case, however, my job is much simpler and more narrow than that. In ruling on the defendants' motion to dismiss, I must only decide if this court has jurisdiction to consider some of the plaintiffs' claims, and whether each of the counts of the amended complaint states a plausible claim for relief.

Vinson's opinion was limited to deciding whether the case could proceed and expressed no opinions on the merits of the claim. "I am only saying that (with respect to two of the particular causes of action discussed above) the plaintiffs have at least stated a plausible claim that the line has been crossed." With that crossing of the legal Rubicon, Obamacare was on the run.

THE FIRST VICTORY

On November 18, 2010, exactly a year to the day after the fateful meeting in the Mayflower Hotel, the Federalist Society held its annual meeting. This time the challenge to the ACA was not a mere glimmer in the eyes. It had garnered victories in federal court in Virginia and Florida. Ken Cuccinelli, triumphant after his victory in Richmond, appeared on a panel with Professors John Eastman and Jeffrey Rosen, moderated by Sixth Circuit Judge Jeffrey Sutton. In introducing Cuccinelli, Sutton, a well-known and respected jurist appointed by President George W. Bush, said that "Cuccinelli has taken the lead in the fight against Obamacare." At the time I blogged that it was odd that a federal judge called the law "Obamacare." In 2010, "Obamacare" was still considered an insulting label by some. Cuccinelli stressed that "this case is not about health insurance. It is about liberty." With his sights set on the Supreme Court, he told those in attendance that he expected Judge Hudson to rule on the case very soon. Beyond that, "we have started talking with the Department of Justice about expediting the case because of the uncertainty of this litigation hanging over this legislation."

Rosen, who has for years urged the Roberts Court to take the path of judicial restraint, issued a warning to the Federalist Society crowd. "It is now Democrats, liberals who are more committed to upholding laws of Congress. . . . If the Roberts Court strikes down as unconstitutional the health care law, then that Court runs the risk of being tarred in history as the same type of conservative activists [as] in the 1930s. Remember judicial restraint."

Judge Sutton asked, "Is Rosen right that the traditional role of liberal and conservative views on judicial restraint has been switched? Are conservatives advocating aggressive roles for the courts?" The judge asked Cuccinelli whether "we can be principled in advocating for judicial restraint." In a mark of self-introspective prescience, Sutton replied to Rosen, "I don't know whether you've shown that conservatives represent a big tent, or how easily they can be divided and conquered." Less than one year later, trumpeting the cause of judicial restraint, Judge Sutton would cast an unexpected vote to save the ACA.

A few weeks later, on December 13, Judge Hudson gave Cuccinelli the decisive victory he was waiting for when he ruled that the individual mandate was unconstitutional. In the past, Hudson wrote, "every application of Commerce Clause power found to be constitutionally sound by the Supreme Court involved some form of action, transaction, or deed placed in motion by an individual or legal entity." The individual mandate's constitutionality "turns on whether or not a person's decision to refuse to purchase health care insurance is such an *activity* [emphasis added]." Hudson observed that neither "the Supreme Court nor any federal circuit court of appeals has extended Commerce Clause powers to compel an individual to involuntarily enter the stream of commerce by purchasing a commodity in the private market." Hudson concluded: "On careful review, this Court must conclude that Section 1501 of the Patient Protection and Affordable Care Act—specifically the Minimum Essential Coverage Provision— exceeds the constitutional boundaries of congressional power."

Rather than rejecting the entire ACA, however, Hudson "severed," or struck out, only the individual mandate from the rest of the 2,700-page law. "This Court will hew closely to the time-honored rule to sever with circumspection," excising any "problematic portions while leaving the remainder intact." The rest would remain on the books.

In damage-control mode, the Obama administration stressed that Hudson's opinion was only one of many cases pending. A Justice

Department spokesperson said, "We are disappointed in today's ruling but continue to believe—as other federal courts in Virginia and Michigan have found—that the ACA is constitutional." Indeed, other courts in Virginia, Michigan, and elsewhere had found the law was constitutional—though these were lower-profile cases. But with Hudson's judgment, constitutional arguments were headed to the court of appeals, which would now have to resolve these disputes. The DOJ said in a statement, "We are confident that we will ultimately prevail."

At the end of Hudson's opinion, he augured where the case was going. "This case, however, turns on atypical and uncharted applications of constitutional law interwoven with subtle political undercurrents. The outcome of this case has significant public policy implications. And the final word will undoubtedly reside with a higher court." But with a federal court now accepting the constitutional arguments of the challengers, the public discourse had definitively changed. The challenge could no longer be confidently dismissed as "frivolous."

The midterm elections dealt the administration another setback. In January 2011, the Republicans regained the majority in the House of Representatives. As their first order of business, the GOP brought for debate a bill to repeal Obamacare. Before the vote, the House held over thirteen hours of debate, and representatives from across the country voiced arguments about why the ACA was unconstitutional.

John Boehner, newly sworn in as Speaker of the House, urged his fellow Republicans to honor their promise to repeal Obamacare. "Repeal means paving the way for better solutions that will lower the cost without destroying jobs or bankrupting our government. Repeal means keeping a promise. This is what we said we would do." Indeed, Boehner owed his new Speaker position to the widespread Republican opposition to Obamacare. Past and future Republican presidential candidate Ron Paul was "pleased the Constitution has received a lot of attention in recent weeks" and sent his "thanks to the Tea Party movement." Paul was encouraged by a growing grassroots interest in the Constitution, especially on the part of the younger generation. "I'm glad Congress is becoming aware of it."

Democrats unsurprisingly rejected the repeal efforts. Representative Jerrold Nadler of New York brushed off the Republican argument that "the bill is an unprecedented or unconstitutional expansion of constitutional power. They are wrong. There is nothing radical, dangerous, or unconstitutional about the act. We have the power to enact this comprehensive plan, including its minimum coverage requirement under the commerce, necessary and proper, and general welfare clauses of article 1, section 8 of the Constitution." He didn't mention the taxing power.

On January 19, 2011, the repeal bill passed 245–189, a wider margin than Nancy Pelosi had garnered to pass the bill one year earlier. Three Democrats crossed the aisle to vote for the repeal—though they had also voted against the ACA the previous year. The only abstention was Representative Gabby Giffords, a recent victim of a horrific shooting in Arizona.

A similar effort was made in the Senate, to no avail. On January 25, Senator Hatch introduced the American Liberty Restoration Act, which would repeal the individual mandate of the ACA. The bill was referred to the Senate Finance Committee and obtained thirty cosponsors, but never made it anywhere.

Given Democratic control of the Senate, the House vote was largely symbolic. However, repealing the law was not the purpose of the vote. But as the *New York Times* reported, "The House vote was the first stage of a Republican plan to use the party's momentum coming out of the midterm elections to keep the White House on the defensive, and will be followed by a push to scale back federal spending. In response, the administration struck a more aggressive posture than it had during the campaign to sell the health care law to the public."

This vote also kept the issue of the law's constitutionality in the forefront and kept the president "on the defensive," so that his efforts on other initiatives would be diverted to defending the health care law. This vote was consistent with Senate Majority Leader Mitch Mc-Connell's October 23, 2010, statement: "The single most important thing we want to achieve is for President Obama to be a one-term president." After the 2010 election, McConnell elaborated on his message. "But the fact is, if our primary legislative goals are to repeal and replace the health spending bill; to end the bailouts; cut spending; and shrink the size and scope of government, the only way to do all these things is to put someone in the White House who won't veto any of these things. We can hope the president will start listening to the electorate after Tuesday's election. But we can't plan on it. And it would be foolish to expect that Republicans will be able to completely reverse the damage Democrats have done as long as a Democrat holds the veto pen." This vote, no doubt, was part of a concerted Republican strategy to challenge Obama's efficacy as a president and force him to defend his record leading up to the 2012 presidential election.

President Obama coolly rejected the vote to repeal the ACA. "I'm willing and eager to work with both Democrats and Republicans to improve the Affordable Care Act. But we can't go backward." The fight for Obamacare would continue going forward.

On the same day the repeal bill passed the House, six additional states joined the Florida litigation: Kansas, Wyoming, Wisconsin, Maine, Iowa, and Ohio.

"THE ENTIRE ACT MUST BE DECLARED VOID"

Less than two weeks later, on January 31, 2011, the phone rang at the Solicitor General's office at the Department of Justice. A reporter from the Fox News Channel was on the line. He heard that Judge

Vinson "was going to rule on the case in thirty minutes" and was "calling for a statement." No one in the office had even read Judge Vinson's opinion, or knew when it would be released. That is how the government "found out there was going to be a decision." Someone tipped off Fox that the opinion was forthcoming. The Solicitor General's office found this call "unbelievable." It was fitting, perhaps, that the Fox News Channel, the preferred cable network of the Tea Party, knew about the decision before the government. This wouldn't be the last time Fox reported on an opinion before the administration knew about it.

Minutes later, Judge Vinson's opinion was announced. The Affordable Care Act was struck down in its entirety.

Vinson's opinion began by noting the narrow, yet broad scope of this case. "This case is not about whether the Act is wise or unwise legislation, or whether it will solve or exacerbate the myriad problems in our health care system. In fact, it is not really about our health care system at all." With ample citations to the *Federalist Papers*, Vinson declared that this case was "principally about our federalist system, and it raises very important issues regarding the Constitutional role of the federal government." The opinion was crisp, easy to understand, and brutally candid in its skepticism about this unbridled and unprecedented assertion of federal power.

First, Vinson emphatically rejected the idea that Congress had the "power to compel an otherwise passive individual into a commercial transaction." If the Constitution gave Congress this power, "it is not hyperbolizing to suggest that Congress could do almost anything it wanted." The mandate was "unprecedented" because it regulated inactivity. "Until now, Congress had never attempted to exercise its Commerce Clause power in such a way before." The ACA represented an "unprecedented" expansion of federal authority.

Vinson's opinion looked back to the original understanding of the Commerce Clause when it was written in 1787. Vinson noted that modern Supreme Court doctrine had broadly expanded the Founders' conception of it—and he cited the scholarship of Professor Randy Barnett.

Appealing directly to the original Boston Tea Party that helped give rise to the American Revolution, Vinson noted that it was "difficult to imagine" that the Founders meant to create a government "with the power to force people to buy tea." (Yale law professor Akhil Amar would later fault Vinson for this "clumsy wave to today's 'tea party' groups.")

Vinson concluded that the individual mandate regulated economic inactivity, which is the very opposite of economic activity. "Because activity is required under the Commerce Clause, the individual mandate exceeds Congress's commerce power."

Unlike Judge Hudson's opinion—which found that only the mandate was unconstitutional while upholding the remainder of the 2,700-page ACA—Judge Vinson jettisoned the entire Act. To do so, he again turned Obama's own words against him. "In speech after speech President Obama emphasized that the legislative goal was 'health insurance reform' and stressed how important it was that Congress fundamentally reform how health insurance companies do business." To do so, the mandate was indispensable. "In the final analysis, this Act has been analogized to a finely crafted watch, and that seems to fit." Of course, Vinson himself had made that analogy during oral arguments. Like a watch, it was impossible to just remove only a single gear and "try and dissect out the proper from the improper" portions of the law. The whole ACA had to fall.

Vinson gave a resounding victory to the challengers. "Because the individual mandate is unconstitutional and not severable, the entire Act must be declared void. This has been a difficult decision to reach, and I am aware that it will have indeterminable implications." The victory, however, was not complete.

Vinson then rejected arguments that the Medicaid expansion was unconstitutional, as "there is simply no support" in existing case law for the coercion argument put forth by the state plaintiffs.

The reaction to Vinson's opinion was immediate. One attorney in the Florida Attorney General's office told me that they went "from thinking victory at the Supreme Court was a possibility to something that is extremely likely." As Professor Andrew Koppelman wrote in *The Tough Luck Constitution,* "these decisions transformed the debate, lending the objections judicial approval."

Senator Orrin Hatch, who had long been one of the few voices questioning the ACA's constitutionality, took to the Senate floor to praise Vinson's opinion. "Yesterday, barely thirteen months after Obamacare passed the Senate, and less than one year since it became law, the entire scheme was struck down in federal court. In a triumph for both personal liberty and the American Constitution, the individual mandate was found unconstitutional and Obamacare was struck down." Senator Cornyn of Texas observed that the tides were turning. "We also know that on at least two occasions now a federal judge has found that this bill violates the Constitution of the United States because both these judges have said Congress has overreached its authority under the Constitution." Senator DeMint continued the call to "repeal the bill in its entirety. Because at the very heart of it, which makes all of the other parts work, that very heart, that individual mandate, violates the highest law of our land."

Democrats, of course, saw things differently. Senator Max Baucus, the chairman of the Finance Committee who had shepherded the ACA through the Senate, declared the decision "one of the most specious and inadvisable arguments I have heard in a long time." Senator Patrick Leahy of Vermont counted the score. "A dozen federal courts have dismissed challenges to the law. Another four courts have heard arguments about its constitutionality; two have upheld the law as constitutional, and two have not. Legal challenges to the law are expected to reach the U.S. Supreme Court."

The reaction from the professoriate was vicious. Harvard's Laurence Tribe, who had emailed then-Solicitor General Kagan to celebrate the Democrats' securing the votes for passage of the ACA, wrote: "Only a crude prediction that justices will vote based on politics rather than principle would lead anybody to imagine that Chief Justice John Roberts or Justice Samuel Alito would agree with the judges in Florida and Virginia who have ruled against the health care law." Tribe described the case as "a political objection in legal garb," and concluded that "there is every reason to believe that a strong, nonpartisan majority of justices will do their constitutional duty, set aside how they might have voted had they been members of Congress," and uphold the law, which is "clearly within Congress's power."

Akhil Amar was even harsher. He likened Vinson's opinion to that of another judge with the name of Roger: Supreme Court Justice Roger Taney, author of the infamous *Dred Scott* decision, which ruled that slaves were not people protected by the U.S. Constitution. "In 1857, another judge named Roger distorted the Constitution, disregarded precedent, disrespected Congress and proclaimed that the basic platform of one of America's two major political parties was unconstitutional. . . . History has not been kind to that judge. Roger Vinson, meet Roger Taney." I suppose another nominal comparison to Justice Fred Vinson (chief justice from 1946-1953) would not have been as rhetorically powerful.

Two days after Vinson's ruling, on February 2, 2011, the Senate held its first hearing on the constitutionality of the ACA. It is odd, of course, that this hearing was held almost a year *after* the law was enacted.

Testifying against its constitutionality was Michael Carvin, the attorney who would soon take over the case on behalf of the National Federation of Independent Businesses. Joining him was Randy Barnett, who had become the leading academic voice against the ACA. Through his editorials, law review articles, blog posts, and media appearances, Barnett had personally brought the constitutional argument against the ACA to the masses. He would soon become an adviser to the NFIB. Before the Senate, Barnett testified that the individual mandate unconstitutionally turned "citizens into subjects."

Opposing Barnett was his former professor, Charles Fried, who was President Reagan's solicitor general and a well-respected conservative, albeit one from a different jurisprudential generation. Fried adhered to a vision of judicial restraint in which courts should be highly deferential to the democratic process and go to great lengths to save a law's constitutionality. During his testimony, Fried argued vehemently that the mandate was constitutional. Elsewhere, Fried thought that supporters of the challenge were "either ignorant—I mean, deeply ignorant—or just grandstanding in a preposterous way. It is simply a political ploy and a pathetic one at that." The lawsuits, he later told me, were funded by "very rich donors who don't give a damn about the things they say they do" and who "sold a bill of goods" to Tea Partiers. Fried criticized his former student—who, he stressed had not been his constitutional law student (Barnett had Fried for torts and constitutional law with Tribe)—and said that Barnett's argument was "made up out of thin air."

During the hearing, Fried conceded that, in his view, the government could force people to purchase broccoli under its commerce powers. To underscore his seriousness, during an interview on *Fox News*, Fried said he would eat his "kangaroo skin hat" if the ACA was struck down. In fact, Fried found a chef who would bake a cake in the shape of his "kangaroo skin hat," just in case. Based on his reading of the ACA decision, Fried wrote that he did not have to eat either the cake or the hat (which he had given to his daughter-in-law).

EXECUTIVE CONFUSION

Two weeks after Judge Vinson's opinion striking down the entire ACA, the United States remained confused.

On February 17, 2011, the government filed what is known as a "motion for clarification," asking the court to explain whether the United States could continue to take steps to implement Obamacare while the case was appealed, even though Vinson had struck down the entire law.

Some in the Florida Attorney General's office speculated that this may have been a strategic tactic to delay the litigation. One attorney in that office said that the government's motion to clarify could be interpreted as "stalling, and dragging their feet." Another involved in the case concurred, describing the motion as an "exercise in futility" and insisting that the government was trying to "delay things."

The government wasn't stalling. A former DOJ attorney explained that Vinson's order "was framed with such breadth that it would be incredibly disruptive with regard to the portions of the Act that were already in force." The government would not even have been able to comply with the order. The lawyer speculated that Vinson "did not appreciate the full consequences of his order," and the motion to clarify "was able to call the disruption to the court's attention." In any event, Judge Vinson was none too pleased with this request and saw it as a pointless delay.

Vinson ruled that, since his opinion, the government has "continued to move forward and implement the Act." Somewhat skeptically, Vinson mused, "While I believe that my order was as clear and unambiguous as it could be, it is possible that the defendants may have perhaps been confused or misunderstood its import."

Seemingly insulted, Vinson had not expected that the government "would effectively ignore the order." He implied that the motion for clarification was a stalling method. "The sooner this issue is finally decided by the Supreme Court, the better off the entire nation will be. And yet, it has been more than one month from the entry of my order and judgment and still the defendants have not filed their notice of appeal [to the Court of Appeals]."

Vinson made the government's decision for them. He put his order finding the law was unconstitutional on hold, conditional on "defendants filing their anticipated appeal within seven . . . days of this order and seeking an expedited appellate review, either in the Court of Appeals or with the Supreme Court." In other words, he was telling the government to get the matter to a higher court as soon as possible, or else his opinion would go into effect, halting the federal government's ability to implement Obamacare: "Almost everyone agrees that the Constitutionality of the Act is an issue that will ultimately have to be decided by the Supreme Court of the United States. It is very important to everyone in this country that this case move forward as soon as practically possible."

Vinson also took this occasion to shoot back at the testimony before the Senate Judiciary Committee, specifically responding to Fried's admission that he believed Congress could force everyone to purchase broccoli. "This testimony only highlights my concern because it directly undercuts the defendants' principal argument for why an economic mandate is justified here."

The government filed its notice of appeal to the Eleventh Circuit Court of Appeals in Atlanta on the sixth day—with one day to spare. Vinson had struck the first blow against the ACA. It would not be the last.

PART IV

Coercing the States

(February 1–November 13, 2011)

Following victories in Virginia and Florida, the challengers moved on from the district courts to the courts of appeals as the inevitable clash with the justices drew closer. With this leap, new faces entered the litigation. Neal Katyal would take over the appeals as acting solicitor general and bring in "rock-solid" constitutional limiting principles. Paul Clement, who was the solicitor general under President Bush, would take over for the states. The law firm of Jones Day would represent the National Federation of Independent Business.

NEW FACES

By now, the government had secured victories in Ohio, Michigan, and the District of Columbia, but had suffered decisive losses in the two most prominent cases: Virginia and Florida. Within the Department of Justice, the Civil Division handles all cases at the trial court level. The Solicitor General's office had been involved in the litigation, participating in meetings and planning, but so far had offered a "voice but not a vote."

Now that the cases were on appeal, however, the Solicitor General's office was in full control. By the time the appeals made their way to the courts of appeals, the office had been without a solicitor general for nearly a year since Elena Kagan's resignation on May 17, 2010. In truth, it had been without a real solicitor general on this matter since even earlier, as Kagan had walled herself off from any discussions about the Health Care Cases. Throughout this entire time, Neal Katyal had been the top government lawyer in the Solicitor General's office on this matter, and now, with the cases at the courts of appeals, Acting Solicitor General Katyal was in charge and running the show.

There would also be new attorneys for the challengers.

The next change of faces, like many pivotal decisions in the history of law, began over cocktails. It was the night before Judge Vinson's hearing in Pensacola. Randy Barnett was to have breakfast with Florida Attorney General Bill McCollum the next morning. Trying to calm his nerves before the argument, Randy Barnett stopped by the hotel bar (he prefers Cognac). Also at the bar was Karen Harned, the executive director of the NFIB Small Business Legal Center. The two began to chat about the case, the Constitution, and the impending appeal. Though they had never met before, Harned took a liking to Barnett and listened intently to his advice. Harned would come to see Barnett as her "confidant" and "sounding board," and she credits him with creating the theory that would be the "genesis of this lawsuit."

The NFIB, which had been brought on as an "accommodation plaintiff" to make the case stronger than Virginia's, had not been involved in the litigation in any meaningful sense before. But after Judge Vinson had denied the government's motion to dismiss, handing the challengers their first big victory, Harned realized that the case was "bound for the Supreme Court." Barnett agreed and told her that the NFIB should get separate representation—namely, not David Rivkin.

Barnett was not a fan of Rivkin's work on this case. Early on, Rivkin, who developed many of the arguments ultimately presented to the Supreme Court, rejected Barnett's suggestions. Rivkin gave little credit to Barnett's theory that the federal government could not "commandeer," or force, individuals to purchase health insurance. Barnett's "commandeering" argument, which would also be resisted by appellate counsel, was only advanced somewhat indirectly. Rivkin described this as the difference between "academic writing and brief writing," and added, "Barnett was very skeptical about making traditional arguments" following his defeat in *Gonzales v. Raich*. Barnett later insisted to me that he was strongly committed to making *only* traditional legal arguments, as he already had in a law review article. The two men disagreed profoundly.

Though Harned told me that she was satisfied with the representation of David Rivkin, she knew that the NFIB needed "Supreme Court experience," and Rivkin had never argued before the U.S. Supreme Court. Specifically, they wanted the "best Supreme Court litigator," and they wanted that person now—they did not want to "parachute" in a lawyer after the court of appeals. Largely on Barnett's advice, the NFIB decided to drop David Rivkin and hire its own lawyer.

Soon, the NFIB hosted what is known in Supreme Court parlance as a "beauty contest." At this lawyerly pageant, attorneys competing to take the case make "the pitch" and try to persuade the client that their firm is the best suitor. Several leading appellate firms in Washington, D.C., were in contention, including Gibson, Dunn, & Crutcher; King & Spalding; Jones Day; and others.

Initially, the case was "presumptively" going to Gibson, but after Jones Day's pitch, which approached the case from the "ground floor," Harned changed her mind. Harned told me she "didn't really know the attorneys at Jones Day" before the interview, but was "blown away at the level of thought they had already given the case—a lot more than from other firms." Harned was also impressed by the breadth of experience at Jones Day, which had recently hired a large number of Supreme Court clerks from both conservative and liberal justices. Barnett advised Harned that Jones Day had the "right strategy" and was the "best choice." Barnett favored Jones Day because he "wanted a firm that was least likely to follow his lead, and most likely to contribute their own theories. This is exactly what happened."

Harned did consider Paul Clement, who at the time was working at King & Spalding but would soon depart for Bancroft. Clement was "fantastic," but "Jones Day had more resources," Harned recalled. Ultimately, on Barnett's recommendation, she chose Jones Day—led by partners Michael Carvin, Gregory Katsas, and C. Kevin Marshall, and associates Hashim Mooppan and Yaakov Roth.

Harned acknowledged that there was some tension between Carvin and Barnett. Barnett approached the case with "broad strokes," provided "nice conceptual points," and "made significant comments," some of which were incorporated. Carvin determined that some of Barnett's theories would not play well before the Court. Ultimately, Harned told me, Carvin, who had the Supreme Court experience, made the final call. Barnett "always seemed receptive," as Jones Day provided "strong reasons for their decisions." Carvin told me that while Barnett's "insights were important, [at] the end of the day, our brief was no different than if Randy had not been involved." Barnett acknowledged that the NFIB brief was "Jones Day's brief," not his.

Soon Florida would host its own beauty contest, but it had an election to hold first.

Florida Attorney General Bill McCollum left office on January 3, 2011. Five months earlier, he had lost the Florida Republican gubernatorial primary to the eventual winner, Rick Scott. His bid to win the governor's mansion by opposing Obamacare didn't pan out. In fact, most of the attorneys general who joined the suit in Florida in 2010 were unsuccessful in obtaining higher office. South Carolina Attorney General Henry McMaster, who began the initial challenge against the Cornhusker Kickback, lost his bid for the governorship in 2010. Nebraska Attorney General Jon Bruning withdrew his candidacy for the Senate. Washington Attorney General Robert McKenna was defeated in the governor's race in 2012. Only Pennsylvania

Attorney General Tom Corbett would go on to win the governor's mansion in Harrisburg in 2010.

McCollum was replaced by the newly elected Pam Bondi. Shortly before Vinson's opinion was issued, Bondi was faced with her first decision: should the twenty-six states involved in the suit obtain new counsel or stick with David Rivkin? For Bondi, the NFIB's hiring of Jones Day "accelerated the decision to switch." Looking ahead to the eventual end game, an attorney from the Florida Attorney General's office told me that the key question would be "who would argue at the Supreme Court."

Bondi was not as fond of Rivkin as McCollum was. More importantly to Bondi, Rivkin had never argued before the Supreme Court. Though it was an "agonizing decision" to "switch horses," the attorney general decided "it was not going to be Rivkin." All of the other attorneys general agreed to change counsel. Rivkin understood the decision and took it graciously, calling it a "typical Washington thing."

Bondi wanted "the best chance to win" the case with a top Supreme Court litigator. At its beauty contest, Florida interviewed over a dozen potential Supreme Court advocates. Florida did not consider Ted Olson of Gibson, Dunn, & Crutcher, who was President Bush's solicitor general and had argued *Bush v. Gore* and dozens of other cases before the Court. Despite his prolific record for conservative legal causes, Olson's work in challenging the constitutionality of Proposition 8 and supporting same-sex marriage was a red flag and cause for concern among the Republican attorneys general. Otherwise, Olson "would have certainly been in the running." Florida considered Maureen Mahoney and Gregory Garre of Latham & Watkins, as well as Bartow Farr (who would ultimately be appointed by the Supreme Court to argue an issue the government abandoned).

Eventually, the contest was narrowed down to three finalists: Paul Clement of Bancroft PLLC; Miguel Estrada of Gibson, Dunn & Crutcher; and Chuck Cooper of Cooper & Kirk.

Bondi flew to Washington to personally interview Clement. She "really liked [Clement's] demeanor" and thought he "had it all." With fifty arguments before the Court and an "incredibly eloquent" style, he was the "package deal." There was "no question" that Clement, and his superlative associate Erin Murphy at Bancroft, would be the team. Bondi told Supreme Court reporter Joan Biskupic that Clement "shared our passion, and he was confident we could win." And he came with an attractive price tag. The states gave Clement a flat fee of $250,000 to be shared by the twenty-six states.

Clement had become the top Supreme Court advocate of his generation. National Public Radio reporter Nina Totenberg referred to him as the "legal wunderkind." Clement had clerked for Justice Antonin Scalia. By the age of thirty-four, he became the deputy solicitor general to, of all people, Ted Olson. Shortly thereafter, President Bush promoted Clement to be the solicitor general, the youngest attorney to hold that office in over one hundred years. (Perhaps fittingly, Olson, Cooper, and Clement would square off before the Supreme Court in 2013 to argue on opposite sides of the same-sex marriage cases.) By the time he was forty-five, Clement had argued fifty-seven cases before the Supreme Court. Katyal considered Clement the "preeminent advocate in his generation." Solicitor General Donald Verrilli agreed, calling Clement "an extraordinary, extraordinary lawyer."

In government service, Clement argued key cases involving the war on terror, the Second Amendment, abortion, affirmative action, and, most saliently, the scope of federal power.

Ironically, one of Clement's victories had come in *Gonzales v. Raich,* where he faced off against none other than Randy Barnett (Washington is a very small world, after all). In *Raich,* Clement successfully persuaded the Court that possessing marijuana grown on one's own farm constitutes "economic activity" having an effect on interstate commerce. Even under *Lopez*, Congress could regulate this activity. For the ACA, Clement would have to flip the script and now convince the justices that the individual mandate was outside the scope of congressional power. Barnett found it "amusing" that he was now on the same side as Clement. Likewise, Clement found it "very amusing that he was opposite" Barnett on *Raich*. The pair became much closer during the next two years as they united in their common effort against Obamacare.

Once Clement was selected, Rivkin "just sort of dropped out." His name was on the briefs, but he was not involved. Rivkin, who was expecting to at least argue in the Eleventh Circuit, said that he was "not particularly happy that I didn't argue," but was magnanimous about the decision to drop him. Describing himself as a "soldier," Rivkin said that he had to be "disciplined" and that he would "salute" the clients and respect their decision.

FROM RICHMOND TO WASHINGTON

Katyal's first brief as acting solicitor general was filed in the appeal from Judge Hudson's decision to the Fourth Circuit Court of Appeals on January 18, 2011. On January 26, the parties filed a joint motion to expedite the case and hear it at the same time as another challenge brought by Liberty University. In that case, Liberty University, founded by evangelist Jerry Falwell, had challenged the ACA as a violation of Congress's Commerce Clause powers, as well as an infringement of its religious liberties. The district court had dismissed Liberty's case outright.

But Virginia was not planning to follow the normal course of appeals. Cuccinelli was going to hopscotch the court of appeals and leap straight to the Supreme Court.

On February 8, 2011, he filed with the Supreme Court of the United States a "petition for a writ of certiorari before judgment." This unorthodox motion asks the justices to consider a case before it has wound its way through the court of appeals. Court rules permit an appeal directly from a district court while an appeal is pending before the court of appeals, "upon a showing that the case is of such imperative public importance as to justify deviation from normal appellate practice and to require immediate determination in this Court."

This relief is seldom granted. It has been used sparingly over the last century in cases involving the convictions of Nazi saboteurs in front of a military tribunal (*Ex parte Quirin*), President Nixon's exercise of executive power in the wake of the Watergate scandal (*United States v. Nixon*), and the distribution of frozen assets in the aftermath of the Iran hostage crisis (*Dames & Moore v. Regan*). In any event, this was the first opportunity for the justices to consider Obamacare.

The brief was sent to the printers at the eleventh hour, and Virginia insisted that it had to be filed immediately. Virginia also requested that no one at the printer's office disclose any information about the petition until after the press conference that was scheduled for later that day.

Virginia's petition took an ominously partisan tone that was unlikely to curry favor from the justices. The ACA, the petition declared, "has roiled America. The party that unanimously opposed the PPACA in the House of Representatives has just seen its largest electoral gains in over seventy years. With the intervention of six additional states in the Florida suit on January 19, 2011, it became possible for the first time in American history to count a clear majority of states in litigation with the federal government, each claiming that the federal government has exceeded its enumerated powers."

Virginia asked the justices to review the case immediately. "There is a palpable consensus in this country that the question of PPACA's constitutionality must be and will be decided in this Court. Under these circumstances, the issues presented here should be considered to be at least as important as those presented in many of the cases where immediate review has been permitted." Virginia even suggested that the Supreme Court consolidate the Virginia petition with the appeal from Florida—a particularly ironic idea in light of the fact that Virginia had broken off from the Florida litigation and sought to go it alone. This richness was not lost on those in the Florida Attorney General's office, who smirked at this petition.

The government, in a brief signed by Katyal, opposed Cuccinelli's motion and dismissed allegations of Virginia's urgency: "Indeed, because [Virginia] has not sought expedition of its request for certiorari before judgment, even were its petition granted, this case would not be heard until next Term." In other words, Virginia's failure to follow the Supreme Court's procedures undercut the fast-track strategy.

The Supreme Court, to no one's surprise, denied Cuccinelli's petition. The Court considered this petition during its April 15, 2011, conference (fittingly, on the second anniversary of the first major Tax Day Tea Party protests), and again at its April 22 conference, but denied it on April 25, with one sentence: "The petition for a writ of certiorari before judgment is denied." However, this brief order offered an important clue. Usually, if justices recuse themselves from a case, they indicate in the order that they did not participate. Neither Justice Kagan nor any other justice offered any indication of a plan to recuse. It would not be long before the justices would have to get into the fray.

Shortly after Virginia's petition was denied, there was a flurry of activity in Florida to meet Judge Vinson's order. On March 9, 2011, the day before Vinson's deadline, the government appealed the case to the Eleventh Circuit Court of Appeals. Immediately after filing the notice of appeal, the government filed a "motion for expedition." Acting Solicitor General Neal Katyal asked the court to hear the government's appeal on an expedited basis, citing Judge Vinson's "unprecedented severability ruling."

The very next day, on March 10, the twenty-six states filed their own appeal. Likewise, Jones Day filed its first brief on behalf of the National Federation of Independent Business, appealing to the Eleventh Circuit.

While the attorney general of Virginia hoped to fast-track the case directly to the Supreme Court, the attorney general of Florida took a different path. Bondi asked that all eleven judges on the court of appeals, in what is known as an "en banc" hearing, consider the case right away. Usually an en banc hearing is only held following a decision by a three-judge panel—but to Florida this would take too long. Bondi thought this strategy could get the case to the Supreme Court faster. One lawyer for the challengers told me that it was aimed at "getting an answer sooner rather than later." The government did not actively oppose this motion.

However, the petition for an en banc hearing was denied. Oral argument was set for "Wednesday, June 8, 2011, at 9:30 AM, in Atlanta, Georgia, before a three-judge panel randomly selected." The appeals were set.

Strings Attached

The ACA aimed to expand health insurance coverage in two primary ways. First, the mandate required that those who could afford to purchase health insurance must do so. Second, those who were not well off financially would be covered under an expanded Medicaid provision. Medicaid began in 1965 as a cooperative program between the federal government and the states to provide health insurance to low-income people. States that agreed to create a Medicaid program for needy residents would receive federal money to pay for part of it.

The Constitution gives the Congress the power to "lay and collect Taxes, Duties, Imposts, and Excises, to pay the Debts and provide for the common Defence and general Welfare of the United States."

This authority is commonly known as the "spending power." It was through the spending power, and not the Commerce Clause, that Congress authorized Medicaid in 1965.

As with most things in life, there is no such thing as a free lunch—or free federal grants. In order for the states to receive the Medicaid money under the ACA, Congress attached certain strings, or "conditions," to the funding. Beginning in January 2014, the states would be required to provide Medicaid to people whose income is below 133 percent of the poverty line (for a family of four with two children, an annual household income of $30,000 would likely qualify for the Medicaid expansion). To help states absorb the cost of extending coverage to millions of new people who had not been covered before, the federal government would cover 100 percent of the costs of these newly eligible individuals from 2014 to 2016. During this period, the states would have to incur "significant administrative expenses." However, that coverage would decrease to 90 percent over the next several years. The states feared that covering this additional 10 percent would break their already strained budgets.

The challenging states objected, arguing that the Medicaid expansion was more than they had bargained for when they entered into the Medicaid program starting in 1965. Simply put, it would be too expensive to operate, and the states wanted to opt out. The so-called Cornhusker Kickback would have provided additional funding to Nebraska alone under this program. This is why South Carolina and other states initially got involved in opposing the ACA. It wasn't fair that one state got a freer lunch.

The only problem with declining the new funding, the challengers argued, was that failure to accept this new Medicaid program would also eliminate *all* the previous funding they had grown accustomed to receiving. In other words, to continue to receive *existing* Medicaid dollars, the states would have to accept the *new* funding, with all of the strings attached. Florida could not simply maintain the status quo. Florida wrote, "Congress has given the States no practical choice but to comply" and that the expansion "transforms Medicaid well beyond anything the States volunteered to implement" in 1965.

In court, Florida argued that the expansion violated what has become known as the "coercion doctrine" that arose from the principles of federalism protected by the Tenth Amendment. The Supreme Court articulated this concept in a 1987 case, *South Dakota v. Dole:* "In some circumstances the financial inducement offered by Congress might be so coercive as to pass the point at which 'pressure turns into compulsion.'" If the federal government places too many conditions on a federal grant, it becomes coercive—the states have no real choice but to accept the money. The states contended that the ACA crossed this line. They "quite literally cannot afford to sacrifice billions in federal funds" and "therefore have no real choice as to whether to accept these new conditions." Yet the Supreme Court had never found a law unconstitutional under the "coercion doctrine." As Judge Vinson noted early, "The 'coercion' theory has never advanced beyond a hypothetical exception to the spending power."

Until the case reached the Supreme Court, all of the courts consistently held that the Medicaid expansion passed muster. But the claim still lurked in the background as the case made its way up the ladder.

A New Limiting Principle, but Still a Tax

With new leadership in charge of the litigation came a shift in strategy. Neal Katyal felt that the only way to win this case was to give the Supreme Court clear limits on the scope of federal power. Not everyone in the government agreed. Many of the old guard, who came of age and went to law school in the 1970s and 1980s, thought that federal power was without limit. They determined that the cases from the 1990s known as the "Federalism Revolution"—including *Lopez* and *Morrison,* in which the Rehnquist Court placed limits on federal power—were mere aberrations. Further, to the extent that these cases were valid, the old guard believed that they had been repudiated by *Gonzales v. Raich,* the medical marijuana case where Paul Clement smoked Randy Barnett's vision of limited federal power. Katyal, who came of age during the Rehnquist Court, had a different view. He was very keen to reconcile the individual mandate with these federalism opinions while avoiding an argument that would open the door to unlimited federal authority. This divergence of views was described as a "generational issue."

Katyal believed that the government had to embrace these precedents and offer a coherent limiting principle in order to win. Within the government, there was a resistance to Katyal even articulating limiting principles. One DOJ lawyer told me that the difficulty with answering the question "Can the government do X" (such as, can the government make you buy broccoli?) "is that maybe one day Congress will try to do X." The government "never wants to give an answer whether something in the abstract is constitutional or not." Doing so may preclude future governmental action. This explains Solicitor General Drew Days's strategy not to answer questions about limiting principles in *United States v. Lopez,* the gun-free school zone case. This principle is also probably why Attorney General Eric Holder would later equivocate over Senator Rand Paul's question about whether the president can order a lethal drone strike of a U.S. citizen on American soil. Only after a twelve-hour filibuster did Holder answer clearly, "No." The government is loath to disclaim any power in advance of using it, no matter how unlikely it is that the power will ever be exercised (whether it be to approve domestic drone strikes or impose broccoli mandates).

Acting as solicitor general, Katyal had free rein to implement this strategy at the courts of appeals. While the attorney in the district court litigation had taken a circuitous route to avoid answering questions about the limiting principle to the government's power, the

Solicitor General's office under Katyal's stewardship opted to answer this question directly.

To Katyal, this was the "only way to get to five votes on the Commerce Clause." One former DOJ lawyer told me that Katyal was "100 percent convinced he was going to lose unless the answer was built around *Lopez* and *Morrison*," as these cases provided "ironclad" limits on federal power. Katyal would not make the mistake that he had witnessed Solicitor General Drew Days make years earlier in *Lopez*.

Katyal consistently answered the question about the limiting principle in the same way. In the Fourth Circuit, when Judge Diana Motz asked, "The Supreme Court in recent years has been very concerned about limits. Are we not just opening up to an unlimited congressional power here? What limit would remain?," Katyal offered a prepared, two-factored limiting principle that he would give in every court. "We agree completely with *Lopez* and *Morrison*. There are two rock-solid limits on [the] ability of [the] federal government to act on commerce power. First, it can't act in attenuated ways, [as in] *Morrison*. Second, it can't infringe on areas of traditional state responsibility. There is a distinction between what is truly local and truly national. This is a market that is truly national in scope."

Under the first rationale, there must be a close link between the federal government's powers to regulate interstate commerce and the regulated market at hand. Katyal believed there was a strong link between Congress's goal of limiting rising health care costs, which is interstate commerce, and the individual mandate, which is aimed at reducing those costs. Under the second rationale, the matter being regulated is within the authority of the federal rather than the state government. For most of the twentieth century, health insurance has been subject to federal regulations.

This question-and-answer was duplicated in the Sixth Circuit, when Judge James Graham asked Katyal, "I am having difficulty seeing how there is any limit to the [commerce] clause as you are defining it. Every human function has some economic consequences. If [the] power to regulate commerce includes [the] power to regulate economic activity, [i]f every human activity can be aggregated, where ultimately is [the] limit on Congress's power? [H]ow can courts begin to restrain Congress when it begins to do something invasive, such as to require someone to purchase a product or service they don't want?" Katyal replied, with ease, "We are not here saying that there are unlimited powers under commerce. We think *Lopez* and *Morrison* establish prohibitions that forbid the type of adding up.... That is the limit."

Katyal's calculus about the Supreme Court accepting this argument would prove, however, to be wrong. Ultimately, the limits that Katyal advanced would not persuade a single conservative justice. Solicitor General Verrilli, to his credit, would decide to de-emphasize this argument.

One of the lawyers for the challengers told me that Katyal was "ineffective" because he "refused to engage with the hostile questions" about the limiting principles. He simply "stuck to talking points." There was no way "to get to five votes with that position." The import of Katyal's arguments, another attorney for the challengers told me, was that "there were no limits" to the power to impose economic mandates.

Beyond the Commerce Clause, along with the Necessary and Proper Clause, the alternate basis for the law's constitutionality was under the taxing power. The Constitution gives Congress the power to "lay and collect Taxes." As Justice Stone had whispered into the ear of Francis Perkins decades earlier, the taxing power is much, much broader than Congress's power to regulate interstate commerce.

But the courts had so far consistently rejected the argument that the individual mandate was a tax. Judges seized on the fact that the law Congress wrote referred to the enforcement provision of the mandate as a penalty, not as a tax. In other places, Congress called provisions of the ACA a tax (such as the infamous "Snooki tax" on tanning). Yet the mandate was clearly labeled a "penalty."

This decision was not inadvertent. In his opinion finding the ACA constitutional, Sixth Circuit Judge Jeffrey Sutton noted that Congress chose not to style the mandate as a tax. "Words matter, and it is fair to assume that Congress knows the difference between a tax and a penalty, between its taxing and commerce powers, making it appropriate to take Congress at its word." In his opinion upholding the law's constitutionality, D.C. Circuit Court of Appeals Judge Laurence Silberman wrote: "That Congress called numerous other provisions in the Act 'taxes' indicates that its decision to use the word 'penalty' here was deliberate." Congress chose to call the mandate a penalty and not a tax.

Plus, the government still had to deal with President Obama's statement that the ACA did not raise taxes. During oral argument before the judge, Silberman asked Katyal: didn't the president "say over and over again he was not imposing a tax?" Judge Sutton stressed the politics of the matter: "Elected officials are not known for casually discussing, much less casually increasing, taxes. When was the last time a candidate for elective office promised not to raise 'penalties'?"

Although the taxing power argument became the darling of many in the professoriate, championed by law professors Jack Balkin, Neil Siegel, and others, administration lawyers became disenchanted by repeated defeats and turned against it. During Katyal's practice moot court sessions, when he led off with the taxing power, everyone "shut him down" and told him to concentrate on the Commerce Clause. Notwithstanding the letter that Katyal had sent to the White House citing the need to rely on the tax argument, many in the government were still concerned about its implications. Katyal agreed to make the commerce argument first and the tax argument second. At the courts of appeals, that proved to be a wise strategy.

The Eleventh Circuit Court of Appeals aptly summarized the record of the taxing power argument: "Beginning with the district court in this case, all [judges] have found, without exception, that the individual mandate operates as a regulatory penalty, not a tax." And so it would remain, until Chief Justice Roberts's opinion.

THE QUEEN CITY

The first court of appeals to decide the constitutionality of Obamacare was the Sixth Circuit, based in Cincinnati, Ohio. (I began clerking on the Sixth Circuit after this case was decided and had no involvement with it.) On June 1, 2011, the court heard the appeal from a district court in Michigan that had ruled that the ACA was constitutional in its entirety.

Yet, before the case was even argued, supporters of the ACA became leery. The three-judge panel would consist of one judge appointed by President Carter and two appointed by Republican presidents. One of the Republican-appointed judges was Judge Jeffrey Sutton, who six months earlier had moderated the debate with Cuccinelli at the Federalist Society's National Lawyers Convention. Sutton was seen by many as a possible Republican nominee for the Supreme Court in a Romney administration.

Many progressives panicked. As *Slate* columnist Dahlia Lithwick wrote, tongue in cheek, "If liberals want to get a head start on their own freak-outs over the lawsuits, they might well note that the just-announced panel for the June 1 hearings on the Affordable Care Act at the 6th Circuit Court of Appeals in Cincinnati includes a George W. Bush appointee, a Reagan appointee, and a Carter appointee. So we can already start writing that 2–1 decision."

Yet the arguments went surprisingly well for the government. Only twenty-eight days later, the court issued a split opinion with two votes in favor of upholding the mandate. On June 29, 2011, the Sixth Circuit became the first court of appeals to decide in favor of the Obama administration.

The majority opinion was authored by Judge Boyce Martin, who wrote, "At the outset, it is important to note that our elected officials and the public hotly debated the merits and weaknesses of the Act before Congress voted, and will undoubtedly continue to in the future. However, it is not this Court's role to pass on the wisdom of Congress's choice." Martin reasoned, "Virtually everyone will need health care services at some point, including, in the aggregate, those without health insurance." Thus, "by regulating the practice of self-insuring for the cost of health care delivery, the minimum coverage provision is facially constitutional under the Commerce Clause."

Judge James Graham, a district court judge who had been appointed by President Reagan and was temporarily sitting "by designation" on the court of appeals, dissented. "The ACA represents Congress's attempt to solve national problems in the health insurance market. That problems are felt nationwide does not mean that Congress can try to solve them in any fashion it pleases. Congress must choose from the limited powers granted to it by the Constitution, and federal courts have a duty to uphold the Constitution when Congress has exceeded its authority."

But the most significant jurisprudential aspect of the opinion was what Judge Sutton wrote separately. The fact that the law might "be unconstitutional as applied to some individuals, [but] not to all of them," he found, was sufficient to defeat a challenge to the law on its face. Sutton was able to save the individual mandate without having to base his ruling on the deeper grounds on which it might be unconstitutional. He found that because the individual mandate was constitutional as applied to some people who already had insurance, the court should not find it unconstitutional as applied to all people.

Judge Sutton, a prominent conservative jurist, shocked many by voting to uphold the ACA. As Lithwick noted, before Sutton's vote, "no judge appointed by a Democratic president has had a problem with it, while no Republican appointee has voted to uphold it."

The challengers would get several more bites at the apple. The ACA road trip was now headed to the Fourth Circuit in Richmond,

Virginia, the Eleventh Circuit in Atlanta, Georgia, and finally to the D.C. Circuit Court of Appeals in our nation's capital.

RETURNING TO RICHMOND

Because Cuccinelli's attempts to fast-track his case to the Supreme Court failed, he first had to make his arguments to the Fourth Circuit Court of Appeals in Richmond, Virginia, a few blocks away from his office. If the composition of the panel in Cincinnati augured well for the challengers, the three judges assigned to the case in Richmond looked good for the government—all three had been appointed by Democratic presidents.

Dahlia Lithwick channeled the confidence: "Even before oral arguments started last week over the constitutionality of President Obama's health care reform law at the federal appeals court in Richmond, Va., some conservatives were complaining that the result was preordained because the three-judge panel consisted of two Obama appointees and a Clinton appointee." The most senior judge on the panel, Diana Motz, was married to another federal judge, J. Frederick Motz, who was appointed by President Ronald Reagan. Motz quipped, "Yes, it's true: He's a Republican. It's his only flaw."

Arguments were held on May 10, 2011. Things did not go well for Virginia, and it became clear that the court would rule for the government. On his way out of the Lewis F. Powell Jr. U.S. Courthouse, Ilya Shapiro, a senior fellow in constitutional studies at the libertarian Cato Institute, shook his head. Shapiro joked to Cuccinelli, "Time to start writing the Cert petition."

Shapiro knew better than perhaps anyone what was at stake. His prediction to Cuccinelli was prescient. On March 31, 2010, weeks after the law passed, Shapiro had issued a challenge: he would debate anyone, anywhere, anytime about the constitutionality of Obamacare (as long as they paid his travel expenses). At the time, nearly all academics thought that the law was clearly constitutional. During the next two-and-a-half years Shapiro engaged in over one hundred debates across the country with law professors, attorneys, and anyone else who was up for the challenge. He and Barnett were the only people to attend all arguments at the courts of appeals, often sitting together and exchanging written notes.

Virginia's attempt to challenge the federal law by means of the Virginia Health Care Freedom Act failed. First and foremost the Fourth Circuit held that Virginia, "the sole plaintiff here, lacks standing to bring this action." Because the mandate "imposes no obligations" on Virginia, the Commonwealth did not have an interest in bringing the case. The court specifically rejected the validity of the VHCFA, which was in essence a "smokescreen for Virginia's attempted vindication of its citizens' interests." As Judge Andre Davis noted during oral argument, "How can there be standing if all it takes is for a state to pass a statute?" Harkening back to the Commonwealth's uneasy history with the federal government, the court concluded, "Virginia lacks the sovereign authority to nullify federal law." Cuccinelli's suit was stopped in its tracks and would never make it to the Supreme Court.

With favorable rulings in Ohio and Virginia, the government was 2–0. But the most important case was in Georgia—the appeal of that case united twenty-six states against the ACA. The Eleventh Circuit, which hears appeals from Florida, Georgia, and Alabama, held oral argument on June 8, 2011. The judges assigned to the case did not seem auspicious for Florida: Chief Judge Joel Dubina was appointed by President George H. W. Bush, but Judges Frank Hull and Stanley Marcus were both appointed by President Bill Clinton.

Arguing for the states was their advocate of choice, Paul Clement. After taking the same flight from Washington to Atlanta, Barnett and Clement shared a cab, along with Clement's associate, Erin Murphy. Barnett took that opportunity to ask Clement how he planned to handle the Necessary and Proper Clause—the issue that had so divided Barnett and Rivkin. Barnett was pleased and relieved when he learned Clement's approach. Mike Carvin was arguing on behalf of the National Federation of Independent Business. Each would receive thirty minutes of argument time. Neal Katyal would make his last argument on behalf of the government.

Arguments were held during a nationwide heat wave. It was an oppressive day in Atlanta, with a high of ninety-four degrees. Waiting in the thick humidity, the line of spectators trying to get into the courthouse—which included Barnett, Harned, Shapiro, and Supreme Court reporters like Joan Biskupic—snaked around the block. Chief Judge Dubina welcomed the advocates in his strong, southern drawl, and began, "I have read all the Supreme Court cases from the very beginning that talk about the Commerce Clause." Dubina noted that he could not "find any case [the Supreme Court has] written that's just like this. . . . There's no case out there just like this." He asked Katyal, "Would you agree with that?"

It was time for Katyal to make the government's most important argument to date. He wryly answered, "Depending on what you mean by 'just like this,' yes." During a follow-up question, Katyal clarified that "while there isn't a case that is exactly like this one, this case and what Congress is doing falls within a long line of Supreme Court authority." In other words, while the Supreme Court had not considered a case like this, what Congress did with the ACA was within the bounds of what the Court had allowed before.

Then Judge Dubina asked what had been the most difficult question for the government to answer: "If we uphold the individual mandate, are there any limits on Congress's power left?"

Katyal offered his stock response: "Absolutely there are limits. *Lopez* and *Morrison* established rock-hard limits on the power of the federal government, and nothing that we are saying here puts those decisions into question in any way." Later, Chief Judge Dubina asked Katyal again, unsatisfied with his previous answer, "If we uphold the individual mandate in this case, are there any limits on Congress's power left?" Katyal avoided answering the question directly and postured that health care is unique among all other areas that Congress can legislate on. "Our point is that people are seeking this good already in untold numbers, the good of health care, that it is almost a universal feature of our existence and that the failure to pay for that good when they seek it is what causes the cost-shifting."

Judge Hull did not seem satisfied with Katyal's argument, which implied that any law aimed at solving a "national problem" was constitutional. "You're basically saying, if it's within the ambit of the very broad national economy, which almost everything is, Congress can regulate it in a way as long as it's part and parcel of the national economy . . . and it substantially affects interstate commerce."

Katyal answered candidly, "Yes." The skepticism from the bench illustrates why Katyal's argument would later be deemed by his successor to be too "capacious." Paul Clement successfully persuaded the court that the government's "biggest problem on the Commerce Clause is the lack of a limiting principle."

Next, the questions turned to whether the government could force people to buy health insurance. Throughout the litigation, the government took great pains to argue that people were not being compelled to purchase health insurance, even though this was the crux of the challengers' case. Judge Marcus asked, "Is there any case out there that has sustained, on Commerce Clause grounds, the power to compel the purchase of a product on the open market?" Katyal replied, "That's not the power we're asserting here."

Paul Clement rejected this understanding of the mandate. "There's a great deal about this case that's complicated, but I think that the constitutional issue at the heart of it with respect to the individual mandate is actually quite simple. It boils down to the question of whether or not the federal government can compel an individual to engage in commerce the better to regulate the individual."

When Judge Hull asked, "Is it fair to say this is an economic mandate?" Katyal answered negatively. "I don't know exactly what the words 'economic mandate' mean. I would prefer to use the words Congress used—which are—'minimum coverage provision.' It is purely about financing." Katyal's implication was that there was in fact no actual mandate. This answer served as a precursor to the solicitor general's argument before the Supreme Court that there was no individual mandate, but merely a tax on those who choose not to buy health insurance.

After arguments, the challengers were confident. Ilya Shapiro felt pretty good and wrote, "In the most important appeal of the Obamacare constitutional saga, today was the best day yet for individual freedom. The government's lawyer, Neal Katyal, spent most of the hearing on the ropes."

On August 12, 2011, the Eleventh Circuit dealt President Obama his most decisive defeat to date, ruling the individual mandate unconstitutional. The court issued 307 pages of opinions, consisting of a 207-page majority opinion jointly authored by Judges Hull and Dubina—an odd practice in appellate judging—and a 100-page dissent from Judge Marcus.

What made this alignment even more significant was that for the first time Judge Hull, nominated by a Democratic president, voted to strike down the mandate (Hull was deemed to be more of a moderate).

First, the court rejected the government's argument that the mandate was supported under Congress's taxing power. "The individual mandate was enacted as a regulatory penalty, not a revenue-raising tax, and cannot be sustained as an exercise of Congress's power under the Taxing and Spending Clause. The mandate is denominated as a penalty in the Act itself, and the legislative history and relevant case law confirm this reading of its function." In other words, Congress had called it a penalty, not a tax, and so would the court.

Second, the court held that the mandate exceeded Congress's Commerce Clause power: "The individual mandate exceeds Congress's enumerated commerce power and is unconstitutional." The court labeled the mandate a "wholly novel and potentially unbounded assertion of congressional authority: the ability to compel Americans to purchase an expensive health insurance product they have elected not to buy, and to make them re-purchase that insurance product every month for their entire lives." It was, in every sense, unprecedented.

The court rejected Katyal's limiting principle: "We have not found any generally applicable, judicially enforceable limiting principle that would permit us to uphold the mandate without obliterating the boundaries inherent in the system of enumerated congressional powers." The court specifically shot down Katyal's position that the health care market was in fact unique: "'Uniqueness' is not a constitutional principle in any . . . Supreme Court decision." Katyal's "rock-solid" limiting principle was pulverized into constitutional dust.

Third, the Eleventh Circuit, like all other courts before it, held that the expansion provisions of Medicaid were constitutional. "Existing Supreme Court precedent does not establish that Congress's inducements are unconstitutionally coercive, especially when the federal government will bear nearly all the costs of the program's amplified enrollments." It would take the Supreme Court to change that doctrine, not an "inferior court."

Unlike Judge Vinson, who had compared the ACA to a Swiss watch that could not be disassembled into pieces, the Eleventh Circuit decided that it could simply cut out the mandate from the remainder of the 2,700-page bill. "The individual mandate, however, can be severed from the remainder of the Act's myriad reforms. The presumption of severability is rooted in notions of judicial restraint and respect for the separation of powers in our constitutional system. The Act's other provisions remain legally operative after the mandate's excision."

Yet, in aiming for judicial restraint, the Eleventh Circuit created a chimera-ACA. Without a mandate, premiums would skyrocket. The guaranteed issue and community rating provisions, in the absence of the individual mandate, would create an unsustainable death spiral of costs, thus crippling the entire law.

The dissent from Judge Marcus challenged the majority's engaged approach to the power of judicial review. "The approach taken by the majority has . . . disregarded the powerful admonitions that acts of Congress are to be examined with a heavy presumption of constitutionality, that the task at hand must be approached with caution, restraint, and great humility, and that we may not lightly conclude that an act of Congress exceeds its enumerated powers."

The Eleventh Circuit's decision created a split among the circuits. The Eleventh Circuit had found the law to be unconstitutional, while the Sixth Circuit—joined by the Fourth and D.C. Circuits—had found the law to be constitutional. It was now certain that this case was headed to the Supreme Court. As law professor Ilya Somin wrote, "It is now extremely likely that the Supreme Court will end up hearing the case, as the Court cannot allow a situation where the mandate is valid in some parts of the country but not in others."

But before the appeal to the Supreme Court, there was some procedural drama. The judgment from the Eleventh Circuit was about to go into effect, and the government had to make a choice. It could seek en banc review, which would have put the issue in front of all eleven judges on the court of appeals. This choice would have delayed the case and pushed the Supreme Court's consideration until after the 2012 election—by which time President Obama might be a former president. Or the government could go directly to the Supreme Court, which would virtually guarantee a decision from the justices by June 2012, placing the ACA center stage in the heat of the upcoming election.

Initially, the government "kept the states in the dark" about whether it would "go for cert" right away or seek en banc review by the Eleventh Circuit. If the government dragged its feet, it could effectively push the argument in the case to after the election. With such uncertainty, NFIB considered filing its own petition on all issues, even though it had won in the lower courts and had nothing to appeal—a plausible argument in light of the Court's precedents. NFIB's petition was drafted but never sent to the printers.

Clement went "back and forth with the government," inquiring about how they would proceed. Eventually NFIB learned from Clement that the solicitor general was soon going to file. The Obama administration decided to seek immediate review by the Supreme Court. At the "eleventh hour," a lawyer from Florida told me, "Paul worked it out" with the government. Everyone would file cert petitions on the issues they lost. Both the United States and Florida would file their appeals "on the same day." A lawyer for NFIB told me that "Paul has pretty good connections."

Randy Barnett praised the government's decision to go directly to the Supreme Court. "The president and solicitor general deserve full credit for refusing to employ delaying tactics in this pressing constitutional controversy." Jennifer Haberkorn of Politico added a more cynical take. "The Justice Department did not explain its decision, but there were strong reasons for it not to pursue the en banc hearing. There are only five judges appointed by Democrats on the 11-judge circuit, and one them has already ruled to strike down the mandate."

The next, and final, stop on the ACA road trip was One First Street, NE—the address of the Supreme Court.

ROMNEYCARE RETURNS

As November 2012 approached, the race for the Republican nomination became fiercer. At the GOP primary debate on September

12, 2011, in Tampa, Florida, Governor Mitt Romney was under fire about the health insurance mandate in Massachusetts, which had been dubbed "Romneycare." At another debate, former Minnesota Governor Tim Pawlenty famously referred to the ACA as "Obamney-care." In a response to a point from Herman Cain, Romney—in order to explain how Romneycare differed from Obamacare—said: "It was good for the state, but not the federal government. And with regards to Massachusetts care, I'm not running for governor. I'm running for president. And if I'm president, on day one I'll direct the secretary of Health and Human Services to grant a waiver from Obamacare to all fifty states. It's a problem that's bad law, it's not constitutional. I'll get rid of it."

Texas governor Rick Perry, who had announced his candidacy for president a month earlier with some fanfare, shot right back. Romneycare was the "plan that President Obama has said himself was the model for Obamacare." Representative Michele Bachmann agreed. "We are never going to get rid of [Obamacare] unless we have a president committed to getting rid of it. And if you believe that states can have it and that it's constitutional, you're not committed. If you've implemented this in your state, you're not committed. I'm committed to repealing Obamacare."

Romney had attempted to explain away Romneycare, with little success. In a May 12, 2011, address at the University of Michigan, Romney released a report and accompanying soporific PowerPoint slides. "Our plan was a state solution to a state problem," Romney said. In contrast, Obamacare "is a power grab by the federal government to put in place a 'one-size-fits-all' plan across the nation. . . . They fundamentally distrust free enterprise and distrust the idea that states are where the power of government resides," said Romney. In an editorial, the *Wall Street Journal* tartly called Romney "Obama's Running Mate," adding: "More immediately for his Republican candidacy, the debate over ObamaCare and the larger entitlement state may be the central question of the 2012 election. On that question, Mr. Romney is compromised and not credible. If he does not change his message, he might as well try to knock off Joe Biden and get on the Obama ticket." Romney's inability to articulate an opposing vision on Obamacare would be a key setback for his ill-fated campaign.

A CAPITAL CASE

Before the ACA made its way to One First Street NE, it had one final pit stop to make in Washington, D.C., about half a mile down Constitution Avenue at the E. Barrett Prettyman U.S. Courthouse. There the D.C. Circuit Court of Appeals would be the final arbiter to weigh in on the ACA before the Supreme Court took over.

The D.C. Circuit held oral argument on September 23, 2011. The panel was loaded with two conservative all-stars: Judges Laurence Silberman and Brett Kavanaugh. Silberman, who had been appointed by President Reagan, was seen as a possible candidate for the Supreme Court in the late 1980s and early 1990s. He had delighted conservatives with his significant opinion in *Parker v. District of Columbia,* finding that the Second Amendment protects an individual right to keep and bear arms. The Supreme Court would agree with Silberman the next year in *District of Columbia v. Heller.* Paul Clement had clerked for Silberman before clerking for Justice Scalia. Kavanaugh served as senior counsel to President George W. Bush before being appointed to the D.C. Circuit at the young age of forty-one. Like Sutton, Kavanaugh consistently "fed" clerks to the justices of the Supreme Court and was viewed as a possible Supreme Court nominee in a Romney administration. The third jurist was Judge Harry Edwards, a well-respected and distinguished Carter appointee. Randy Barnett praised the "intellectual fire power of the panel."

For the first time, Neal Katyal did not present the government's case at a court of appeals. This time, the briefs were signed by Solicitor General Donald Verrilli.

Beth Brinkmann would argue this case for the United States. Unlike her predecessor, Katyal, Brinkmann evaded any effort to identify a limiting principle. Her strategy was a dry run for Verrilli's approach before the Supreme Court.

When Judge Silberman asked, "Let's go right to what is your more, most difficult problem: what limiting principle do you articulate?" Brinkmann answered, "Certainly, here, Your Honor, this is a regulation of economic activity, it's the means by which people finance their health care services, and it is using insurance, which is the customary means." Silberman interrupted. "Counsel, you're telling me what the facts of this case [are], but you know the difficult question for you is what kind of mandate . . . could Congress come up with under the Commerce Clause which would be unconstitutional? What kind of requirement that persons buy services or products would be unconstitutional?"

Following the office's new strategy, Brinkmann avoided answering the question directly. "Well, certainly it would depend. . . . " Frustrated, Silberman cut her off midsentence: "Just give me an example. Give me an example." She wouldn't. Silberman pressed. "Is it you're unwilling to give me any example of a mandate that would be unconstitutional?" If so, he continued, did that "then feed into your opponent, who says you have no limiting principle?" Brinkmann replied, "Far from it, Your Honor. Not at all. I think it's difficult." She stuck closely to her plan.

Like Silberman, Kavanaugh was also concerned about the limiting principle. "Another major concern I have . . . is in 220 years, with a whole lot of laws and a lot of crises, Congress has never once mandated a purchase." But even when Silberman asked Brinkmann again, "Give me an example of something that would be unconstitutional," she didn't answer the question. Brinkmann wasn't unprepared—she simply did not have the authority to answer that query.

Brinkmann's evasiveness was a preview of what her new boss, Solicitor General Verrilli, would do at the Supreme Court. Her circuitous answers were not sloppy—rather, they were part of a concerted effort not to identify the limiting principle. The arguments at the D.C. Circuit were a walk-through—a moot court, if you will—for the Supreme Court. Ilya Shapiro "cautiously predict[ed] a 2–1 ruling in favor" of striking the mandate.

The D.C. Circuit's opinion was released on November 8, 2011, one week before the Supreme Court would grant review of the Florida case. In a shocking development, all three judges voted to uphold the mandate, though for different reasons.

Judge Silberman, joined by Judge Edwards, decided that Congress had the authority under its commerce powers to enact the mandate.

Unlike Judge Sutton, Silberman thought he was "obliged to confront the gravamen of appellants' argument as to the scope of the Commerce Clause." He rejected the challengers' argument that the mandate was unprecedented. "The mandate, it should be recognized, is indeed somewhat novel, but so too, for all its elegance, is appellants' argument." Further, Silberman would not read an activity requirement into the Supreme Court's cases. "In short, we do not believe these cases endorse the view that an existing activity is some kind of touchstone or a necessary precursor to Commerce Clause regulation."

Verrilli's strategy not to provide a limiting principle had proved successful. Silberman wrote, "We acknowledge some discomfort with the Government's failure to advance any clear doctrinal principles limiting congressional mandates that any American purchase any product or service in interstate commerce." But he was not discomforted enough to strike down the law. Instead, Silberman stressed that Congress should receive the benefit of the doubt. "We are obliged— and this might well be our most important consideration—to presume that acts of Congress are constitutional." This strategy would prove decisive to Chief Justice Roberts.

Judge Kavanaugh did not join Silberman's opinion. Instead, he wrote a sixty-five-page opinion that argued that the court could not even decide this case—his opinion intentionally did not resolve the case on the merits.

Kavanaugh's opinion was premised on an 1876 law called the Anti-Injunction Act (AIA) as applied to an arcane section of the tax code. Even though the government did not rely on this provision of the tax code, Kavanaugh still applied it. In fact, his highly technical analysis came out of left field (or is it right field?). No one anticipated it. During the oral argument, Judge Edwards asked Brinkmann if she had read the obscure provision that Judge Kavanaugh was asking about, and would ultimately hang his opinion on: "You haven't read it yet, have you?" Brinkmann, who had been involved with the litigation since March 2010, replied, "No." Judge Silberman asked her to "read it, please." Kavanaugh joked in his opinion, "The Tax Code is never a walk in the park."

The purpose of the Anti-Injunction Act is to prevent taxpayers from challenging a tax in court before it is assessed. Instead, they must first pay a tax under protest and challenge it after the fact by seeking a refund. The penalty under the ACA would not be assessed until 2014. In the district court, the government used the AIA as a defense. If the AIA applied, the challengers would have to wait until the tax was assessed in 2014 before challenging it. Almost every court had rejected this notion, finding that the mandate was not a "tax," as defined by the AIA.

When Neal Katyal had assumed control of the case, he abandoned this losing position. Judge Silberman wrote of this change in his opinion: "Earlier in this litigation, the Government argued that the Anti-Injunction Act barred this suit because the shared responsibility payment is a 'tax.' . . . The Government has since abandoned that position." Likewise, as Judge Motz noted for the Fourth Circuit Court of Appeals, "Both the Secretary and plaintiffs contend that the AIA does not bar this action." Judge Kavanaugh counted ten district courts in which the government argued that the "Anti-Injunction

Act barred these cases." No one, not even the president, wanted to delay this case until 2014—when he might no longer be in office, Judge Kavanaugh reasoned. Katyal explained that the administration "changed its mind about the Anti-Injunction Act . . . presumably because of an understandable policy desire to have courts resolve the constitutional question about the individual mandate sooner rather than later." He concluded, "We don't think AIA applies, even if it is favorable to the government."

One lawyer for the challengers told me that it was "remarkable" that the government conceded that the Anti-Injunction Act did not apply. It was "pretty powerful" for the government to abandon the AIA issue, as the federal government had a strong "institutional interest in having it apply." Indeed, internally many in the Treasury Department vigorously opposed this decision. Former commissioners of the Internal Revenue Service filed a brief with the D.C. Circuit arguing that the AIA should apply. The "government saying it does not apply, and you should reach the merits" now, was significant. The administration "wanted a decision sooner rather than later." They simply did not want to wait.

Yet Katyal's choice put the government in an awkward position. Like Janus, he was looking both ways, and arguing simultaneously that the mandate was *not* a tax for purposes of the Anti-Injunction Act, and that it *was* a tax for purposes of the Constitution's taxing power.

If the mandate was a tax under the AIA, the case could not be heard until 2014. This is known as a "jurisdictional" rule, meaning that courts have no discretion—it cannot be heard early. The government did not want this to happen—it wanted the case to be heard right away—so the government waived the AIA argument and gave it up. (It is impossible for the government to waive a jurisdictional rule. By finding that the penalty was not a tax for purposes of the AIA, the Court did not need to reach the issue of the government's waiver.)

However, in order for the AIA not to apply, the mandate could not be a tax. So long as the mandate was not a tax, the suit could be brought before 2014. What complicated this situation was the government's simultaneous assertion that the mandate was a tax, for purposes of Congress's broad power to lay and collect taxes. But if the mandate was not a tax, the government could not rely on the taxing power to support it. This head-scratching contradiction would be fully explored at the Supreme Court. If you're confused, don't worry—Chief Justice Roberts would untie this Gordian knot.

Kavanaugh concluded, "In any event, in my judgment, the relevant prudential considerations favor our waiting until 2014." Kavanaugh looked beyond the upcoming presidential election. "If we do not decide the constitutional issue now, we may never have to decide it."

JUDICIAL RESTRAINT

Both Judges Sutton and Kavanaugh found ways to uphold the ACA while avoiding the constitutional question and to send this dispute back to the elected branches of government. Both opinions evinced the principles of judicial restraint. Rather than engaging the constitutional issues, Kavanaugh's and Sutton's opinions chose to avoid them. Both sought to avoid deciding the constitutional issue today, and either require the suits to be brought in the future or, even better, place their hope in the political process to fix the mess. But they reached these conclusions in different ways.

Judge Kavanaugh expressed his sentiments of restraint during argument, tempering the "notion that [judges] all feel powerful." He stated, "You know, we're courts of judicial restraint. It's a delicate act to declare an Act of Congress unconstitutional." Kavanaugh harkened back to the New Deal clash between the Supreme Court and President Roosevelt—opposition that led Roosevelt to threaten "packing the Court" with justices of his choosing. In the future, "there could be a lot of that going on, depending on the constitutionality and the policy judgments, but why should a court get in the middle of that and risk being another 1935 situation where you're in the middle of a change going on in how commerce is thought of in terms of the Government?" DOJ lawyers would often speak of a "sense of historical déjà vu" with the New Deal.

During oral argument in the Sixth Circuit, Judge Sutton also expressed his preference for allowing the law to go into effect before a court considered its constitutionality. Under this approach, "We don't have to reach that issue today." His approach allowed for "judicial restraint," so we only "reach the hardest issues when we really have to reach them. . . . We can answer that some other day." Sutton wrote, "Nothing prevents such individuals from bringing as-applied challenges to the mandate down the road."

Sutton took a very humble posture in his opinion, noting that it was "not the job of a middle-management judge to abandon the distinction between taxes and penalties." Sutton was "mindful that we at the court of appeals are not just fallible but utterly non-final in this case." He was invoking the famous maxim from Justice Robert Jackson about the Supreme Court: "We are not final because we are infallible, but we are infallible because we are final."

Sutton preferred to wait. "Time assuredly will bring to light the policy strengths and weaknesses of using the individual mandate as part of this national legislation, allowing the people's political representatives, rather than their judges, to have the primary say over its utility." In an article, Judge Sutton reiterated the sentiment. "In close cases, it thus makes sense for courts to err on the side of democracy— to allow the elected branches of government to monitor, adjust to, and ultimately solve, as best they can, difficult social and economic problems."

A year earlier, at the 2010 Federalist Society National Lawyers Convention, when Sutton had moderated a panel on Obamacare with

Cuccinelli and Rosen, he had said, presciently, "We can be principled in advocating for judicial restraint." His opinion fulfilled that aspiration.

Obamacare opponents were not so sanguine about Sutton's opinion. Ilya Shapiro wrote that "it is shocking that an avowed constitutionalist like Judge Sutton" would uphold the law in the manner he did. . . . If the [Supreme] Court joins the Sixth Circuit and goes there, it would mean putting the final nail in federalism's coffin." Over cocktails at the Madison Club reception during the following Federalist Society National Lawyers Convention, the two reached a rapprochement.

Michael Carvin, lead counsel for the NFIB, had worked with Sutton while he was an attorney at Jones Day. Carvin recalled that Sutton was "not a [Justice Antonin] Scalia type of a conservative," but "more of a [Justice] Lewis Powell type of a guy." In right-wing circles, those are fighting words. Powell was a moderate Nixon appointee who voted in favor of abortion rights, affirmative action, and other progressive issues. Even in his time at the Supreme Court, Sutton was pulled between those two poles. Sutton was hired to clerk for the then-retired Powell but would often be detailed to the chambers of Justice Scalia. One longtime Supreme Court follower told me that "Sutton's opinion was written as memo to John Roberts of why you need to uphold the mandate." Yet no other judge would adopt Judge Sutton's reasoning.

Kavanaugh also articulated his vision of restraint. "To be clear, federal courts do not wait to decide constitutional cases simply because of the possibility of congressional change to the legislation or presidential non-enforcement of what the President concludes is an unconstitutional law. Delay on that basis would constitute judicial abdication, not judicial restraint. But the discussion here has been addressing the question whether there are compelling prudential considerations that would justify overriding the limits of the Anti-Injunction Act and deciding this case now."

Kavanaugh, however, made a point in passing that was not lost on the solicitor general. A statute similar to the one Congress enacted, but without the individual mandate, said the judge, would be absolutely constitutional. Kavanaugh reasoned that a "minor tweak to the current statutory language would definitively establish the law's constitutionality under the Taxing Clause (and thereby moot any need to consider the Commerce Clause)."

By "eliminat[ing] the legal mandate language"—that is, by deleting a single sentence—the statute would be transformed from a command on people to purchase insurance to a mere tax on those who do not have insurance. The former was of dubious constitutionality, but the latter would be well within Congress's powers. Kavanaugh was echoing Justice Stone's whisper to Frances Perkins, "The taxing power of the Federal Government, my dear, the taxing power is sufficient for everything you want and need." Like Frances Perkins before him, the solicitor general listened carefully.

Simply eliminating one sentence—the mandate—would save the law. With an assist from Judge Kavanaugh, the solicitor general advanced this very argument at the Supreme Court.

PART V

Strategizing for the Supreme Court

(November 14, 2011–March 25, 2012)

On March 26, 2012, when oral arguments began before the Supreme Court, this constitutional challenge would reach its crescendo. But first, the parties had to prepare for the clash. Under the leadership of Donald Verrilli, the new solicitor general, the government made several pivotal strategic decisions. Verrilli de-emphasized Katyal's limiting principle, which was deemed too "capacious." Under that principle, the government could enact any economic regulation that implicated a national problem; that did not limit nearly enough. Departing from the previous strategy, the solicitor general insisted that the office take another, closer look at the taxing power argument, which he felt had only been perfunctorily advanced. As a fallback strategy, if the Commerce Clause argument did not work, Verrilli chose to argue that the ACA should be understood as an incentive-enforced-by-taxes rather than a mandate-enforced-by-penalties. The latter is of dubious constitutionality, but until this case even an "incentive" tax on inactivity was unprecedented. That was new law by the Chief Justice. With this alternate strategy, the Solicitor General's office felt that Chief Justice Roberts could be persuaded to become the pivotal "fifth vote."

THE CHANGING OF THE GENERALS

Before the case arrived at the Supreme Court, there was first a changing of the generals in the Solicitor General's office. On June 6, 2011, Verrilli was confirmed by a 72–16 vote. Acting Solicitor General Neal Katyal would argue the appeal before the Eleventh Circuit Court of Appeals two days later on June 8, but that would be his last task in the office. Verrilli was sworn into office on June 10. The next day Katyal submitted his letter of resignation, to be effective at the end of June. Many questioned the administration's choice to replace Katyal with Verrilli shortly before the case would wind up at the Supreme Court. However, Obama's decision to appoint Verrilli made clear to Katyal that he would not be the one to argue the ACA case before the Supreme Court. Tony Mauro reported for BLT: The Blog of Legal Times, "Katyal's departure was rumored for months after Verrilli was nominated to the position, though he publicly indicated his support for Verrilli." Though he still teaches constitutional law at Georgetown, after being approached by over thirty firms, Katyal joined Hogan Lovells—the same firm that previously employed John G. Roberts.

Coming to the case late, Verrilli had to get up to speed quickly. Arguments were less than ten months away. From the outset, Verrilli made this case his top priority. Normally, the solicitor general only reviews a draft of a brief to the Supreme Court four or five days before it is due, leaving deputies to write and edit. If it is an important case, the solicitor general may be involved early on in discussions. For the health care cases, however, Verrilli was deeply involved with strategic decisions from the outset and in shaping the arguments that would be made. He would work closely with his deputies on the briefs, reading and rereading them up to eight times before submission. In the Solicitor General's office, it was said, preparing for this case was "just like any other case, just more so."

Everyone was on high alert. Whereas usually assistant general counsels of the various cabinet-level departments might attend strategy meetings with the Department of Justice, for this case the general counsel of each agency crowded each meeting along with all the other attorneys working the case.

Solicitor General Donald Verrilli was now in charge—and with that office came a reappraisal of the strategy before the Supreme Court, which led to several important decisions.

Verrilli first had to decide whether to argue that the Anti-Injunction Act would bar consideration of the case until 2014. The argument that the AIA applied was rejected in many of the lower courts. After considering views from the various government departments, cabinet secretaries, and the Justice Department, the Solicitor General's office "made a judgment to stay where we were." One lawyer stressed that, as an "initial matter," it might have been better not to give up that issue, but that it would "risk our credibility to switch positions on this issue not once, but twice." This might seem "opportunistic." The "best course of action was to argue that the Anti-Injunction Act did not apply." So the solicitor general stayed the course with respect to the AIA. Yet that position raised the same conundrum that Katyal had confronted in the lower courts: how could the mandate both not be a tax, for purposes of AIA, and be a tax, for purposes of the taxing power?

Verrilli's second big decision was to depart from the limiting principle that Katyal had advanced in the lower courts—but not for the expected reasons. The attorneys in the Solicitor General's office were "under no illusion from the outset that the Commerce Clause argument was not going to be challenging." Internally, the government conceded that there "wasn't anything quite like the individual mandate." Even they knew it was unprecedented.

After "careful consideration," Verrilli thought Katyal's argument "ultimately was not going to be helpful as a limiting principle." The "rock-solid" limits that Katyal located in *Lopez* and *Morrison* "wouldn't seem robust enough [as] a limiting principle under these circumstances." More importantly, Katyal's position could not answer the hard hypotheticals—including, of course, the broccoli horrible example. Deeming the principles in *Lopez* and *Morrison* too "capacious," the Solicitor General's office came to the conclusion that those cases "were not going to be enough, and they needed to give a narrower answer." If *Lopez* and *Morrison* represented the outer bounds of government power, the government could impose any economic mandate that addressed a national problem. If the government drew the line at these cases, the justices, potentially worried that the government could do too much, might not buy the argument.

In the end, Justices Scalia, Kennedy, Thomas, and Alito did obliterate the argument advanced by Katyal, writing that the Constitution does not give Congress the "whatever-it-takes-to-solve-a-national-problem power." Notwithstanding the Necessary and Proper Clause, the mere fact that a national problem—such as health care—exists does not give Congress additional powers. The Constitution "enumerates not federally soluble problems, but federally available powers." Chief Justice Roberts's opinion on the Commerce Clause would concur with this view. After the case was decided, a government lawyer told me that this section in the joint opinion validated the decision not to continue with Katyal's argument. It did not persuade a single conservative justice, let alone result in five votes.

Third, Verrilli prepared for a fallback argument in the event the Court rejected the leading commerce clause position. After arriving at the office, the solicitor general thought that the government's taxing power argument had not been made as well as it could be. One government attorney characterized the taxing power argument as "just going through the motions," almost as if "we didn't really believe it. This could be a ground on which the statute was upheld." The D.C. Circuit Court of Appeals' order requesting additional briefing from the government on the taxing issue underscored that the Solicitor General's office wasn't "conveying enough in [its] briefs." The sentiment grew that the taxing argument was merely being raised to "preserve it," but that it "wasn't integral to the analysis."

The decision to take a second look at the taxing power came from the top. One reporter who covers the Supreme Court told me that Verrilli personally "insisted on pushing" it. Of course, the "obvious problem" was that the word "tax" was not in the individual mandate provision. The word used was "penalty." "Apart from that," I was told by a senior DOJ official with no irony, that the tax argument "had a lot going for it." Judge Kavanaugh's opinion convinced the Solicitor General's office that the "tax argument might be a more conservative and judicially restrained basis to act to uphold as a tax." The "nomenclature was the only serious impediment to winning." Despite this problem, the solicitor general believed that characterizing the mandate as a choice between maintaining insurance and paying a tax was not only a way of avoiding a serious constitutional question, but indeed the best reading of the law. Though it "wasn't ideal," the government determined that it "could manage" this argument. And the key to solving that problem of nomenclature fell directly on the shoulders of Donald Verrilli, with Judge Kavanaugh being credited with the "assist." In what should be a permanent exhibit in the Washington Museum of Doublespeak, Verrilli persuasively argued that the mandate was, at the same time, not a tax and a tax.

In the course of preparing for the filings before the Supreme Court, the solicitor general reread *New York v. United States*. In this 1992 opinion, the Supreme Court held that the federal government could not force New York to take title, or possession of, radioactive waste. Such an order would violate the Tenth Amendment and principles of federalism and states' rights. The case was one of the important precedents in the so-called Federalism Revolution of the Rehnquist Court.

But in a more obscure portion of the case, Verrilli saw what turned out to be the key to the Chief Justice's controlling opinion. The statute at issue in *New York* stated that "each state *shall* be responsible for providing" for the disposal of radioactive waste. This was a *mandate*. New York's refusal would result in "penalties for failure to comply." The solicitor general had a "holy cow" moment: he realized how similar the statute in *New York* was to the ACA. The individual mandate in the ACA used similar language: "An applicable individual *shall* . . . ensure" that she is "covered under minimum essential coverage." If a person failed to obtain that level of coverage, "a penalty [would be] imposed on the taxpayer." Both laws, on their face, created a mandate with associated penalties. The similarities were striking—and this argument had not been made anywhere in the government's briefs up to that point.

In *New York v. United States,* Justice Sandra Day O'Connor, writing for the Court, found that to view the statute as a mandate on the states would render it unconstitutional. Rather than reading it in a way that would make it unconstitutional, O'Connor chose instead to read the statute in a way that would preserve its constitutionality. She transformed the mandate into a "series of incentives." Verrilli realized that this case was a novel way to explain how the mandate could be saved. If he could use this precedent to persuade the Court to read the ACA's minimum coverage provision as a series of incentives premised on a tax, as Justice O'Connor did, rather than a mandate premised on a penalty, he was home free. After all, the "tax power was so attractive," as one DOJ lawyer described it, and illustrated "much more of a gestalt of the breadth of congressional powers."

If the Court rejected the government's commerce clause arguments— their primary position—I was told the fallback saving construction had the "best chance of winning over Chief Justice Roberts's vote." The government thought that this argument, "premised on notions of judicial modesty," would appeal most to Roberts. One administration lawyer told me that Verrilli was "one of the few people who saw that the chief justice could be the fifth, and not the sixth, vote." Although this argument was only presented in passing in the solicitor general's briefs, it predominated the government's time during the first day of oral arguments concerning the Anti-Injunction Act—not the second day of arguments about the commerce and taxing power. Months later, in his opinion, Chief Justice Roberts adopted the saving construction. Relying on Justice O'Connor's opinion in *New York*, and citing the solicitor general's brief, as well as the transcript from the solicitor general's oral argument, Roberts concluded, "We see no insurmountable obstacle to a similar approach here."

Fourth, in preparing the case before the Supreme Court, Verrilli, after careful consideration, rejected many of the arguments of leading academics. Under the previous stewardship of Neal Katyal, a constitutional law professor at Georgetown, academics had been given much greater access to the government's strategy and had a greater impact on it. Much to their disappointment, Verrilli clamped down on that access.

On April 27, 2012, Yale Law School hosted a conference on constitutional law, focusing on a recent book by Professor Jack Balkin. Over the past two years, Balkin had been Barnett's progressive foil, leading the intellectual movement on the left in defense of the ACA. (The two are, in fact, excellent friends.) Balkin had been developing arguments in support of the individual mandate's constitutionality since the fall of 2009. Held a month after oral arguments, the conference doubled as a venting session for many who were frustrated with the litigation, and in particular Verrilli's approach to the case. Many academics felt "frustrated" and "cut out" because the solicitor general did not allow their participation at all. In contrast, Katyal had had a "footing with the academy." The attendees also were not happy with Verrilli's strategy. One professor said that Verrilli was leaving the best possible arguments "on the table." Some attributed Verrilli's poor performance in the argument to his rejection of academic assistance. The sentiment became, "It was Don's fault. If someone decent was arguing the case, it would have gone better." Or more precisely, "If Don would have just listened to us, he wouldn't have messed up."

Yet the solicitor general apparently did not "lose any sleep" over discounting the professors' opinions. Many of their arguments, especially those based on mandates in early America, were, I was told, at best, "footnote material." The fact that Verrilli was unwilling to adopt these popular limiting principles is evidence that the leading arguments from academics were not nearly as airtight and conclusive as many argued. A lawyer who served in the administration and later returned to academia told me that Verrilli's choice "was spot on and was absolutely right." Though many professors, including Balkin and Siegel, consistently advanced the taxing power argument, ultimately it was Verrilli's formulation of the fallback saving construction that would win the day.

Certiorari Is Granted

Serving as a justice on the Supreme Court is a cushy gig. Justices are guaranteed lifetime tenure during "good behavior," and their salaries cannot be decreased. They set their own hours, usually meeting three to four days a week between the first Monday in October (the official start to the term as set by Congress) and the last week in June (right before summer vacation commences). One of the biggest perks is that the justices decide for themselves what cases they will consider. They can choose, with limited exceptions, what appeals they will review. Parties who are unsatisfied with a judgment of a federal Court of Appeals or a state Supreme Court can file a petition for a writ of certiorari, asking the Supreme Court to review their case, but granting this writ is purely discretionary. On the Court, the so-called Rule of Four provides that if any four justices want to review a case, certiorari—or "cert," as it is commonly known—is granted.

In November 2011, the cert petition from the Eleventh Circuit's judgment came before the justices. Most agreed that the Court would have to take the case to resolve this monumental issue, especially given the split between the lower courts. And it did. On November 14, 2011, the Court granted certiorari and agreed to hear the case.

But the justices did more: they broke up the massive dispute into four concrete issues, each to be argued separately. More astonishingly, the Court granted almost six hours of argument time over the span of three days, an unprecedented amount of time for the modern era. Most cases receive a mere hour of argument time. After certiorari was granted, Senator Mike Johanns of Nebraska stressed the significance of the extended time: "It is one of the most important cases reviewed in recent history. The Court has set aside a remarkable six hours for oral arguments, more time than has been devoted to a case in over four decades."

McConnell v. FEC, an important campaign finance case, had received four hours of argument in 2003. The landmark criminal procedure case of *Miranda v. Arizona* received six in 1966. The seminal school segregation case *Brown v. Board of Education* was allotted fifteen hours over the course of two arguments, one in 1952 and another in 1953. But most others, including such blockbusters as *Roe v. Wade,* the landmark Supreme Court case involving abortion, got only one hour of argument time.

Ultimately, even six hours would prove insufficient. On the final day, Chief Justice Roberts would add thirty more minutes. Roberts was more generous with time than his predecessor, Chief Justice William Rehnquist, who would notoriously cut off advocates in midsentence when their time was over.

By granting so much time to the appeal, the justices signaled that they were going to take the case very seriously and air out all possible issues. This did not bode well for the administration. An attorney for NFIB told me that he could not "imagine that the government was thrilled with that much argument" time. The "unprecedented length of argument underscored the point about the importance of the case [and] the seriousness of the challenge." The lengthy time granted "made quite foolish the people pontificating" about the inevitability of the government's success. That dismissive position "became patently absurd in the face of six hours of oral argument" time. With the cert grant, Randy Barnett felt vindicated and became more "optimistic."

The first day was scheduled for Monday, March 26, 2012. On that day, the justices would consider whether the Anti-Injunction Act prevented the Court from hearing the case until the mandate was actually enforced in 2014.

The second day would be the key day. The justices would consider whether Congress could pass the individual mandate under its commerce or taxing power.

The third day would be a doubleheader. In the morning, the justices would listen to arguments about whether, if the individual mandate was unconstitutional, the rest of the ACA could survive. This was the "severability" argument. After a very brief lunch break, everyone would return to hear arguments concerning the constitutionality of the Medicaid expansion.

Faced with the need to divvy up their time between the states and NFIB, the challengers decided that Clement would argue the Medicaid issue on Wednesday afternoon on behalf of the states, and that Clement and Carvin would each argue on Tuesday about the commerce and taxing power authority. It remained unclear, however, who would argue on Monday and Wednesday mornings. Carvin and Clement asked the Court for "divided argument time" for the Anti-Injunction Act and severability issues. To their "unpleasant surprise," this motion was denied. Karen Harned told me that after "casual conversations with Clement," they decided that each side would get "equal time." Because the states wanted Clement to argue severability on Wednesday, NFIB "acquiesced." Carvin's partner, Gregory Katsas, was assigned to argue the AIA issue.

Solicitor General Verrilli was to personally argue three out of the four arguments: Monday on the Anti-Injunction Act, Tuesday on the Commerce Clause and taxing power authority, and Wednesday afternoon on the Medicaid expansion. Edwin Kneedler, a veteran in the Solicitor General's office, would argue the severability issue on Wednesday morning.

The Supreme Court appointed two Washington, D.C., attorneys— Robert A. Long and Bartow H. Farr III—to argue on behalf of the positions the government had abandoned: the Anti-Injunction Act and severability, respectively. This was done to ensure that the justices were presented with the best arguments on all points.

The dates were set. The issues were set. The lawyers were set. The main event would soon begin.

J'ACCUSE RECUSE

Throughout 2011, there were calls for two justices—Clarence Thomas and Elena Kagan—to recuse and not hear the case. The politics of the calls for recusal were transparent on both sides. With only eight votes, the likely outcomes would be a 5–3 vote or a 4–4 tie. Without Kagan, a 5–3 vote, assuming Kennedy voted with the conservatives, would kill Obamacare. A 4–4 tie would affirm the Eleventh Circuit, resulting in the invalidation of Obamacare. Senator Orrin Hatch implied as much when he noted, somewhat optimistically, that with a tie, "the lower court decision will be the acting law." Without Thomas, a five-vote conservative bloc would be impossible. Yet, all three prognostications assumed that the swing vote would be, as usual, Anthony Kennedy. In fact, it would be Chief Justice Roberts who would cast the deciding vote.

In February 2011, seventy-four House Democrats, led by soon-to-be-former-representative (and future mayoral candidate) Anthony

Weiner, wrote a letter asking Justice Thomas to recuse himself. The letter cited the involvement of his wife, Ginni Thomas, with Liberty Central, a Tea Party group that she directed. Ginni Thomas claimed that her name had inadvertently appeared on a Liberty Central memo asserting that Obamacare was unconstitutional. Although she had resigned from Liberty Central in November 2010, she had become a lobbyist in February 2011. "The appearance of a conflict of interest merits recusal under federal law," the Democrats wrote. "Your spouse is advertising herself as a lobbyist who has 'experience and connections' and appeals to clients who want a particular decision—they want to overturn health-care reform." The letter closed, "We urge you to recuse yourself from this case. If the U.S. Supreme Court's decision is to be viewed as legitimate by the American people, this is the only correct path."

As fiercely as Democrats urged Thomas to recuse, Republicans urged Kagan to recuse. Senator Hatch said, "I think that Kagan, who was the solicitor general at the time this was all done, probably should recuse herself, which means it might not be resolved by the Supreme Court." A number of conservative groups, including Judicial Watch and the Judicial Crisis Network, echoed Hatch's call. They cited the emails exchanged between Kagan, Tribe, and Katyal as evidence that the justice had been involved in the case and had expressed enthusiasm about the ACA. Remember, Kagan told Tribe, "I hear they have the votes, Larry!!"

However, Kagan did not make this error. From an early age, she was very cognizant of where she was headed in life. In her eighth-grade yearbook, Kagan famously posed for a photograph wearing a judicial robe and holding a gavel. She added a quotation from Supreme Court Justice Felix Frankfurter in her caption: "Government is itself an art, one of the subtlest of the arts."

Kagan understood very well the "art of government" and deftly navigated her way through the system: from Princeton, to Harvard Law School, to the chambers of Justice Thurgood Marshall (he called her "Shorty"), to an academic career, to the Clinton White House, back to Harvard Law School, first as a professor and then as a dean, to the Solicitor General's office, and to her final destination on the Supreme Court. Kagan has a reputation for being uniquely skilled at this "subtlest of arts." She knew better than to be involved in this case. As Kagan famously told Neal Katyal, "You should do it." Dahlia Lithwick aptly wrote, "She was at pains to distance herself from this case because it would have looked bad." Kagan did not recuse.

Thomas also did not recuse. At a February 2011 Federalist Society dinner at the University of Virginia, which I attended, Politico reported that Justice Thomas praised his wife, saying that they both "believe in the same thing" and "are focused on defending liberty." Thomas also passionately assailed his critics—presumably those who called for his recusal. Addressing the crowd of law students, Thomas proclaimed, "You all are going to be, unfortunately, the recipients of the fallout from [this situation]. There's going to be a day when you need these institutions to be credible and to be fully functioning to protect your liberties." Thomas implied that the Court, as an institution, may not be there for them.

Thomas closed with a quotation from Reverend Martin Luther King Jr.: "In the end, we will remember not the words of our enemies, but the silence of our friends. And what I think is important for you all, is that when you see people standing in defense of what's right, that you make sure that your voice is not remembered as one of the silent."

Thomas is notoriously taciturn on the bench. He did not say a word from the bench for over seven years. That streak was broken in January 2013 in order to make a joke at the expense of his alma mater, Yale Law School. However, he is a passionate and engaged speaker.

All nine justices would hear this case: Chief Justice John Roberts, and Justices Antonin Scalia, Anthony Kennedy, Clarence Thomas, Ruth Bader Ginsburg, Stephen Breyer, Samuel Alito, Sonia Sotomayor, and Elena Kagan. The "Nine" were ready.

Walk the Line

The Supreme Court is one of the last places on earth where cameras are not allowed. The justices do not permit any recording devices inside the courtroom, nor do they permit a live audio feed to be broadcast. The only way to witness the proceedings live is to be physically present in the Court.

The Supreme Court releases a small number of tickets for the general public, usually fifty, on the day of arguments. Typically, the only way to obtain tickets is to arrive at the Supreme Court at the crack of dawn and wait on the sidewalk outside. For higher-profile cases, it is necessary to arrive the night before and camp out on the sidewalk. I have done this several times, once waiting over twelve hours in 2009 for arguments in *McDonald v. Chicago,* which considered whether Chicago's handgun ban violated the right to keep and bear arms.

The most unsettling aspect of such a campout, aside from the possibility of rain or cold weather, is the sprinklers. They come on every morning around 3:00 AM and give all sleeping spectators a wet wake-up call. For the most part, social norms develop that allow people to get up, move around, make a run for Union Station (the only bathroom open at night), or get some food or coffee at the nearby Au Bon Pain. However, the Supreme Court police (don't call them security guards!) do nothing to enforce the line. If you leave the line, you may lose your spot.

This was the most important case in a generation. To witness history, a dedicated group of spectators braved the blistering cold, scattered thunderstorms, and freezing rain. They camped outside the Supreme Court for up to ninety-two hours to secure one of the fifty coveted tickets set aside for the public.

The first person in the line was Kathie McClure, a trial lawyer from Atlanta; she arrived on Friday at 2:00 PM, three days before arguments were scheduled to begin on Monday. Kathie said, "I wanted to see the

Supreme Court's health care arguments with my own two eyes because my kids are sick with incurable illnesses, type 1 diabetes and epilepsy, and are uninsurable in the private insurance market." She would camp outside the Court for ninety-two hours. "I've never pulled four all-nighters in a row—not in law school or child-rearing—much less outside in rain and freezing temps with a pop-up chair, flimsy sleeping bag, and a tarp," she recalled. When a reporter from the *Washington Post* asked her if the "92 variously wet, cold and sleepless hours" were worth it, she replied that they were. "Because for me liberty is the right to see very personal justice being dispensed with my own two eyes." By Friday afternoon, three days before arguments would begin, seven other people had joined McClure on the line. A nearby church allowed them to take showers.

The second person in line was Monica Haymond, who kept an invaluable blog of her experiences on the line. She complained about "midnight sandblasting at the Capitol building that kept us awake," but "most of us," she said, "were able to sleep until it started sprinkling around 5:30." By Saturday morning, there were clashes with the hired line-waiters, many of whom were paid minimum wage to sit outside for days. The line-waiting companies, a common fixture on Capitol Hill, charged thousands of dollars for the service. Ironically, Haymond recalled, one of the paid "line standers" was a "40-year-old man who has never had health insurance in his life."

On Saturday night, Haymond wrote, a "heavy rain unleashed itself on the crowd at 2:00 AM, waking everyone who had managed to fall asleep sitting upright in their chairs . . . [and] at 4:00 AM the coup de grâce—just as the rain had stopped the automatic sprinklers shot to life and drenched everyone from behind." The company that hired the line-waiters "never delivered their promised rain supplies, and most had few ways to protect themselves."

Haymond wrote on her blog that by early Sunday morning the line had "quadrupled in size, rounding the corner on East Capitol [Street].

A count at 8:00 put the number at approximately 47." The early ar-
rivals tended to be more in favor of the ACA. The line continued
to snake down First Street toward the Library of Congress. After an
"abrupt 3:00 AM shower" on Monday morning, the "line had grown to
80 participants over night."

Argument day had finally arrived. Hundreds of protesters turned
the plaza outside the Court into a circus. At the Court, the "free
speech zone" extends along the sidewalks and the plaza—but not
onto the Court's iconic steps. Protest there and you get arrested.

Tea Partiers competed with progressives for media attention.
C-SPAN cameras were trained on the festivities all day long, since
the action inside the Court was off-limits. HEALTH CARE IS A HUMAN
RIGHT read one sign. Another person waved American and Gadsden
flags and screamed that "for the federal government to infringe on
every person is unconstitutional." The demonstrations would continue throughout all three days of argument.

Haymond recalled that, "at 7:30 [on Monday morning], the police instructed the line that 60 people would be admitted [to the first
day], and no one would be allowed a second viewing." Many of those
in line went in to hear the first day of argument. However, McClure,
Haymond, Daniel Rice, and a few others chose not to go inside with
the crowd and to continue to brave the elements on the line for one
day more. They wanted to be in the Court for the historic second day.

And so, on March 26, 2012, almost two years to the day after the
law's enactment, the Supreme Court heard oral arguments on the
constitutionality of the ACA. After two years of litigation, political
wrangling, and punditry from the ivory tower to the beltway to the
Tea Party, the case had finally reached its crescendo before the nine
justices.

PART VI

In the Supreme Court

(March 26–28, 2012)

The drama that would unfold at the Supreme Court over the three days of argument was a worthy encapsulation of the roller-coaster ride that was the constitutional challenge to the Affordable Care Act. With Donald Verrilli confirmed as the new solicitor general, the government would test out its new strategy before the nine justices. On the first day, Verrilli attempted to persuade the Court that the individual mandate was both a tax and not a tax—and that, by the way, there was actually no mandate. On the second day, Paul Clement skillfully argued that Congress lacked the powers under the Commerce Clause to compel people to buy insurance. On day three, Clement and Verrilli clashed over whether the federal government could take away Medicaid funding from states that did not want to comply with the new conditions. By the end of the third day, the outcome was looking favorable to the challengers. Though this resolution would not remain for long—the votes on the Court would soon switch.

Day One: Tomorrow It's a Tax, but Today It's Not

On the first day, the justices would consider whether the Anti-Injunction Act allowed the Court to consider the suit before the mandate was actually enforced in 2014. But the solicitor general had an ulterior motive—to convince the Court that there was in fact no mandate, but merely a tax on an individual's failure to obtain health insurance.

The solicitor general began the most important series of arguments of his life by saying, "This case presents issues of great moment." While most onlookers and analysts felt that the arguments on the second day would be the most dramatic, the first day proved to be the most important—to Chief Justice Roberts at least.

The solicitor general had a very curious argument. First, for purposes of the Anti-Injunction Act, the individual mandate, which he referred to as the "minimum coverage provision," was not a tax. If it were a tax for purposes of the AIA, the Court could not hear any challenges to it until it was assessed—and this would not happen until 2014. The following day, however, Verrilli would have to argue that the mandate was in fact a tax, for purposes of Congress's power to lay and collect taxes. What was not a tax on Monday would be a tax on Tuesday.

The justices were very skeptical about how the same law could be a tax under the Constitution but not a tax under the AIA statute.

Right off the bat, Justice Alito challenged the solicitor general. "Today you are arguing that the penalty is not a tax. Tomorrow you are going to be back and you will be arguing that the penalty is a tax. Has the Court ever held that something that is a tax for purposes of the taxing power under the Constitution is not a tax under the Anti-Injunction Act?" The solicitor general replied, "No, Justice Alito," and tried to explain how the same provision could be a tax tomorrow but not today. (In an odd moment of déjà vu, exactly one year later during oral arguments about the constitutionality of the Defense of Marriage Act, Justice Alito would ask Verrilli virtually the same exact question, substituting "standing" for "tax": "Well, tomorrow you're going to be making a standing argument that some parties think is rather tenuous, but today, you're—you're very strong for Article III standing?")

Justice Scalia was not persuaded that the penalty was a tax for any purposes. On the next day, he asked Verrilli directly, "The president said it wasn't a tax, didn't he? . . . Is it a tax or not a tax? The president didn't think it was." Verrilli, no doubt frustrated by this question, evaded it with some Washington-spin: the president, Verrilli noted, had said that the penalty "wasn't a *tax increase*," but he didn't say it wasn't a *tax*. A new tax must logically be a tax increase.

Chief Justice Roberts was skeptical. "You're telling me [Congress] thought of it as a tax; they defended it on the tax power. Why didn't they say it was a tax?" Verrilli did not answer the question, but insisted, "This Court has got an obligation to construe it as an exercise of the tax power, if it can be upheld on that basis." This would become Verrilli's consistent argument throughout the entire case. Speaking to the chief justice, Verrilli said that the Court "has a solemn obligation to respect the judgments of the democratically accountable branches of government, and because this statute can be construed in a manner that allows it to be upheld in that way, I respectfully submit that it is this Court's duty to do so." Even if Congress structured the mandate as a penalty, if the Court could read it as a constitutional tax, it should. This argument echoed a point that Verrilli had made in his briefs. "Congress enacted the Affordable Care Act, and chose to include the minimum coverage provision, after years of careful consideration and after a vigorous national debate. That was a policy choice the Constitution entrusts the democratically accountable branches to make, and the Court should respect it."

Despite the justices' skepticism, the solicitor general, keeping with his strategy, urged the Court again and again to construe the penalty as a tax, even if that was not what Congress intended, in order to avoid finding that Congress lacked the constitutional power to enact it. In response to a question from Justice Alito about whether the mandate was to be viewed as a tax, Verrilli said over and over again, "If there's any doubt . . . *the right way* to handle this case [is to] read [it] that way."

Likewise, when Justice Kagan remarked, "Congress determinedly said this is not a tax," Verrilli replied, again, "Not only is it fair to read this as an exercise of the tax power, but this Court has got an obligation to construe it as an exercise of the tax power, if it can be upheld on that basis."

In his closing arguments on the final day, Verrilli repeated himself again: "But if there is any doubt about that under the Commerce Clause, then I urge this Court to uphold the minimum coverage provision as an exercise of the taxing power."

Verrilli had made the argument that would save the ACA. Everyone had been so distracted with the Commerce and Necessary and Proper Clauses on day two that the most pivotal argument remained right under their noses but had gone almost unnoticed on day one.

If the minimum coverage provision was a tax, as Verrilli argued, how would the justices treat the separate statutory command to purchase insurance, which provided that a covered person must "ensure" that she "is covered under minimum essential coverage"? This legal requirement was distinct from the penalty and could not independently be justified by the taxing power. In order for the Court to accept the solicitor general's argument that the minimum coverage provision was simply a tax—even though Congress had not called it a tax—the Court would have to make one huge inferential leap. To buy Verrilli's argument, the justices would have to disregard the fact that the individual mandate was a separate compulsion to purchase health insurance.

The hardest part of the theory was persuading the Court that despite two years of litigation over the individual mandate, there was in fact no mandate and no punishment for failing to comply with the provision. To Verrilli, the health care law did not compel people to buy insurance. Rather, the law only required that those who did not buy insurance to pay a tax. Such a law could more easily be justified by the taxing power. The only problem with this argument was that it did not reflect the statute that Congress wrote. This construction effectively read several words out of the ACA.

Verrilli pushed back against any questions about the mandate and rejected any assertions that it was an "entirely stand-alone" requirement to buy insurance. As the government noted in its brief, citing the opinion of Judge Kavanaugh from the D.C. Circuit, "To the extent the constitutionality of [the act] depends on whether [the minimum coverage provision] creates an independent legal obligation [a mandate], the Court should construe it not to do so." In other words, in order to save the ACA, the Court should read the mandate to not be an actual mandate.

When Justice Alito asked if people are "not under an obligation to maintain the minimum essential coverage," Verrilli responded, "That's correct." Returning to his fallback argument, he repeated the refrain that this was "the stronger reading of the statute."

But if there was no mandate, what would happen if a person failed to purchase insurance? Justice Sotomayor asked the solicitor general whether there was any "collateral consequence for the failure to buy" health insurance—that is, would there be any criminal penalties for not buying insurance? The solicitor general responded, emphatically, "No." The only consequence would be that the person would have to pay a tax.

Further probing this issue, Justice Kagan asked whether people who failed to obtain insurance would have "violated any federal law"? Verrilli answered clearly, "No," adding that, as long as "they pay the tax, then they are in compliance with the law." Verrilli misspoke. Justice Breyer jumped in, "Why do you keep saying 'tax'?" Verrilli corrected himself and said, "Penalty." It was a Freudian slip—Verrilli really meant "tax," because that was what he wanted the Court to see it as.

Verrilli then offered an important "representation" to the Court on how the Obama administration viewed the law. This representation proved pivotal. The "only consequence" of not having health insurance was the "tax penalty." Verrilli noted that the government "made a representation, and it was a carefully made representation, in our brief that it is the interpretation of the agencies charged with interpreting this statute, the Treasury Department and the Department of Health and Human Services, that there is no other consequence apart from the tax penalty." In other words, there was no mandate or legal requirement to buy insurance, despite the statute stating that there was such a requirement.

In his brief, the solicitor general wrote that the minimum coverage provision "does not operate separately from the tax penalty" and that those who did not comply would *not* be "regarded as violators of a freestanding statutory requirement." At this moment, it became clear why Verrilli personally was making the arguments on the first day. As one veteran Supreme Court litigator told me, the solicitor general "needed to personally invoke" this theory because he "represents the authority of the federal government." No one else carried the same authority.

The solicitor general recognized that this representation was critical. It was "indispensable" that for his taxing power argument to work, the provision had to only be a tax. There "couldn't be any separate legal consequences." Senior officials at the Treasury Department were unhappy with this representation. They did not want to abandon the power to compel people through mandates in other circumstances. Remember, the federal government is loath to disclaim any power. Internally within the Obama administration, this was "not an easy decision to make." I was told by a senior DOJ attorney that it was "not normal for government lawyers to say something is not actually a legal requirement," but the solicitor general knew this was pivotal to winning the case.

This argument was devised by the solicitor general in response to a point that Michael Carvin had stressed throughout the litigation—the Anti-Injunction Act did not apply because they were not challenging the tax; rather, they were challenging the mandate. This position implied that there were two separate provisions, the mandate and the tax. No one was challenging the tax, Carvin contended. Likewise, Paul Clement argued, "the challenge here is to the mandate, and not the penalty that enforces it. The two are distinct provisions with distinct exemptions."

The solicitor general, in response to these strong arguments, advanced the position that in fact there was no free-standing mandate. A DOJ lawyer told me that NFIB's argument on Monday about the separate provisions "presented an opening" and a "way to gain advantage on Monday, before the Court got to it on Tuesday." At the Court, the solicitor general made the conscious decision to spend his final minutes nailing down the point that there was no separate mandate apart from the tax.

The states opposed the government's effort to "jettison both the mandate and the penalty and replace them with a tax." Clement urged the Court not to "reconceptualize the mandate as a tax statute that Congress made a deliberate decision not to enact." Clement's brief reminded the Court that "Constitutional avoidance is a powerful doctrine, but it is not a license to rewrite a statute in a way that bears no resemblance to the enacted text." This was the very argument that the chief justice would ultimately accept. Roberts would rewrite the statute in exactly that manner, citing Verrilli's brief and oral argument statement, where the representation was made.

Later in the day Roberts seemed to have accepted Verrilli's position. In questioning Gregory Katsas, the lawyer for NFIB, Roberts said that it "doesn't seem to make much sense" that "the mandate is something separate from" the penalty—that is, they were one and the same. Katsas tried to explain, but the chief justice persisted, asking, "What happens if you don't follow the mandate, and the answer is nothing?" That was Verrilli's crucial representation: nothing would happen for failing to comply with the mandate. Thus, Roberts continued, "it seems very artificial to separate the punishment from the crime." After this question, an NFIB attorney told me that he worried that if Roberts accepted this argument, the "door was wide open" for him to find that mandate was a tax. Once the chief justice made this "legal interpretive move, then the argument that it is a tax was pretty solid." Roberts, on the first day of argument, while everyone was so intently focused on the Commerce Clause, was already forecasting his ultimate vote.

Because no punishment was associated with refusing to buy insurance, the best reading of the statute was to say that those who failed to maintain insurance were subject to the tax penalty and were not lawbreakers in any sense—unless they failed to pay the tax. The mandate could not be a freestanding obligation, separate from the penalty. An NFIB attorney later told me that if they lost on the taxing power, he was willing "to bet every dime he had that they lost the way the solicitor general argued it." That was the "*only* way to rule for the government."

Three years of arguing over whether the individual mandate was constitutional boiled down to the claim that there was no mandate after all.

Perhaps the only pundit who realized the ingenuity of Verrilli's strategy was Harvard Law School professor Larry Tribe—the same professor Kagan had exchanged celebratory emails with on the day the law was enacted. On Thursday, March 29, 2012, in his "Thinking About the Constitution" class for Harvard undergraduates, Tribe made prescient comments:

> There was an interesting point that Roberts made a couple of times on Monday, and that was this: did he think it made any sense to view the mandate as a free-standing obligation to purchase insurance separate and apart from the tax penalty for not doing so? Interestingly, the chief justice says, "Look, I don't understand the idea that the mandate is a free-standing obligation; the mandate says, Purchase health insurance, or else, or else what? Or else you have to pay a penalty." And if the chief succeeds in persuading others on the Court, and maybe all that's needed is that he, himself may be persuaded, that the mandate and the tax penalty are part of an inseverable whole and that the law simply says to people, "You have a choice, it's not really a mandate even though it's called one, you have a choice to either buy insurance or see your tax bill go up a little bit to compensate for the fact that you didn't buy it and are thereby imposing costs on others"—if it's seen as a choice, and if you're not viewed as a law-breaker as long as you pay the penalty, though you don't comply with the so-called mandate, then the taxing power becomes a much more readily available basis to uphold what Congress did in the Affordable Care Act.

Tribe went on to comment on the solicitor general's response to Roberts's question: "What if somebody for example is on probation, and is asked, 'Have you violated any federal law lately?' could the person truthfully answer, 'No, I haven't,' even though the person didn't purchase the required insurance but merely paid the penalty?"

> The Solicitor General said, "I assure the Court"—and he's in a position to do so given his pivotal place in the Justice Department and in the government—"I assure the Court that anyone who pays the penalty when required will not be deemed a lawbreaker from the perspective of the United States government." Well, given that assurance, it becomes considerably more plausible to see the law being upheld under the taxing power, as Judge Kavanaugh suggested it would be [as] if the law were interpreted this way. Kavanaugh is in the D.C. Circuit in the case that I emphasized earlier. So that's one straw in the wind that I think is sort of more or less overlooked in the media discussions but that I think could be very important.

Tribe nailed it less than twenty-four hours after the arguments concluded and before the justices even met at the pivotal conference. But for the moment, it would be one of Tribe's former constitutional law students who reveled in the spotlight.

THE "INTELLECTUAL GODFATHER"

The big day had arrived. On Tuesday, the Court would hear arguments about whether Congress had the power to enact the individual mandate. That morning, the *New York Times* ran on the front page a glowing profile of Randy Barnett—authored by Sheryl Gay Stolberg and Charlie Savage—featuring a photo of the grinning professor in front of the Supreme Court.

Titled "Vindication for Challenger of Health Care Law," the profile was a tribute to Barnett's leadership in advancing this case from a mere idea to the Supreme Court. Over the two preceding years, "through his prolific writings, speaking engagements and television appearances, Professor Barnett has helped drive the question of the health care law's constitutionality from the fringes of academia into the mainstream of American legal debate and right onto the agenda of the United States Supreme Court." Previously, the *Times* had referred to Barnett as the "intellectual godfather" of the challenge. The profile concluded that Barnett, "more than any other legal academic," was associated with the challenge. Barnett was very pleased with the piece and called it quite "favorable."

The profile also drew attention to many who doubted the merit of this argument. When Barnett first began challenging the health care law, "many of his colleagues, on both the left and the right, dismissed the idea as ridiculous—and still do." Typifying this dismissiveness was University of Virginia law professor Douglas Laycock, who deemed Barnett's challenge frivolous: "He's gotten an amazing amount of attention for an argument that he created out of whole cloth." Laycock wondered why anyone was even paying attention to Barnett: "Under existing case law this is a very easy case; this is obviously constitutional. I think he's going to lose eight to one."

Many supporters of the ACA sneered at the profile, which they claimed gave gushing treatment to what they deemed to be a frivolous argument. Instead, they argued, the *Times* should have focused on the conservative judges who struck down the law and who, in their opinion, had acted politically rather than apply any constitutional doctrine.

Linda Greenhouse, the Pulitzer Prize–winning reporter who covered the Supreme Court for the *Times* from 1978 to 2007, was not pleased with the coverage of the case in the paper of record. At the same Yale Law School event in April where law professors faulted Verrilli, Greenhouse criticized the reporting on the ACA by her successor at the *Times*, Adam Liptak. Greenhouse, who now writes on the *Times* Opinionator blog, asserted that Liptak and others at the

Times, by giving the challengers so much attention, created a "false equivalency." Greenhouse claimed that Liptak validated Barnett and his frivolous ideas. Smirking, Barnett relayed to me what other professors were saying: "Randy Barnett was the creation of the *New York Times.*"

Liptak emphatically rejected Greenhouse's "false equivalence" allegation. At the conference, he quipped, "Do I sense some hostility?" Later, Liptak would tell me that he was "taken aback by what I perceived to be harsh and heartfelt criticism from people I respect at my alma mater" (Yale Law School). He added that at the conference "There was something like a consensus that the press in general and perhaps the *New York Times* in particular had fallen down on the job by unduly dignifying the arguments in support of the Commerce Clause challenge to the Affordable Care Act." Liptak felt, however, that he had "present[ed] both sides of the argument." Courts are a "poor place to make the 'false equivalency' criticism," Liptak explained. "The critique is weaker still when the arguments on one side were made by a majority of the states and had divided the lower courts." Liptak added, "As it turned out, there was reason to present fairly an argument that would end up capturing five votes on the Supreme Court"—contrary to the "consensus in the legal academy that the Commerce Clause argument was frivolous and would be rejected by a lopsided vote."

Charlie Savage, who coauthored the profile of Barnett for the *Times,* told me that the story was "one of many articles about the biggest D.C. news event of the moment," and that the editors at the *Times* "decided to commission [it] in order to add some human interest to the mix. It was a moment of major drama, and [Barnett] was a driving force behind it, so he merited the scrutiny." Kevin Sack, who covered the ACA litigation for the *New York Times* during the early stages, told me that he "enjoyed his relationship with Randy Barnett. Barnett, in addition to many other scholars and attorneys, took a lot of time to walk me through things. It was a fascinating legal education." Sack related that, at first, most progressives were dismissive and told him the case was "preposterous," no doubt hoping the press would agree. However, as favorable rulings came in, ACA supporters "started to talk more seriously" as "it became clear this was going to be a legitimate legal argument."

The members of the Supreme Court press corps, a close group of colleagues who have been covering the beat for a long time, largely disagreed with the assertion that the media was setting up a "false equivalency." Joan Biskupic, legal affairs reporter for Reuters, told me that, as a journalist, the "false equivalency" argument didn't make sense to her. She had to "treat the argument as if it was legitimate because the courts were treating it as legitimate." Robert Barnes, the Supreme Court correspondent for the *Washington Post,* told me that the challengers made "compelling arguments" that struck him as "certainly plausible" and that warranted attention. He was "surprised by how others dismissed the challenge." The challengers' initial legal victories were given prominent front-page coverage because "they really made people think differently about what was going on" with the law. David Savage of the *Los Angeles Times* also disputed the allegations of a "false equivalency," noting that, from the outset, the challengers "had the makings of a reasonable argument," since the government was "crossing a line" by telling people they had to buy a product. Savage added that it is "wrong to start with the premise that there is no argument on the other side." The job of journalists, he said, "is to explain and lay out the arguments on both sides, not to say one side is baloney." Ilya Shapiro, who was in close contact with the media throughout the litigation, told me that this case represented a "changing of the guard. Greenhouse out, Liptak in." While waiting in line to enter the court that day, Barnett saw his former constitutional law professor, Larry Tribe. Tribe, who was quoted in the *New York Times* piece, told Barnett that he only had good things to say about his former student. Barnett thanked him for his generous words.

Day two at the Supreme Court would be Barnett's moment to shine—though decision day would prove to be bittersweet.

Day Two: "He Choked"

Back at One First Street, it was pandemonium. The *Wall Street Journal* called the scene outside "sidewalk theater." But the real show would begin promptly at 10:00 AM inside the Court.

At the stroke of 10:00, Chief Justice John G. Roberts announced: "We will continue argument this morning in Case 11–398, the *Department of Health and Human Services v. Florida.*" Roberts asked Solicitor General Donald Verrilli to begin.

The solicitor general, dressed in the customary morning coat with tails, rose to the lectern and declared, as is tradition, "Mr. Chief Justice, and may it please the Court.

"The Affordable Care Act addresses a fundamental and enduring problem in our health care system and our economy. Insurance has become the predominant means of paying for health care in this country." Then he suddenly stopped.

On the biggest stage of his life, and in the midst of the most significant case argued before the Court in decades, the solicitor general unexpectedly and uncharacteristically paused during his opening remarks. Visibly nervous, he coughed, twice. After recovering, he repeated his last sentence—which had certainly been committed to memory—verbatim. He continued: "For most Americans, for more than 80 percent of Americans, the insurance system does provide effective access."

He paused again. This time for about six seconds, though it felt like an eternity.

Sitting in the packed-to-capacity courtroom were the attorney general, countless members of Congress, cabinet members, other dignitaries, and the curious spectators who had spent up to ninety-two hours sleeping outside the Court to ensure a seat to witness history. Everyone was waiting for the solicitor general to continue.

Amid the six seconds of quiet, the solicitor general reached for a glass of water. He took a sip. In the hush of the room, everyone could hear the ice cubes clinking against the glass. One Supreme Court reporter told me that Verrilli's coughing "was bad" and "very noticeable."

It is the practice of the solicitor general to argue before a moot court twice for each case, so he can test out ideas and field questions from other attorneys acting as judges. Verrilli was scheduled to argue three cases, which required six moots. Each had lasted several hours. After all of that talking the previous week, his throat was sore. As a result, he would take an ill-advised sip of water right before he rose to speak. Unfortunately, it went down the wrong pipe. It's happened to the best of us. The solicitor general would later tell friends that he was actually choking—he could not breathe at all. Verrilli would concede, I was told, that the hour started "horrendously." Though he would recover, it was an inauspicious start for the government's case.

The solicitor general resumed his argument, with all eyes on him. Verrilli would soon be barraged by hostile questioning from across the bench about this unprecedented assertion of federal power.

All eyes turned to Justice Kennedy, who began by asking Verrilli about the Commerce Clause: "Assume for the moment that this is unprecedented, this is a step beyond what our cases have allowed, the affirmative duty to act to go into commerce. If that is so, do you not have a heavy burden of justification?" Kennedy had said unprecedented—and it was the burden of the government, and not the challengers, to convince the Court that this expansion of federal authority should be allowed. In constitutional law, the party with the burden of persuasion usually loses.

Everyone in the packed courtroom listened with rapt attention.

Kennedy continued: "I understand that we must presume laws are constitutional, but, even so, when you are changing the relation of the individual to the government in this, what we can stipulate is, I think, a unique way, do you not have a heavy burden of justification to show authorization under the Constitution?" To Kennedy, the government had to prove why, despite the law going beyond any other the Supreme Court had upheld, it ought to be sustained regardless. In other words, contrary to what Katyal had argued in the lower courts, this case would not be controlled by simply applying the Court's earlier precedents, such as *Lopez* and *Morrison*.

Verrilli stumbled to a response, arguing, first, that the "health care market is unique" because "virtually everybody in society is in this market," and second, that the law did not compel people to engage in commerce.

This was not the answer Kennedy was looking for. His response stunned the room: "Here the government is saying that the federal government has a duty to tell the individual citizen that [he] must act, and that is different from what we have [upheld] in previous cases." Then Kennedy dropped the second bombshell of the day. Such a law "changes the relationship of the federal government to the individual in the very fundamental way."

When Kennedy said this, Barnett's jaw "dropped to the floor." This was a point he had been making for years. With this law, Kennedy saw an unprecedented expansion of the federal government's ability to command what individuals do. In Barnett's words, this response was a "game-changer."

Justice Scalia, smirking, finally posed the broccoli *question.* "Everybody has to buy food sooner or later, so [if] you define the market as food, therefore, everybody is in the market; therefore, [can] you . . . make people buy broccoli?"

Verrilli, almost certainly anticipating that question, promptly shot back that the health care market was different from the food market. "It is quite different. The food market, while it shares that trait that everybody's in it, it is not a market in which your participation is often unpredictable and often involuntary." In other words, everyone knows when they will need food, but they don't know when they will need medical treatment. Also, a hospital can't turn away a poor patient, but a grocery store can turn away a customer with no money.

Justice Scalia was not persuaded. Nor was Chief Justice Roberts buying this argument. "You say health insurance is not purchased for its own sake, like a car or broccoli; it is a means of financing health care consumption and covering universal risks. Well, a car or broccoli aren't purchased for their own sake either. They are purchased for the sake of transportation or in [the case of] broccoli, covering the need for food."

Justice Sotomayor repeated the question. If the government could "force [people] into commerce," was there no limit to that power? The solicitor general answered, "No," explaining that economic activity was already in existence and no one had been forced to buy insurance.

Justice Kennedy rejoined the barrage of questions, turning to the issue of compulsion. "Can you create commerce in order to regulate it?" Verrilli wouldn't take the bait. "That's not what's going on here, Justice Kennedy, and we are not seeking to defend the law on that basis." The solicitor general repeated his refrain from the previous day—there was no individual mandate, and no one was being compelled to engage in commerce. The only thing being regulated was the "method of financing health [care]." When Chief Justice Roberts asked Verrilli if Congress could "require you to buy a cell phone because that would facilitate responding when you need emergency services," Verrilli again rejected the premise of the question. This case did not involve a mandate but was merely "an issue of market regulation."

Next, the arguments would turn from leafy produce to limiting principles.

It was Justice Kennedy who posed the million-dollar question. "Well then, your question is whether or not there are any limits on the Commerce Clause. Can you identify for us some limits on the Commerce Clause?"

The solicitor general stuck closely to his plan. "Yes. The rationale purely under the Commerce Clause that we're advocating here would not justify forced purchases of commodities for the purpose of stimulating demand."

Justice Kennedy was not persuaded. "But why not? If Congress says that the interstate commerce is affected, isn't, according to your view, that the end of the analysis?"

Verrilli stumbled, arguing that the line should be drawn at economic activity already in existence. "No. . . . Here Congress is regulating existing commerce, economic activity that is already going on."

Chief Justice Roberts tried to pin down the solicitor general on a limiting principle. "But what I'm concerned about is, once we accept the principle that everybody is in this market, I don't see why Congress's power is limited. . . . Once you're in the interstate commerce and [Congress] can regulate it, pretty much all bets are off. . . . The question is, is there a limit to the authority that we're advocating here under the commerce power?"

The justices were growing very frustrated by Verrilli's evasiveness, but remaining evasive was part of his plan.

Justice Alito gave the solicitor general a clear opportunity to state his limiting principle. "Could you express your limiting principle as succinctly as you possibly can?"

Verrilli's answer would be scrutinized and criticized relentlessly for the next three months. Here it is in its entirety:

> We got two and they're—they're different. Let me state them.
> First, with respect to the comprehensive scheme. When Congress is regulating—is enacting a comprehensive scheme that it has the authority to enact, that the Necessary and Proper Clause gives it the authority to include regulation, including

a regulation of this kind, if it is necessary to counteract risks attributable to the scheme itself that people engage in economic activity that would undercut the scheme. It's like—it's very much like *Wickard* in that respect. Very much like *Raich* in that respect. With respect to the—with respect to the—considering the Commerce Clause alone and not embedded in the comprehensive scheme, our position is that Congress can regulate the method of payment by imposing an insurance requirement in advance of the time in which the—the service is consumed when the class to which that requirement applies either is, or virtually most certain to be, in that market, when the timing of one's entry into that market and what you will need when you enter that market is uncertain, and when—when you will get the care in that market, whether you can afford to pay for it or not and shift costs to other market participants. So, those—those are our views as to—those are the principles we're advocating for, and it's, in fact, the conjunction of the two of them here that makes this, we think, a strong case under the Commerce Clause.

Verrilli's response was winding, circuitous, and unsatisfactory to nearly everyone in the Court. It was definitely not "succinct," but that was no accident.

Alito had tossed Verrilli a softball, a question that any first-year law student should have been able to knock out of the ballpark. But after realizing that the Court was not buying his leading Commerce Clause argument, Verrilli laid down a sacrifice bunt to advance his other arguments. The government's litigation strategy was to *not* provide what would have been an unsatisfactory limiting principle. Lisa Blatt, a veteran Supreme Court litigator, remarked at the time that "it may be that there was a strategic decision not to give a crisp and clear answer." Paul Smith, Verrilli's former partner at Jenner Block, told me,

"I don't think anything happened accidentally in that process." It was not in the government's interest to state whether laws other than the mandate were constitutional. It was enough to distinguish the mandate from the broccoli horrible.

Verrilli was prepared to rope-a-dope, like Muhammad Ali, taking punch after punch, so that he could avoid giving a limiting principle that would not limit enough. Although Verrilli swung and missed with his effort at providing a satisfactory limiting principle, he would land a knockout punch with his fallback argument that the mandate should be saved as a tax. Verrilli's response was based on his understanding that there was no satisfying answer to Alito's question. That was the trap—Alito posed a question that could not be answered. Any incomplete answer would give the Court a reason to strike down the law.

Though Verrilli certainly stumbled through his answer to Alito's question, what he said was no different from what he had stated in his briefs, where he offered two discernible standards. First, pursuant to Congress's powers under the Necessary and Proper Clause, Congress could impose the mandate to ensure that essential provisions of the ACA—guaranteed issue and community rating—would be effective. Second, under its commerce power, Congress could regulate how people choose to finance the purchase of health care. That is, Congress could ensure that people purchase health insurance before they need it, as virtually everyone will need health care.

Yet neither of these standards would satisfy the justices. Indeed, for the reason Paul Clement articulated in response, Verrilli had not offered a limiting principle but rather "simply a description of the insurance market. It's not a limiting principle, because the justification for why this is a valid regulation of commerce is in no way limited to this market." A limiting principle must limit.

Recognizing this, the solicitor general hung his hopes on the fallback argument—that the Court should read the statute as imposing a tax rather than as mandating the purchase of insurance.

After the solicitor general's frustrating and stultifying performance, Paul Clement rose to the podium with a clear message—and a clear throat. He didn't choke, in any sense of the word. His performance was described by one reporter as the greatest oration before the Court in decades.

> Mr. Chief Justice, and may it please the Court. The mandate represents an unprecedented effort by Congress to compel individuals to enter commerce in order to better regulate commerce. The Commerce Clause gives Congress the power to regulate existing commerce. It does not give Congress the far greater power to compel people to enter commerce to create commerce essentially in the first place. Now, Congress, when it passed the statute, did make findings about why it thought it could regulate the commerce here, and it justified the mandate as a regulation of the economic decision to forgo the purchase of health insurance. That is a theory without any limiting principle.

Clement's argument was devastatingly simple, but effective. "The whole problem is that everybody is not in that market, and [Congress] want[s] to make everybody get into that market." Clement's brief—drafted with his co-counsel Erin Murphy—was flawless, described by a well-known Supreme Court watcher as "written in the voice of Anthony Kennedy."

After skillfully answering questions from both sides of the bench, Clement closed: "The individual mandate is an unprecedented law that rests on an extraordinary and unbounded assertion of federal power. Under any faithful reading of the Constitution's enumeration of limited federal powers, the mandate cannot survive constitutional scrutiny."

With barely a minute left, the yellow light on the podium lit up to tell him he had to wrap up. Without even giving the justices a chance to ask a follow-up question, Clement quickly changed course:

"I would like to say two very brief things about the taxing power, if I could." This law was not a tax, he said, and the law was not proper. Neither Clement nor Michael Carvin, who would argue next, spent any meaningful time discussing the taxing power argument. The entire day had been dominated by the Commerce Clause arguments.

The chief justice closed: "Thank you, Mr. Clement." The Court recessed at 12:05, more than two hours after arguments began. The punditry began immediately.

Jeffrey Toobin, legal affairs reporter for CNN, raced from the Court to the waiting camera on First Street. Toobin ominously proclaimed, "This was a train wreck for the Obama administration. This law looks like it's going to be struck down. I'm telling you, all of the predictions, including mine, that the justices would not have a problem with this law were wrong." He would later say, "This still looks like a train wreck for the Obama administration, and it may also be a plane wreck. But this entire law is now in serious trouble. It's hard to imagine how things could be going much worse for the Obama administration." Paul Smith, Verrilli's former law firm partner, told me that Toobin's comments "set the tone" for the rest of the media. Blaming the solicitor general for the law's failure became the media template.

The Drudge Report blasted a picture of Verrilli with the headline "Obama's Lawyer Chokes Again." Within hours after the audio of the arguments was released, the Republican National Committee released a YouTube advertisement attacking Verrilli's performance. The advertisement took the audio of Verrilli choking at the podium and doctored it to make the awkward silence last longer than it actually did. Over a stark picture of the Supreme Court, the headline "ObamaCare: It's a Tough Sell" appeared. The import was clear—not even the government could justify this law. The Obama administration rallied to defend Verrilli. Obama's deputy campaign manager, Stephanie Cutter, said that the attack on Verrilli was a "low blow" and that he was "one of the most talented attorneys in this country. He made a very forceful argument and we knew these arguments were going to be tough."

Tom Goldstein, a frequent Supreme Court litigant and the founder of SCOTUSBlog, described the advertisement as "the single most classless and misleading thing I've ever seen related to the Court. It is as if the RNC decided to take an incredibly serious and successful argument that has the chance to produce a pathbreaking legal victory for a conservative interpretation of the Constitution, drag it through the mud, and vomit on it."

Politicians also emerged from the Court to seize the moment. Characteristically, New York senator Chuck Schumer was the first to the microphone, barely ten minutes after the Court recessed. Schumer assailed Mitt Romney and other Republicans for changing their positions on the mandate. Texas senator Kay Bailey Hutchison, who had raised the initial constitutional point of order in the Senate two years earlier, said—ironically, in hindsight—that Chief Justice Roberts had emphatically rejected the taxing power argument.

Utah senator Mike Lee, who had clerked for Justice Alito and whose father was the solicitor general for President Reagan, was cautiously optimistic about Justice Kennedy's vote. "Based on the questions he asked, based on demeanor, body language, facial expressions, in the wake of answers to those questions, I think he was leaning towards the proposition that the individual mandate is unconstitutional. That conclusion becomes more compelling when reviewed in the context of his writings on structural federalism." Lee cautioned, however, that "I don't want to describe any justice as predictable." Florida senator Marco Rubio said he was "proud that Florida has taken the lead on challenging the constitutionality of this law. Hopefully the Supreme Court will see it as we do." He was "hopeful it will turn out on the side of the Constitution."

A DOJ lawyer told me that Verrilli had "started off in a deep hole, but fought his way out of it," and that it was not until the last fifteen minutes that he started to "land points." The government thought it was a "jump ball" leaving the Court.

As for the criticisms, Verrilli recognized that he was a public official and that the First Amendment guarantees that the press and citizens can criticize public officials. Paul Smith told me that Verrilli was a "grown-up" and could take the criticism. Ultimately, the solicitor general had to live with the judgments he made on how to litigate the case. Yet he did not have much time to reflect on his performance. After all, he had another argument to make the next morning.

Usually cases are argued before the Supreme Court in one hour and advocates have to wait months before they can receive any validation. This case, stretched over three days, was different. The second day provided an opportunity for instant feedback. Randy Barnett told me that the "most significant thing about the second day was that the justices were every bit as critical as they were on the first day. They didn't take any back. They doubled down." One day more.

Day Three, the Morning: A "Hollow Shell"

By the third day, fatigue was beginning to set in. Wednesday's arguments would be a doubleheader. In the morning, the justices would hear arguments about whether the entire ACA—all 2,700 pages of it—should fall if the individual mandate was found unconstitutional. Because the government argued that the mandate could not survive without the guaranteed issue and community rating provisions (which prevented denial of coverage for preexisting conditions), if the mandate was unconstitutional, then these other provisions would also have to fall.

Verrilli took a breather while longtime Deputy Solicitor General Edwin Kneedler was making the government's argument that the guaranteed issue and community rating provisions could not stand alone. These provisions prevented insurance companies from charging higher premiums to those with preexisting conditions. The Court appointed a friend of the Court, Washington lawyer Bartow Farr, to argue that the mandate could be severed and the ACA could survive without the two related provisions. Paul Clement was arguing, once again, for the states.

In the afternoon, Verrilli would return to the podium against Paul Clement to argue whether the Medicaid expansion violated the Constitution.

Clement began his argument in the morning by going for broke. Rather than strategically giving the justices the easier option to only kill the mandate and leave the rest of President Obama's signature legislation on the books, Clement sought to slaughter the entire bill. "If the individual mandate is unconstitutional, then the rest of the act cannot stand. As Congress found and the federal government concedes, the community rating and guaranteed issue provisions of the act cannot stand without the individual mandate."

But who should decide how to fix the ACA if the mandate was found unconstitutional? The Court? Or Congress? Justice Sotomayor asked, "Why shouldn't we let Congress do that, if in fact the economists [are] right that prices will spiral? What's wrong with leaving it . . . in the hands of the people who should be fixing this, not us?"

Congress had in fact considered the question of severability. Back in 2009, during a committee markup of the bill, Democratic Senator Max Baucus, the chairman of the Senate Finance Committee and one of the prime movers of the ACA, rejected Kentucky senator Jim Bunning's proposal that would have allowed individuals to opt out of the mandate. Baucus said, "It's a mortally wounding amendment because . . . individuals will opt themselves out [by not buying insurance] and that's going to undermine this whole system here. It clearly is going to undermine the system. The system won't work if this amendment passes." In other words, the ACA could not operate without the mandate.

In response to a similar amendment from Senator Mike Crapo of Idaho, Senator Baucus replied, strongly, "This is a killer amendment. This is an amendment which guts and kills health reform." For Baucus in 2009, the mandate could not be severed from the rest of the bill. The mandate was the heart of the law. Of course, this history also inconveniently undercut Verrilli's argument that there was no mandate. Everyone from Stuart Butler to Hillary Clinton to Barack Obama to Mitt Romney knew what this law did—forced people to buy health insurance against their will. That was the point. But in the Supreme Court in 2012, the law would take on a new life of its own and transform from a legal command to a tax.

On December 8, 2011, during a discussion of the pending litigation, Republican Senator Chuck Grassley of Iowa, recalling "that original legislative bargain," reminded his colleagues that, under the bargain, "the individual mandate was very critical to the ability to pass this law. . . . The people promoting this legislation that passed on a partisan vote knew the whole operation of the law depended upon the compulsion of the individual mandate. . . . Congress could not have enacted any part of this law without the individual mandate or any other provision."

To Justice Scalia, the most reasonable path was to strike down the entire law and let Congress fix it from a clean slate. "Whether we strike it all down or leave some of it in place, the congressional process will never be the same. One way or another, Congress is going to have to reconsider this." Scalia asked, "Why isn't it better to have them reconsider [the act in its entirety] rather than having some things already in the law which you have to eliminate before you can move on to consider everything on balance?"

Clement argued that the ACA gutted of the individual mandate would be nothing but a "hollow shell." He told the Court, "You can't possibly think that Congress would have passed that hollow shell without the heart of the act." Without the mandate, the law would have never been enacted.

The morning arguments were over. It seemed clear that if the mandate was unconstitutional, the remainder of the ACA could not survive. There would be a brief break, followed by the finale in the afternoon—when the sleeper issue of the case would make a rousing appearance.

Day Three, the Afternoon: "Your Money or Your Life"

By the afternoon of the third day, everyone was exhausted. The justices had already heard over four hours of arguments. Because of the Court's security processes, most of the reporters who had attended the morning session had only about fifteen minutes to run out, grab lunch, and run back in to be seated before arguments resumed. They were getting groggy. This legal relay race was on its final leg.

The third afternoon was defined by two competing visions of Medicaid. The federal government viewed the ACA's expansion of Medicaid as another successful chapter in the federal-state partnership to provide health care for the poor. The states viewed it as a proverbial gun to their heads that infringed on state sovereignty. The federal government declined to say whether states that rejected the expanded funding would lose all of the original funding. The states insisted that if they did not comply, their entire Medicaid programs would be defunded and bankrupted. The federal government repeatedly refused to state on the record whether the secretary of Health and Human Services (HHS) could actually cut all of the funding. The states insisted that this discretion meant that the entire expansion must be found unconstitutional. The middle ground between these two positions, as described by Justice Ginsburg, would be the "easy repair."

The dynamics on the bench at the Supreme Court are always difficult to gauge, but the arguments on the third afternoon spiraled somewhat out of control.

To illustrate that the Medicaid grant was coercive, Justice Scalia harkened back to "the old Jack Benny thing, 'your money or your life.'" The "your money or your life" bit came from a classic episode of *The Jack Benny Show,* first aired on March 28, 1948—exactly sixty-four years to the day of the Medicaid oral arguments. (I'll assume that Scalia the Originalist knew this.) During the sketch, Jack Benny is approached by a mugger who demands, "Don't make a move, this is a stickup. Now, come on. Your money or your life?" With a gun pointed at him, Benny pauses for several seconds. The studio audience erupts in laughter. The mugger, growing impatient, demands, "Look, bud! I said, your money or your life!" Benny, with his legendary timing, responds, "I'm thinking it over!"

Scalia mused that even though the mugger provided Benny with a choice, there really was no choice. Of course he would hand over the money. Similarly, Scalia reasoned, although the ACA ostensibly gave states the choice of whether to accept the new money, the failure to accept that funding would result in the death of their preexisting Medicaid programs. To Scalia, the states bringing suit after being mugged by the federal leviathan was no different than Jack Benny being robbed by a common criminal. The states could either take the money or give up their lives—that is, their sovereignty as states. The federal government was not a cooperative partner, but a despotic outlaw.

Continuing his own stand-up routine, Justice Scalia added, "You can't refuse your money or your life. But your life or your *wife's,* I could refuse that one."

Chief Justice Roberts, who did not look amused, said, "Let's leave the wife out of this." Justice Sotomayor attempted to join in on the fun. Referring to Clement's wife, she warned that "Mr. Clement, he's not going home tonight." Sotomayor's joke fell flat. (After the silent Justice Thomas, Sotomayor usually garners the fewest laugh lines at the Supreme Court.) Clement began saying something about "Ms. Clement," but was interrupted again by Justice Scalia. The chief justice, who at this point was visibly displeased, cut things short. A dour-looking Roberts exclaimed, "That's enough frivolity for a while."

Those in the court observed that with each barb from Justice Scalia, Chief Justice Roberts became more and more irritated. Dahlia Lithwick remarked that Scalia, who consistently wins the award for the funniest justice (measured by the most laugh lines), "cranked it up about three notches. He was there to brawl." *Huffington Post* reporter Mike Sacks remarked that Scalia's antics were upsetting the chief justice. Lithwick added that at this point Roberts and Scalia "were not on the same page."

Yet Scalia's frivolity was, as usual, not entirely without merit. Five days before the ACA was signed into law, Arizona, under the leadership of Tea Party–backed governor Jan Brewer, had notified the Department of Health and Human Services that it intended to terminate its participation under the KidsCare program. This program, commonly known as CHIP, was one aspect of the ACA's expansion that provided additional funding to the states to provide health insurance for children.

One week after the ACA became law, HHS responded with an ominous and pointed letter: "In order to retain the current level of existing funding, the state would need to comply with the new conditions under the ACA." This observation was followed by a warning: "We want you to be aware that it appears that your request . . . would result in a loss of [all] Medicaid funding for Arizona." If Arizona opted out of CHIP, it could stand to lose almost $8 billion in Medicaid funding. That would probably obliterate the state's budget.

The HHS letter to Arizona contained a not-too-veiled threat of what would happen to other states that did not go along with the

ACA's expansion of Medicaid funding. To Arizona, this letter was the equivalent of HHS secretary Kathleen Sebelius acting out the "your money or your life" bit. There was no real choice. This letter was not attached as an exhibit to the Supreme Court briefings but had been referenced in a single footnote, added by Timothy Osterhaus, in a motion submitted to Judge Vinson back in Florida.

Relying on this letter, Paul Clement argued that what made this expansion so coercive was that Congress was tying "the states' willingness to accept these new funds . . . to their entire participation in" Medicaid. In other words, turning down the new funds would result in opting out of the entire program, including the old funds. From a statutory perspective, as noted by Professor Nicole Huberfeld, there was no real distinction between "new" and "old" funds. However, the Court adopted this distinction.

Despite the 2010 HHS letter, the federal government retreated from this position, though obliquely. The chief justice asked the solicitor general if it would be appropriate for the federal government to say, "States, you can take this or you can leave it, but if you don't take it, you lose every last dollar of federal funding for every program."

Verrilli evaded the question and did not say that this would *not* happen. "Well, but I don't think that this is a case that presents that question, Mr. Chief Justice."

The chief justice returned to this question later, specifically referencing the Arizona letter. "Could you give me some assurance? We heard the question about whether or not the secretary would use this authority to the extent available. [Are] there circumstances where you are willing to say that that would not be permissible?" What was stopping the government, Roberts asked, from taking away all funding from the states if they didn't follow some conditions?

The solicitor general refused to answer the question. "Well, Mr. Chief Justice, it would not be responsible of me to stand here in advance of any particular situation . . . coming before the secretary of

Health and Human Services and commit to how that would be resolved one way or another."

One government lawyer told me that Verrilli knew that this question about the Arizona letter was coming and that "it was an issue," but he did not have the authority to make a "representation about the secretary's discretion." This limitation was described as a "pretty normal thing" in the Department of Justice. Thus, Verrilli had an obligation to answer the question the way he did. As a government lawyer, it is sometimes impossible to make what would be a winning argument. Without understanding the underlying policy rationales for the government's position in court, it is very difficult to blindly criticize the solicitor general's performance. While Verrilli could represent that the ACA did not compel people to buy insurance, he could not represent that the secretary of HHS would not have the discretion to strip a state of all funding.

And then Justice Kagan deftly threw the drowning solicitor general a life preserver. "Has the secretary in fact ever made use of that authority?" Verrilli latched on. "That's correct, Justice Kagan. It's never been used."

Chief Justice Roberts, unsatisfied with the answer, interrupted Verrilli midsentence with indignation in his voice and sharply questioned him: "What about the Arizona letter we just heard about today?"

Verrilli made an audible sigh and attempted to complete his prior thought. "It has never been used to cut off—" The chief justice, this time more animated, with his voice raised several levels, interrupted Verrilli again: "It's been used to threaten [states]." Justice Scalia, under his breath but within reach of the microphone, chimed in sarcastically, "Of course not," as if to say, sarcastically, *Of course the secretary would never cut off the funding.*

Roberts, even more engaged, continued. Evoking the image of Clint Eastwood as Dirty Harry, Roberts declared, "Of course no state is going to say, 'Okay, go ahead, make my day, take it away.'" An uncomfortable laughter trickled out. Roberts pursued the point further. The states, he said, are "going to give in."

Then Justice Breyer joined the pile-on, sharply asking, "Has the secretary gone around threatening people that we will cut off totally unrelated funds. What is the situation?" Again, the solicitor general refused to answer that question. "I don't think it would be responsible of me to commit that the secretary would exercise the discretion uniformly in one way or another."

Before he could even finish his sentence, Chief Justice Roberts interrupted him. Sticking with the Wild West imagery, Roberts said that Verrilli's response to the "your money or your life" analogy was, "There's no evidence that anyone has ever been shot." The chief justice continued: "Well, it's because you have to give up your wallet. You don't have a choice." Again, the solicitor general tried to jump in. "But that—"

The chief justice charged right on. "And you cannot represent that the secretary has never said: 'And if you don't do it, we are going to take away all the funds.' They cite the Arizona example; I suspect there are others, because that is the leverage." A third time, Verrilli tried to interrupt Roberts, stuttering, "But it . . . it . . . it. . . . "

Roberts was not done. "I'm not saying there's anything wrong with it."

Finally, Verrilli was able to finish his thought. "But it's not coercion, Mr. Chief Justice."

Roberts, upset by this last statement, promptly shot back, "Wait a second," and asked, incredulously, "It's not coercion?"

Meekly, the solicitor general spoke over the chief justice, repeating, "It's not coercion." Roberts continued, asking rhetorically, "It's not coercion to say I'm going to take away all your funds, no matter how minor the infringement?" The solicitor general again tried, with no success, to jump in. "But of course."

This time Justice Breyer, intrigued by this exchange, interrupted the solicitor general. "I want you, in other words, to answer the question the chief justice has." Breyer, sensing that the ACA might be in jeopardy, wanted to assuage Roberts's concerns on this all-important issue.

Verrilli punted on the question yet again. Breyer spoke up skeptically: was Verrilli not "privy to what those [discussions] are" within the government? With a slight chuckle, almost as if to say that the question was above his pay grade, the solicitor general said, "I'm not." Verrilli was not authorized to say whether the secretary would ever do this.

The chief justice was not persuaded. "So long as the federal government has that power, it seems to be a significant intrusion on the sovereign interests of the state." Merely to have the gun aimed at them, whether or not the trigger was pulled, infringed on states' rights.

Roberts was willing to live with the secretary having this discretion for new, related funding, but not with the secretary having the discretion to cut off funding for unrelated programs from the past. Verrilli toed the line, saying that this was "different from saying that they are coercive, and that's different from saying that it's unconstitutional."

Breyer pounced, irately asking twice, "Why is it different? Why is it different?" Breyer wanted the solicitor general to give him something to allay the chief justice's concerns, but Verrilli wouldn't do it. When Verrilli attempted to jump in, Breyer continued right along, noting that Clement had said that the secretary "would do it" and withdraw the funding. Breyer said, "I would like a little clarification."

Scalia asked if the secretary had the power to withdraw the funding. Verrilli begrudgingly admitted that "it is possible." But, he continued, "I'm not willing to give that away." In other words, he would not concede that fact.

Kagan would not accept that and asked why Verrilli was not "willing to give [that] away." Breyer chimed in. "What's making you reluctant?" Verrilli, with a slight chuckle, replied, "I'm not trying to be reluctant." He chuckled because he knew from the outset that he was not going to answer the question posed to him.

Scalia interrupted him. "I wouldn't think that is a surprise question." The solicitor general was not unprepared. Rather, consistent with his strategy the previous day regarding questions about his limiting principle, he had made a conscious choice not to answer the question. He told the justices, "I'm trying to be careful about the authority of the secretary of Health and Human Services and how it will apply in the future." Verrilli represented the interests of the United States. He could not pin the government into a position that would bind it in the future. Yet, his risky strategy not to answer this question would backfire, as seven justices would reject his position.

Verrilli had only inflamed the concerns of Roberts, Breyer, and Kagan—the very justices who would soon vote against him on the constitutionality of the Medicaid expansion. The Arizona letter, mentioned only in a footnote in a brief before Judge Vinson in Florida, would prove decisive in the most far-reaching restriction on the spending power in the Court's history.

Like Verrilli's gamble the day before about the mandate, this gamble and his reticence in answering Chief Justice Roberts's question did not pay off. If the government would not disclaim this coercive power, the Court would limit that power for it, as it would do its commerce power.

But how would it be limited? As Paul Clement rose for rebuttal, Justice Ginsburg, who had been uncharacteristically silent for nearly an hour, interjected, in her frail voice, a question that presaged the ultimate outcome of the case. She asked Clement whether he was "asking the Court as relief [to] cure the constitutional infirmity" by saying that the expansion "has to be on a voluntary basis"—in other words, that states that voluntarily chose to accept the new funding would be bound by the conditions, but states that chose not to accept the expanded funding (such as those involved in the lawsuit) would keep their old funding. Ginsburg called this approach the "easy repair." Or, she continued, was Clement asserting "that this whole Medicaid . . . expansion has to be nullified, and moreover, the entire health care act"?

Ginsburg had presented Clement with two options. First, accept a modified version of the statute, where states that did not want the new funding could keep the old funding and states that wanted the new funding would be bound by the ACA's conditions. Second, go for broke and strike down the entire expansion, leaving even those states that wanted the funding without any money.

Clement played it safe and chose door number one. He acknowledged that there was a "need for repair." While his first preference would be to nullify the entire statute, "we would be certainly happy if we got something here, and we got a recognition that the coercion doctrine exists; this is coercive." And that is exactly what he got—the "easy repair."

Two Conceptions of Liberty

After Paul Clement's allotted time elapsed, the chief justice gave him additional time, something his strict predecessor, Chief Justice Rehnquist, would never have done. Later, when Roberts also gave Verrilli additional time, following his rough outing, the solicitor general chuckled out loud, joking, "Lucky me. Lucky me."

At last, with three minutes left from his expanded time, the solicitor general began what has become known as his "closing statement." (If he had finished when his allotted time was up, he would not have had enough time.)

Generally, Supreme Court advocates are given a few seconds at the beginning of their argument to speak without interruption to lay out the roadmap of the case. Then, almost immediately, rapid-fire questions rain down from the bench. However, after three days of argument, Verrilli made the unorthodox decision to provide his final thoughts. The justices would let him speak uninterrupted. The solicitor general, who had been the subject of ridicule on the right and the left, had one final chance to make his case for the Court.

Verrilli's closing statement aimed to encapsulate the wide range of arguments on law, politics, and philosophy that the Court had waded through during the past three roller-coaster days. Interestingly enough, his closing focused on a topic that had been conspicuously absent—liberty.

Verrilli had the idea for his closing statement in his head, though it wasn't prepared. During the three days of argument, something important had been missing from the discussion: namely, the practical consequences for millions of Americans of the law being struck down.

He began, "But if I may just say in conclusion. . . . " He coughed. "I'd like to take half a step back here." His argument wasn't just about "the Medicaid expansion that we're talking about this afternoon," but also the individual mandate provisions discussed the previous day.

Verrilli urged the justices to remember that it was for the elected branches, not the Court, to decide the fate of this law. Health care reform "is something about which the people of the United States can deliberate and they can vote, and if they think it needs to be changed, they can change it. And I would suggest to the Court, with profound respect for the Court's obligation to ensure that the federal government remains a government of enumerated powers, that this is not a case in any of its aspects that calls that into question. That this was a judgment of policy, that democratically accountable branches of this government made by their best lights." This was an argument aimed directly at the chief justice. From the outset, the Solicitor General's office had thought that the chief justice in particular would be open to an argument premised on respect for the outcome of the democratic process. This assessment would prove to be correct.

Verrilli reminded the justices that more than one vision of liberty was at issue. "There is an important connection, . . ." he began, then paused for emphasis. "A profound connection, between that problem and liberty. And I do think it's important that we not lose sight of that. . . . In a very fundamental way, this Medicaid expansion [protects] individual liberty and dignity interests."

One of the attorneys working on the challenge told me that Verrilli's closing argument was a "quintessential example of a liberal trying to use terms Justice Kennedy agrees with, by using words like 'liberty' and 'dignity.' That's how Kennedy speaks, but not what he means." He added that Verrilli was also making "a huge strategic mistake because Clement was going to have a rebuttal." Another lawyer for NFIB told me that "whatever arguments exist in defense of Obamacare, liberty is not high on that list."

Turning to the practical realities at hand, Verrilli continued. "There will be millions of people with chronic conditions like diabetes and heart disease, and as a result of the health care that they will get, they will be unshackled from the disabilities that those diseases put on them." Through this law, we can "secure the blessings of liberty." Here, Verrilli was quoting from the Preamble to the Constitution, which states that our great charter was ratified to "secure the Blessings of Liberty to ourselves and our Posterity."

The relationship between health security and liberty was a sermon that progressives had preached throughout the enactment of the ACA. Upon signing the bill, President Obama declared that it enshrined "the core principle that everybody should have some basic security when it comes to their health care." On March 22, 2010, minutes after the midnight vote in the House that passed the ACA, a jubilant Speaker Nancy Pelosi beamed that "this bill tonight [creates the] opportunity for affordable health care for all Americans [so they] have the freedom to have a healthier life [and] to have the liberty to pursue their own happiness." Pelosi was channeling Thomas

Jefferson's eternal ode to freedom from the Declaration of Independence, which recognizes our "inalienable rights of life, liberty, and the pursuit of happiness." President Obama delivered a similar message in his second inaugural address, also evoking Jefferson. "That they are endowed by their creator with certain unalienable rights, and among these are life, liberty, and the pursuit of happiness. Today we continue a never-ending journey to bridge the meaning of those words with the realities of our time. For history tells us that while these truths may be self-evident, they've never been self-executing. That while freedom is a gift from God, it must be secured by his people here on earth." It is the people, through the collective, not the individual, who must secure these rights. This was President Obama's modern liberty, and Verrilli was its messenger to the Court.

Verrilli concluded: "I would urge this Court to respect that judgment and ask that the Affordable Care Act, in its entirety, be upheld. Thank you."

After years of litigation, criticism, and political wrangling, the government had stated its case.

Without skipping a beat, the chief justice said, "Thank you, General. Mr. Clement, you have five minutes." Paul Clement rose to have the last word and provided an impromptu rebuttal that offered a very different vision of what individual liberty means.

"Let me just finish by saying I certainly appreciate what the solicitor general says, that when you support a policy, you think that the policy spreads the blessings of liberty." After three long, hard-fought days of argument, Clement would have the last word on liberty.

"But I would respectfully suggest that it's a very funny conception of liberty that forces somebody to purchase an insurance policy whether they want it or not." This was not the individual liberty of Justice Kennedy.

Clement echoed a point he had made in his brief: "The Constitution protects and promotes individual liberty, while the mandate's threat to liberty is obvious. The power [of the federal government] to compel a person to enter into an unwanted commercial relationship is not some modest step necessary and proper to perfect Congress's authority to regulate existing commercial intercourse. It is a revolution in the relationship between the central government and the governed." Such a conception of freedom for society as a whole comes at the expense of liberty for the individual. "By making clear that this uncabined authority is not among the limited and enumerated powers granted the federal government, this Court will preserve our basic constitutional structure and the individual liberty, state sovereignty, and government accountability it guarantees. . . . An individual can do very little to avoid the long arm of the federal government other than refrain from entering into the commerce that Congress may regulate." If the Court did not stop this encroachment on the freedom of individuals, Clement contended, our system of constitutional governance would be at risk. Clement had written in his brief, "If this is to remain a system of limited and enumerated federal powers that respects individual liberty, accountability, and the residual dignity and sovereignty of the States, the individual mandate cannot stand."

Clement continued: "And it's a very strange conception of federalism that says that we can simply give the states an offer that they can't refuse." He added that it would be foreign to our federalist republic to "force the states to do whatever we tell them to. . . . That is a direct threat to our federalism." To Clement, individual liberty was the autonomy of the individual and not the collective. Freedom was the sovereignty of the states and not the power of the federal government.

Just as the red light turned on, Clement finished. "Thank you."

"THE CASE IS SUBMITTED"

Chief Justice Roberts brought the proceedings to a close on Wednesday, March 28, 2012, at 2:24 PM. "Thank you, Mr. Clement. And thank you, General Verrilli, Mr. Kneedler, Mr. Carvin, Mr. Katsas, and in particular, of course, Mr. Long and Mr. Farr [the Court-appointed advocates]. The case is submitted."

After three grueling days and six-plus riveting hours of arguments, following three grueling years, the case had come to a close.

That evening the Heritage Foundation hosted a reception for all of the attorneys involved. Mike Carvin, Greg Katsas, Randy Barnett, and many others were there. The mood was festive. They all felt fairly confident about how the arguments had gone. Before the reception, Katsas's wife had emailed Todd Gaziano and told him that a bald eagle had landed in the backyard of their suburban Virginia home. She attached a photo of the bald eagle, the symbol of our nation, proudly perched on their lawn.

Gaziano deemed it an omen of victory. He asked an intern to blow up the picture and put it on a huge poster board at the reception. Everyone at Heritage looked at the eagle and smiled. At that point, many in the room thought they had won. At that point, they *had* won.

PART VII

Outside the Supreme Court

(*March 29–June 27, 2012*)

The Court finished hearing the arguments in the Health Care Cases on March 28, 2012. Although there would not be a decision until the end of June, the traditional end of the term, the battle over the Affordable Care Act was far from over. Soon it would shift from inside the courtroom to outside the Supreme Court as all three branches of the government got involved. Following leaks, attempts to influence the vote of the chief justice would provide another twist to the tale. After two years of arguments before the courts, it would be the final arguments made outside the Court that would define the legacy of *NFIB v. Sebelius*.

THE CONFERENCE

The justices usually do not talk with each other about a case before it is argued. The first opportunity for "the Nine" to express their opinions and discuss how they will vote is at the "conference," usually held a few days after a case is argued. In his memoir *Five Chiefs*, Justice John Paul Stevens noted that "the most important business at conference is the decision of the cases that have been argued and submitted since the prior conference."

The format of the conference is very structured. Only the justices are allowed to attend. No one, not even clerks or staff, is permitted in the conference room during deliberations. Justice Harry Blackmun once stressed the importance of secrecy during conferences. "We could not function as a court if our conferences were public. There are just the nine of us, no more." After exchanging the ritual handshakes—each shakes the hand of all the others (a total of thirty-six handshakes)—the justices are seated in order of seniority along a long table.

The most junior associate justice serves as the "doorkeeper" and is responsible for answering the door when someone knocks. Justice Tom Clark referred to the position as the "the most highly paid doorman in the country." Justice Stevens recalled one time when he committed an "unforgivable error in my first or second conference: I was so absorbed in the discussion that I did not realize that someone had knocked until Bill Brennan on my left and Bill Rehnquist on my right pushed back their chairs and got up to answer the door. That humiliating lesson taught me to keep track of priorities."

Stevens wrote that at conference the "introductory comments" about a case "were made in order of seniority." The chief justice begins, offering his thoughts on the case. Chief Justice Rehnquist said that he would begin by "reviewing the facts and the decision of the lower court, outlining his understanding of the applicable case law, and indicating either that he votes to affirm the decision of the lower court or to reverse it." Then, the most-senior justice would provide his or her comments about the case, then the second-most-senior justice, and so on, until the junior justice spoke. For the voting, however, the order is reversed. The "most junior justice was the first to vote, and the chief was the last." Bernard Schwartz notes in *Decision: How the Supreme Court Decides Cases* that the reason for the switch "is to make it less likely that the juniors will be influenced by how their seniors have voted." But it seldom works that way in practice.

As Chief Justice Rehnquist noted, "I don't believe I have ever seen it happen [that way] at any of the conferences that I have attended." After each justice speaks, it is usually clear how he or she will vote.

Following the vote, the chief justice tallies the votes. If he is in the majority, he can either assign the writing of the opinion to another justice or keep it to write himself. If the chief justice is in the dissent, the most-senior justice in the majority can assign the opinion or keep it for himself or herself.

The conference is usually routine, though in theory it should allow for persuasion. Justice Harry Blackmun recalled that "we can say what we initially believe, only to be proved wrong by the honing effect of conference and agreement and disagreement." Generally speaking, however, not many views are swayed at conference. As Justice Scalia has noted, "Not much conferencing goes on" at the conference. Scalia told Bernard Schwartz, "In fact, to call our discussion of a case a conference is really something of a misnomer, it's much more of a statement of the views of each of the nine Justices, after which the totals are added and the case is assigned."

Yet it is *not* unprecedented for a vote to change after the conference. If a vote changes following the conference, and that realignment flips a five-vote bloc, the authorship of the opinions is reassigned. What was a majority opinion becomes a dissent, and vice versa.

Justice Scalia should know more than any other justice of the modern era how a vote can change after conference—especially in a controversial constitutional law decision. As reporter Jan Crawford documented in *Supreme Conflict,* the votes in the landmark 1992 abortion case *Planned Parenthood v. Casey* flipped. Justices Sandra Day O'Connor and Anthony Kennedy initially voted at conference to uphold the law that placed limitations on access to abortions. Justice David Souter, who had been notoriously silent about abortion during his 1990 confirmation hearing, voted to strike down the law. The votes were tallied, and the law would be upheld in a 6–3 split, dealing a striking blow to *Roe v. Wade.*

Rehnquist assigned the opinion to himself and circulated a draft that effectively overruled *Roe v. Wade*. Two days later, Kennedy wrote to Blackmun, who had been in dissent, saying that he had some "wonderful news" about "developments in *Planned Parenthood v. Casey*." Rehnquist and the other conservatives worried that Kennedy was "wavering." Scalia reached out to Kennedy and invited him on a walk around their suburban Virginia neighborhood. After this stroll, Scalia was "confident that Kennedy was a solid vote." Scalia misjudged his colleague. Following the conference, the troika of O'Connor, Kennedy, and Souter had changed their votes and united with a compromise position.

The next day an opinion landed on Scalia's desk. O'Connor, Kennedy, and Souter had privately coauthored a "joint opinion"—none taking authorship—that found a way to "reaffirm" *Roe* while still placing restrictions on the right to abortion. Kennedy and O'Connor switched their votes, turning a 6–3 reversal of *Roe* into a 5–4 opinion that did just the opposite, and largely saved the law.

Crawford reported that at the annual skit put on by the law clerks that year, the clerk who portrayed Justice Kennedy emerged to the theme song of the television show *Flipper*. On decision day, the triumvirate took turns announcing their opinion. A bitter Scalia, whom Crawford called the "master of burning bridges," stated that with this opinion the "imperial judiciary lives." Kennedy's reputation as a swing vote on the Court had only become more fixed in the two decades that followed. Ironically, two decades later, it would be Kennedy trying to rein in a wavering justice, not the other way around.

THE VOTE

The conference for the Health Care Cases was scheduled for Friday, March 30, 2012. It would be anything but ordinary. Perhaps the vote could have gone something like this:

The justices voted in reverse-seniority order. First up was Justice Elena Kagan, the most junior justice. During argument, she had been very deferential to the government's power to enact the mandate, but seemed somewhat skeptical of Verrilli's refusal to place any limits on whether HHS could withdraw Medicaid funding. She was followed by Justice Sonia Sotomayor, who joined the Court in 2009. Sotomayor had been critical of the solicitor general's argument that the mandate was both not a tax and a tax, but she seemed comfortable with the commerce power. Sotomayor's senior was Justice Samuel Alito, who seemed uneasy about the impact of the Medicaid expansion on federalism and was befuddled by Verrilli's inability to provide a limiting principle.

Justice Stephen Breyer followed. Breyer was finally enjoying some seniority. He had served as the junior justice for a staggering 4,228 days from 1994 to 2006. (He missed Justice Joseph Story's record by thirty days.) Breyer, whose jurisprudence is generally deferential to the scope of federal power and who wrote the leading dissent in *United States v. Morrison*, was a lock for upholding the mandate. But, like Kagan, he seemed annoyed that Verrilli refused to assure the chief justice that HHS would not take away funding for preexisting Medicaid programs from the states.

Justice Ruth Bader Ginsburg, who had been uncharacteristically quiet during the arguments, made clear that she saw the individual mandate as another step in the progressive social compact that stretched from Social Security to Medicare and now to the ACA. And she had proposed the "easy repair" to save Medicaid.

Justice Clarence Thomas hadn't said a word from the bench in nearly seven years, but he made clear in his opinions that he thought much of the Commerce Clause case law of the last seventy years is wrong. He would likely have no trouble striking down the ACA. During argument, Justice Anthony Kennedy had expressed strong doubts about the government's assertion of power, yet tempered his comments in his usual equivocal way. He never showed all of his cards. Justice

Antonin Scalia, of course, made no secret of his opinion that the entire law was unconstitutional and that he would revel in striking it down.

Last to cast his vote at the conference was the most pivotal vote: Chief Justice John G. Roberts. Justice Stevens has praised Chief Justice Roberts's leadership at conferences: "He was always a well-prepared, fair, and effective leader." Stevens recalled that Roberts "welcomed more discussion of the merits of the argued cases than his predecessor," Chief Justice William Rehnquist. When pressed, Roberts would expand on "the reasoning behind his own votes." Yet "he maintained the appropriate impartiality in giving each of us an opportunity to speak." What Roberts would say at this pivotal moment remains one of the most hotly contested secrets in Supreme Court history.

On July 1, 2012, just three days after the decision in *NFIB v. Sebelius,* Jan Crawford released a bombshell story. She reported that at the conference Roberts "initially sided with the Supreme Court's four conservative justices to strike down the heart of President Obama's health care reform law." Roberts had agreed at the conference that Congress did not have the Commerce Clause power to enact the mandate, and "aligned with the four conservatives" to find the mandate unconstitutional on Commerce Clause grounds. Crawford reported that the chief justice was "less clear on whether . . . the rest of the law must fall." Other issues, such as the issue of severability and the Medicaid expansion, were still in play. Because Roberts was the most senior justice in the majority opinion, Crawford reported, "he got to choose which justice would write the court's historic decision. He kept it for himself."

Yet Roberts's vote would remain "in flux."

UNDER PRESSURE

Although the ACA was now in the hands of the nine justices, those in the other branches were not content to sit by and instead insisted on getting involved. For the Supreme Court, the pressure would come from all sides.

On Monday, April 2, 2012, five days after the arguments—and three days after the Court's all-important conference on March 30, 2012, when the votes were cast—President Obama made some off-the-cuff comments to the press about the case. Obama said that it would be "unprecedented" for unelected judges to overturn an act of Congress enacted with popular support.

> Ultimately, I'm confident that the Supreme Court will not take what would be an unprecedented, extraordinary step of overturning a law that was passed by a strong majority of a democratically elected Congress. And I'd just remind conservative commentators that for years what we've heard is, the biggest problem on the bench was judicial activism or a lack of judicial restraint—that an unelected group of people would somehow overturn a duly constituted and passed law. Well, this is a good example. And I'm pretty confident that this Court will recognize that and not take that step.

This statement can be read as calling into question the power of judicial review—that is, the authority of courts to find laws unconstitutional. Professor Andrew Koppelman labeled these "uncharacteristically inarticulate" remarks as "impl[ying] that judicial review itself was unprecedented." Obama, a former constitutional law professor, should have been able to do better than this." However, this was not the import of Obama's words. Instead, the president was making it clear that he did not see the Supreme Court as a body that should be in the business of striking down popularly enacted laws, especially when no clear precedent compelled such a decision. Of course, Obama's view was tempered by the vigorous defense his administration provided for the ACA at every level. The former constitutional law lecturer knew quite well that the Court could strike down the

ACA within the bounds of the Constitution without reversing any of its precedents, yet he hoped it wouldn't.

Republicans were outraged by the president's remarks and accused him of trying to intimidate the justices. Senate Minority Leader Mitch McConnell shot back at Obama: "Only someone who would browbeat the Court during the State of the Union"—referring to the president's comments about *Citizens United*—"and whose administration stifled speech during the health care debate would try to intimidate the Court *while* it's deliberating one of the most consequential cases of our time." McConnell said that "this president's attempt to intimidate the Supreme Court falls well beyond distasteful politics; it demonstrates a fundamental lack of respect for our system of checks and balances."

Representative Lamar Smith of Texas was "disappointed" with the president's comments and noted, "Nothing could be more appropriate for the Supreme Court to decide than whether a bill is constitutional or not. What is unprecedented is . . . the president of the United States trying to intimidate the Supreme Court." Senator Chuck Grassley added, "President Obama wrongly argued [that] it would be unprecedented for the Supreme Court to strike down a law that a large congressional majority passed. . . . The president of the United States knows better because he is a former constitutional law lecturer." Senator Orrin Hatch said that it was a "fantasy" to think that "every law you like is constitutional and every Supreme Court decision you don't is 'activist.' . . . Judicial activism or restraint is not measured by which side wins but by whether the Court correctly applied the law." Mitt Romney chimed in, insisting that striking down the ACA would not be an act of "an activist court—that will be a court following the Constitution."

McConnell would later tell the Rotary Club of Lexington, Kentucky, that the president "looked at the line that wisely separates the three branches of government and stepped right over it. But what the president did this week went even farther. With his words, he was no longer trying to embarrass the Court after a decision; rather, he tried to intimidate it before a decision has been made. And that should be intolerable to all of us."

While all of the drama was unfolding within the beltway, this presidential versus congressional squabble soon bled over into the third branch of government—the courts. The next morning, on April 3, 2012, Judge Jerry Smith, who sat on the Fifth Circuit Court of Appeals in Houston, Texas, was hearing arguments in a case that involved a provision of the ACA unrelated to the individual mandate.

During oral argument, in an apparent response to the president's questioning of the power of judicial review, Judge Smith asked a DOJ lawyer if the government agreed that courts could strike down an unconstitutional law. "Does the Department of Justice recognize that federal courts have the authority in appropriate circumstances to strike federal statutes because of one or more constitutional infirmities?" Stunned, the lawyer recited that ever since Chief Justice John Marshall's 1803 opinion in *Marbury v. Madison,* the courts had this power. Smith was not satisfied with the lawyer's answer. According to reporter Jan Crawford, Smith was "very stern."

In a bold move that Professor Andrew Koppelman labeled a "crude political stunt," Judge Smith ordered Attorney General Eric Holder to personally certify in a three-page, single-spaced letter to the court that he supported the power of judicial review. The judge told the DOJ lawyer, "I would like to have from you by noon on Thursday— that's about forty-eight hours from now—a letter stating what is the position of the attorney general and the Department of Justice in regard to the recent statements by the president. What is the authority of the federal courts in this regard in terms of judicial review?" Crawford reported that "the other two judges on the panel . . . both Republican appointees—remained silent."

Mere hours after Smith's order, the president escalated the tensions by doubling down on a point he had made the previous day. "I have enormous confidence that in looking at this law, not only

is it constitutional, but that the court is going to exercise its jurisprudence carefully because of the profound power that our Supreme
Court has." Now Obama was not merely commenting on the scope
of constitutional power but also addressing the Court's "jurisprudence"—that is, the institutional role of the courts in our tripartite
system of government. This is the branch that Alexander Hamilton
called in Federalist No. 78, the "least dangerous branch." Obama was
subtly telling the Court to respect its place in our democracy and not
to subvert the judgments of the elected branches.

Two days later, Attorney General Holder submitted a letter to
Judge Smith, certifying that the "president's remarks were fully consistent with the principles" of judicial review. In a not-too-subtle jab
at Smith, Holder cited the opinions of Judge Sutton from the Sixth
Circuit Court of Appeals and Judge Silberman from the D.C. Circuit,
both of whom had voted to uphold the ACA. White House spokes-
man Jay Carney later added, "The president believes that the Supreme
Court has the final word on matters of judicial review on the constitutionality of legislation. He would, having been a professor of law."

Judge Smith instantly became the subject of massive attention
from the media and criticisms from the academic world. Law professor Jack Balkin wrote a withering critique: "All of us can sympathize
with the plight of Jerry Smith; all of us, in our own ways, have experi-
enced our own dark nights of the soul. Your Honor—and we use that
term advisedly—we feel your pain." On the other side, Judge Smith
would be praised by conservative talk radio host Rush Limbaugh: "I
saw this and I started cheering. I started laughing. Because it's about
time people started fighting back on this. The American people love
the concept of a team. You have to have the right people on the team,
but we are a team here. There is a team that's opposing this president, and attempting to make him a one-termer this November at
the ballot box." To Limbaugh, Judge Smith was on his team opposing
Obama.

One DOJ lawyer told me that Holder's response made him "look like the grown-up" in the room. A former clerk on the Fifth Circuit recalled that "Judge Smith is a very good judge, a judge's judge," though his comments were "reactionary." Another Fifth Circuit clerk said that what Smith did was "legally justified" but "unwise and unnecessary." A federal judge told me that Smith's behavior was "extraordinary" and that asking for the letter from the attorney general was an "improper judicial request." As a postscript to this internecine conflict, the Fifth Circuit, in an opinion that Smith joined, upheld the ACA provision at issue; finding that the court did in fact have the power to consider the constitutionality of laws. As the coup de grâce, the opinion used the phrase "judicial review" a staggering thirteen times.

Chief Justice Roberts, who had pledged to support and strengthen the Court as a respected institution and avoid the appearance of partisan decisions, could not have appreciated this undue attention to the judiciary at such a critical juncture in the Court's history. I agree with Koppelman that "what the Supreme Court needed above all was the public's perception that the judiciary was above politics. This didn't help." The timing of these barbs was especially apt, as Roberts was at this very time vacillating between striking down the law and finding a way to save it. Crawford reported that, as Roberts "began to craft the decision striking down the mandate" in the weeks after the conference, "the external pressure began to grow." As Crawford noted, "Roberts pays attention to media coverage." These forceful attacks on a federal judge could not have evaded the watchful eyes of the chief justice. Amid the squabbling between the president and Congress, this episode could only have added to the "external pressure" he felt.

Indeed, soon enough, political statements were deliberately aimed at Roberts. On May 14, Senator Patrick Leahy gave a speech on the Senate floor pointed right at Roberts. "I trust that he will be a chief justice for all of us and that he has a strong institutional sense of the proper role of the judicial branch," said Leahy. The "conservative activism" reflected in recent decisions had "not been good for the Court. Given the ideological challenge to the Affordable Care Act and the extensive, supportive precedent, it would be extraordinary for the Supreme Court not to defer to Congress in this matter that so clearly affects interstate commerce."

Senator Jon Kyl of Arizona responded to what he perceived as Leahy's partisan attack on the chief justice: "As everyone knows, a ruling on the constitutionality of Obamacare is expected later this month. I think it is important that it be done in the right context. A lot of our Democratic colleagues have made clear their view that if the ruling doesn't go the way they want it to, it is not because they passed an unconstitutional law but rather, in their view, because it is some kind of a partisan activity by judicial activists and a lot of attention has been specifically focused on Chief Justice Roberts. This should not stand."

Many Republicans viewed the president's remarks, as well as Leahy's, as an attempt to intimidate the Court. While this was probably not Obama's intent, in the words of one longtime Supreme Court reporter, the president "made it clear that striking down the law would throw the Court into a partisan fight." Obama was not afraid to politicize decisions of the Court, as he had done during the State of the Union. With a presidential election coming up in months, Obama signaled that he would react accordingly if the Court were to strike down the law.

The media also turned its attention to Chief Justice Roberts. Perhaps the most prominent media analyst to enter this fray was *The New Republic*'s Jeffrey Rosen, whom legal historian David Garrow has called "the nation's most widely read and influential legal commentator." In an influential column, Rosen presented the stakes for the chief justice's vote: "This, then, is John Roberts's moment of truth: In addition to deciding what kind of chief justice he wants to be, he has to decide what kind of legal conservatism he wants to embrace. Of course, if the Roberts Court strikes down health care reform by a 5–4 vote, then the chief justice's stated goal of presiding over a less divisive Court will be viewed as an irredeemable failure." In her investigation, Jan Crawford alluded to reports by journalists that "suggested that if Roberts struck down the mandate, it would prove he had been deceitful during his confirmation hearings, when he explained a philosophy of judicial restraint." This was likely a veiled reference to Jeffrey Rosen's refrain that Roberts had to remain consistent with his confirmation-hearing pledge to promote the Court as a nonpolitical institution.

Chief Justice Roberts had to decide whether he wanted to swallow that bitter pill if he were to strike down the ACA. No doubt he was well aware of the statements of the president and others, especially since, "as Chief Justice, [he] is keenly aware of his leadership role on the court, and he also is sensitive to how the court is perceived by the public," as Crawford put it. But we may never know for sure whether those statements had an impact on the chief justice.

On the right, however, Rosen's article was seen as the "trigger" that raised conservatives' concerns and led them to "[start] to push back." Just as those on the left were trying to nudge a wavering Roberts, those on the right began a concerted effort to solidify the vote of the "wobbly" chief justice.

A Wobbly "Spine of Steel"

In mid-May, *Washington Post* syndicated conservative columnist George Will hosted a dinner at his home in honor of Judge J. Harvie Wilkinson's new book about the role of the courts and constitutional theory. Among the guests were Jeff Rosen, Randy Barnett, and Chip Mellor, the president of the libertarian public interest law firm, the Institute for Justice. The Health Care Cases, the pending decision, and Wilkinson's theory about judicial restraint were lively topics of

conversation. Barnett related that they "debated these different visions of restraint at . . . a convivial dinner." Rosen, a longtime admirer
of Judge Wilkinson, provided a vigorous defense of the judge's book.
Soon, Barnett, Will, and others would articulate their own responses
to Chief Justice Roberts's judicial restraint in print.

In quick succession, two talking points spread throughout the
right wing—respond to Rosen, and shore up the chief justice. Within
a ninety-six-hour period, a torrential response was unleashed in the
conservative media. All the articles shared two goals: drawing attention to alleged liberal attempts to intimidate the Supreme Court, and
Roberts in particular, and trying to solidify the chief justice's vote.

On May 22, 2012, Kathleen Parker's article "The Public Trial of
Justice Roberts" was published in the *Washington Post*. "Novelist John
Grisham could hardly spin a more provocative fiction: The president
and his surrogates mount an aggressive campaign to intimidate the
chief justice of the United States, implying ruin and ridicule should
he fail to vote in a pivotal case according to the ruling political party's wishes. If only it were fiction." She alleged that the president was
waging a "not-so-stealth campaign to influence the Supreme Court"
that was "obnoxious, if not unethical." Parker closed with a pep talk
to the chief justice: "it's up to the chief justice to hold the bar high."

The next day, the *Post's* conservative blogger Jennifer Rubin added,
"In essence, the left asks Roberts, knowing he believes the law to be
unconstitutional, to nevertheless switch sides and thereby violate his
oath of office. . . . I think the left asks waaay too much. The chief
justice, I am certain, doesn't want to go from umpire to the judicial
equivalent of the 1919 Black Sox."

Later that day on the Volokh Conspiracy blog, Randy Barnett observed that the statements from Obama, Leahy, and Rosen "presup-
pose that the conference vote was to invalidate the mandate, or there
would have been no reason to speak now." In other words, Barnett
implied that Rosen and others may have targeted the chief justice

because they knew his vote was in play: "Hence, the specific pressure on Chief Justice Roberts . . . is implicitly urging him to *change his vote* from that which he cast in the conference."

In an essay in the *Harvard Law Review*'s online forum, titled "The Disdain Campaign," Barnett criticized Rosen's column as an effort to intimidate the chief justice. Barnett understood Rosen's column to be "threaten[ing] that [a] campaign of disdain would focus on Chief Justice Roberts should he decide to invalidate the ACA." He also observed the curiousness of the timing: "At the very time that the Chief Justice began to waver (according to CBS News), George Washington University Law School Professor Jeffrey Rosen trained his fire specifically on Chief Justice Roberts."

On May 23, 2012, Barnett also offered a preview of the criticisms of the chief justice by pondering what would happen if Roberts changed his vote. "Thanks to the President, Senator Leahy and the pundits and professors who have so loudly called upon the Chief Justice to decide this case politically or risk the legitimacy of the Court, should he now decide to uphold the ACA, he will always be suspected of being the second Justice Roberts to switch in time." The first Justice Roberts was Owen J. Roberts, who in 1937 changed his vote in *West Coast Hotel v. Parrish*. By doing so, and supporting a progressive minimum wage law, some historians say that this "switch in time that saved nine" avoided a clash between the Roosevelt administration and the Court. Such a conflict could have led to FDR's attempt to pack the Court with like-minded justices. Others view the switch as a craven abandonment of constitutional principle.

On May 24, the editors of the *National Review* continued the theme. Supporters of the ACA were "threatening dire consequences for the reputation of the Supreme Court and especially for Chief Justice John Roberts if he joins a majority of the justices to strike down the individual mandate." The editorial concluded, "We suspect that Chief Justice Roberts wants his legacy to consist of promoting fidelity to the rule of law, not a few months of liberal approbation followed by further blackmail attempts. He should call a strike, and give his would-be advisers the brush-off they deserve."

Finally, on May 25, 2012, under the headline "Liberals Put the Squeeze to Justice Roberts" in his syndicated column, George Will claimed that progressives were "waging an embarrassingly obvious campaign, hoping [Roberts] will buckle beneath the pressure of their disapproval and declare Obamacare constitutional. . . . They hope to secure it by causing Roberts to worry about his reputation and that of his institution." These "clumsy attempts to bend the chief justice," Will wrote, "are apt to reveal his spine of steel." Rosen speculated to me that Will's intent was to "switch Roberts back." One Supreme Court reporter told me that the motivation of Will's article was "obvious"— to "shore up their side," or at least "raise questions about the other side."

The message from the right was loud and clear: Chief Justice Roberts should not be intimidated by Obama, Leahy, Rosen, and others.

Rosen disputed that he had any goal of pressuring Roberts. His intent was to remind readers of what the chief justice had said and to "express the hope that Roberts would do what he said he would do." Rosen stressed that his motivation for writing the column was "nothing more than meets the eye—to point out what is obvious." Rosen wrote in May, "The idea that I was trying to 'intimidate' or 'bend' the Chief Justice came as a surprise to me. The justices have already voted in the health care case and are hardly influenced, in any event, by legal punditry. On the contrary, I suggested that this is a moment of truth for Chief Justice Roberts because I've been a staunch supporter of the vision of bipartisanship that he articulated when he became Chief Justice." Dahlia Lithwick also disputed the notion that Rosen and others were engaging in a preemptive attack on the Court. She told me that this was "such an obvious normative argument about the Court conducting itself as a Court." Lithwick quipped that it is "funny to accuse wonky Jeff Rosen of intimidating people with life tenure."

However, conservatives were not reacting merely to Rosen's article. Our unpredictable and unprecedented journey took another sharp turn to the right. There were leaks from within the Court that directly influenced this response. Though Crawford's report was published on July 1, 2012, I've been told by those who heard the leaks that this information was known as early as May. Several in the Supreme Court press corps confirmed to me that they heard rumors about the chief justice's shifting position, but "nothing was firm enough for anyone to report on." It was speculative, but some on the right decided it wasn't worth risking it and sprang into action to shift the chief back. With the outcome of the most important case in decades on the line, something had to be done.

Soon after the message trickled from the Court that Roberts's vote was "in flux," a right-wing bat signal went out, with a clear message: we need to tell the chief justice to grow a backbone. George Will and others answered that call. Conservatives, who had been noticeably quiet about the outcome of the case after the conference, suddenly perked up in the home stretch, precisely when the war was being waged within the Court over the final vote. A Supreme Court reporter told me that in May "there seemed to be some sense in the conservative press that maybe this wasn't going to work out. It wasn't Kennedy to worry about. It was Roberts."

On June 2, 2012, *National Review* editor Ramesh Ponnuru implied in a talk he gave at Princeton that he had received a leak when he said, "My understanding is that there was a 5–4 vote to strike down the mandate and maybe some related provisions but not the entire act. Since then, interestingly, there seem to have been some second thoughts. Not on the part of Justice Kennedy, but on the part of Chief Justice Roberts, who seems to be going a little bit wobbly. So right now, I would say, [the case] is a little bit up in the air." Crawford also described the chief as "wobbly" in her report: "It also became clear to the conservative justices that Roberts was, as one put it, 'wobbly.'" Dahlia Lithwick told me that she found it curious that they all used the same word—"wobbly." Rosen agreed that "the timing was interesting."

Oddly enough, the efforts outside the Court to sway the chief justice mirrored the efforts inside the Court to do the same. It was a bizarre replay of the internal fight over *Planned Parenthood v. Casey,* yet in reverse. Unlike *Casey,* where Justice Scalia and the other conservative justices had been trying to sway Justice Kennedy, here, according to Crawford, it was Justice Kennedy leading the "month-long, desperate campaign to bring [Roberts] back to his original position." Like Scalia two decades earlier, Kennedy "was relentless. He was very engaged in this." Kennedy "didn't give up until the end."

Kennedy should have known better, in light of his own changed vote in *Casey.* Crawford reports that Roberts even tried to "persuade at least Justice Kennedy to join his opinion. . . . One justice, a source said, described it as 'arm-twisting.'" The efforts to persuade the chief justice, internally and externally, failed. "Roberts held firm," Crawford concluded. And like Kennedy's flip two decades earlier, Roberts's switch would rock the dynamics on the Court. Crawford relates that the conservative justices realized "that Roberts wanted the court out of the red-hot dispute." Roberts wanted to "draw that line" between what Congress could and could not do "in a way that decided future cases, and not the massive health care case." In the end, the conservative justices told Roberts, "You're on your own." Roberts would have to bear his own cross.

Only after resisting this internal pressure did Roberts begin to focus on how the law could be upheld by construing the mandate's penalty as a tax—exactly what the solicitor general had urged him to do. Several Supreme Court reporters offered differing accounts of how Roberts reached his ultimate opinion. One reporter who covers the Court told me that, after the initial vote, it was clear that the Commerce Clause argument had been lost, though Roberts "had never locked in on the taxing power [argument]." Another told me that after the conference, the chief justice assigned the opinion to himself, focusing only on the Commerce Clause; he wanted to see how the rest of the opinion "would write," but "played his cards very carefully." By May, Roberts was already "suggesting he could find grounds to uphold the law beyond the Commerce Clause."

However he got there, eventually Roberts adopted the solicitor general's solution to save the law. He had signaled his preference for this position during oral arguments. There was nothing new for the chief justice to come up with. The solicitor general's brief was waiting, right where Verrilli left it. The government's instincts, once again, were correct—"the chief justice could be the fifth, and not the sixth, vote."

Roberts knew that there would be "hard feelings" from his vote as he prepared to circulate his draft opinion by June 1. Yet he apparently chose to save the law in the short term in order to preserve what he believed to be the best interests of the Court in the long term. Soon enough, this unprecedented journey would reach its climax.

THE END OF THE TERM

On June 27, 2012, the eve of the final day of the Supreme Court term, everyone had an opinion on what was about to happen. Just about everyone would be wrong. A *Washington Post* poll showed that a majority of Americans, and even a slight plurality of Democrats, wanted the Court to strike down the ACA. An *ABA Journal* survey poll revealed that "85 percent of those surveyed (journalists, lawyers and academics) are predicting that the court will uphold the law." In a poll of fifty-six former Supreme Court clerks, 57 percent predicted that the individual mandate would be overturned. Three months earlier, prior to oral arguments, only 35 percent of the clerks voted in favor of invalidation. One said, "I feel like a dope, because I was one of those who predicted that the Court would uphold the statute by a lopsided majority. . . . It now appears pretty likely that this prediction was way off." Over 80 percent of the voters on InTrade speculated that the Court would find the mandate unconstitutional. On FantasySCOTUS.net, a Supreme Court prediction market and fantasy league I created, the results were not statistically significant and were too close to call.

Representative Ron Paul of Texas wasn't optimistic. "We must recognize that the federal judiciary has an abysmal record when it comes to protecting liberty. It's doubtful the entire law will be struck down." Former Arkansas governor Mike Huckabee had his usual folksy take on it: "I look at this health care bill as a big bowl of stew, and at this point the Supreme Court may say there's some tainted meat in that stew that we're going to take out. I don't know, if you take the tainted meat out, if anybody would still want to eat it." Nancy Pelosi was optimistic. "We believe that this bill constitutionally is ironclad. I expect a 6–3 'aye' verdict from the Supreme Court."

Decision day would come on June 28, 2012. It would be a day unlike any other in Supreme Court history.

PART VIII

Judgment Day

(June 28, 2012)

The Affordable Care Act's day of reckoning came on June 28, 2012. Hollywood could not have scripted a more dramatic minute-by-minute conclusion to this epic saga.

THE QUIET BEFORE THE STORM

On judgment day, all news organizations descended on One First Street NE. Beat Supreme Court reporters—those with the so-called hard press passes—secured coveted seats upstairs inside the Court's main chamber. They were there to witness history. Other reporters were downstairs, in the press room, where they could listen to a closed-circuit audio feed of the proceedings in the Court. As soon as the justices began to announce an opinion, the Public Information Office would distribute printed copies and post a copy of the opinion on the Supreme Court's website. All of the major news organizations stationed "runners" who would sprint with a copy of the opinion to the reporters waiting on the street to file the first live broadcasts.

Reporters had to decide where they wanted to cover the case: upstairs in the courtroom, downstairs in the press room, or outside in front of the cameras. Ironically, those upstairs inside the courtroom would be the last to know what happened.

By 9:30, thirty minutes before the session began, the courtroom was filling to capacity. Senator Orrin Hatch arrived at 9:35. He greeted Tea Party favorite Representative Michele Bachmann of Minnesota, who was seated at the front of the public seating area.

At 9:51, Justice John Paul Stevens entered the court, arriving from the area to the right of the bench. Stevens, who had retired from the Court two years earlier, remained in the public spotlight, frequently speaking about the Court's cases and even criticizing his colleagues for their opinions. He was seated in the Court's VIP section on the right side of the courtroom.

Members of the press stood up to look for more VIPs. In the words of Mark Walsh, the *ABA Journal*'s reporter, "For all the drama, the courtroom [was] a bit short on star power."

At 9:55, an officer of the Court rose and gave the same announcement that is delivered every day when the Supreme Court is in session—everyone must stay in their seat, remain quiet, and follow instructions in case of an emergency. He could rest assured that no one was planning on leaving early.

CNN reported that the atmosphere outside the Court was "lively" as Tea Party patriots and ACA supporters tried to "outdo each other with chants." C-SPAN cameras panned to the gathering protesters outside the Court. One sign said UNIVERSAL COVERAGE FOR ALL. Some protesters held up a Gadsden flag and American flags. Another, dressed up as a Patriot of 1776, railed against the health care law amid chants of "USA, USA." Some elderly belly dancers shook their hips in front of a sign that called for Medicare for all.

10:00:00

At exactly 10:00, almost as if by magic, the nine justices majestically appeared from behind the thick, velvet vermillion curtains. Dahlia Lithwick told me that the chief justice looked "wiped tired," as if he had "gone through a washing machine." Lithwick had never seen Sotomayor appear so tired. Justice Kagan also seemed weary. Mark Walsh recalled that Justice Scalia "look[ed] a bit grim." Lithwick observed that Scalia gently pounded his fists on the bench as he sat down, and the usually composed Justice Kennedy looked "pissed off" and let it show that he was mad. Only Justice Ginsburg looked effervescent.

Immediately, Chief Justice Roberts announced the first opinion of the day. It wasn't the one everybody was waiting for. "Justice Kennedy has the announcement today in Case 11–210, *United States v. Alvarez.*" In this case, Justice Kennedy found that the Stolen Valor Act, a law that punishes those who lie about being awarded military honors, violated the First Amendment's protection of freedom of speech.

At this point, the Supreme Court's website was already being inundated with traffic and became unreliable. As Kennedy continued to read his opinion in *Alvarez,* the scene outside the Court became more vibrant. Chants of "USA, USA," grew stronger, then turned into an impromptu singing of "God Bless America." A man on a bullhorn screamed, "This is our home, and we are going to protect it." That was followed by a rousing chant of "Strike it down, strike it down."

10:03:00

Kennedy concluded with what was an obvious dig at the government's argument in the ACA case. "That governmental power [to punish those who falsely claimed they won military honors] has no clear limiting principle." At the time, no one realized how prescient Kennedy's closing was.

As Kennedy continued to read, Tom Goldstein reported on SCOTUSBlog that the Public Information Office, mere steps away from the press room where the reporters congregate, "has one small box and one very large box of opinions on its desk; presumably the larger one is for [the Health Care Cases]." Goldstein would later recount the play-by-play of the events that unfolded that day, many of which are discussed in this chapter.

Outside, the commotion grew. A protester proudly waved a WE LOVE OBAMACARE sign as a siren wailed. CNN's shot outside the Court blared the headline, "Breaking News: Health Care Ruling Any Minute."

10:06:00

At 10:06, Justice Kennedy finished reading *Alvarez.* Next up was the penultimate case, *First American.* To everyone's surprise, there was no opinion. The chief justice announced in *First American,* "The petition for writ of certiorari is dismissed as improvidently granted." "Dismissed as improvidently granted," or DIG in the lexicon, occurs when the Supreme Court has chosen not to rule on a case, typically because the facts were not what the justices thought when they agreed to hear the dispute, or the law has changed in the interim. In this instance, the speculation was that the justices simply ran out of time after focusing on the health care decision. Instead of holding the case over for the next term, the justices just chucked it out.

There was only one case left to announce.

It was silent inside the Court as everyone waited in suspense. Mark Walsh noted, "If audience members could possibly perk up any more in their seats, they did." Everyone knew what was coming next.

10:06:40

At 10:06 and 40 seconds, the moment everyone had been waiting for arrived.

Chief Justice Roberts declared, "I have the announcement in Case 11393, *National Federation of Independent Business v. Sebelius*." Obamacare was on the block.

Chief Justice Roberts would be deciding the fate of the law. Many had predicted that Roberts would write the opinion no matter what the Court did, as the chief justice can assign himself any opinion in which he votes with the majority. Those in attendance wondered if it would be a 6–3 Roberts opinion upholding the mandate, along with Justice Kennedy, or a 5–4 opinion striking down the mandate. In fact, it would be neither.

At the moment the chief justice began to announce his opinion, the Public Information Office downstairs started to hand out copies of the 194-page opinion. Goldstein recounted that "downstairs in [room] G42, the Court's press room staff opens a huge white box and begins handing out the decision. Every reporter grabs a copy and races out." In a frenzy, reporters quickly grabbed the opinion to start digesting it. The reporters inside the Court would remain in the dark for some time.

The Supreme Court's website quickly crashed. It would not come back online for nearly thirty minutes. The Public Information Office had refused requests to email copies of the opinion to the press. For nearly half an hour, the only people with access to the opinions were those on the first floor of One First Street NE.

At that moment, President Obama was standing in the "Outer Oval" with his chief of staff (and future Treasury secretary) Jack Lew, watching a split-screen TV that showed four different networks, including CNN and Fox News. The president of the United States had no idea if his health care reform act was still the law of the land.

10:06:46

The chief justice began to read his opinion and turned to the question that everyone was waiting for. "The question is whether Congress has the constitutional power to enact the individual mandate. The government advances two arguments that it does. First, the government contends that the Constitution's Commerce Clause authorizes the mandate. Second, the government says that Congress could enact the statute under its constitutional power to lay and collect taxes."

Perceptive minds in the Court wondered why Roberts put the commerce power first and the taxing power second. All of the lower court opinions that had invalidated the law began by finding that the mandate was not a valid tax, and then found that it was not a valid exercise of Congress's commerce power. Tom Goldstein recalled, "Inside G42, the press room staff hear the chief justice say over the speakers that the Court will have to confront the government's arguments under both the commerce power and also the tax power. But none of the reporters hear him; they are all gone." No doubt, they were frantically preparing their instant reports on the case.

At 10:06:46, Bloomberg was the first news outlet to publish that the decision had been released. At 10:07:00, Amy Howe reported on SCOTUSBlog that "we have health care opinion." For Supreme Court aficionados, this was the equivalent of a cardinal at the Vatican declaring "Habemus Papam."

But while Bloomberg and SCOTUSBlog took a conservative approach by not broadcasting the outcome, Fox and CNN decided to try to be first. CNN's producer quickly scanned the opinion and saw that the chief justice's opinion found that the mandate was not a valid exercise of Congress's powers under the Commerce Clause. Goldstein reported that the producer incorrectly concluded that it "looks like" the mandate was unconstitutional. The control room asked if they could "go with it." After a brief pause, the producer said yes. CNN ran with it.

Likewise, the producer at Fox News read the opinion and quickly came to the same erroneous conclusion—that the mandate had been struck down. Goldstein related that the Fox News control room asked the producer to confirm. He responded: "100 percent." The din outside the Court grew louder amid reports that the opinion had been released. Protesters, glued to their phones, waited intently for the news.

10:07:00

Less than fifteen seconds after Chief Justice Roberts began reading his opinion, the first report hit CNN. At exactly 10:07, host Wolf Blitzer cut to a shot of the Supreme Court. Reporter Kate Bolduan, CNN's congressional correspondent, frantically rushed to the camera, fumbling with the 194-page opinion. She began, "This is our first read . . . but I want to bring you the breaking news, according to our producer, [the individual mandate] is not a valid exercise of the Commerce Clause." Bolduan, nervously looking down at her notes and somewhat short of breath, blurted out, "So it appears as if the Supreme Court justices have struck down the individual mandate, the centerpiece of the health care legislation."

As CNN made this initial report, inside the chief justice was still explaining how the law was not constitutional as an exercise of Congress's commerce powers.

At the White House, President Obama watched the reports on CNN. He was, according to ABC News, "crestfallen and anxious."

As Bolduan frantically tried to explain an opinion she had not read, the scene inside the Court was tense. Roberts continued, noting that this was the first time that Congress had tried to force people to buy a product they did not want, and nothing in our constitutional history suggested Congress had this authority. The law had no precedent. It was not looking good for Solicitor General Donald Verrilli, who was sitting in the front row.

10:07:32

At 10:07:32, less than a minute after the chief justice began speaking, Bloomberg issued a contrary report: "Obama's Health-Care Overhaul Upheld by U.S. Supreme Court."

Inside the courtroom, the SCOTUSBlog staff was still reviewing the opinion—they would be "parsing it ASAP." At that moment, the caption "Supreme Ct. Kills Individual Mandate" flashed on CNN.com. That message spread throughout CNN's social media platform on Twitter, Facebook, and in breaking news alerts. CNN tweeted at 10:08:00, "Supreme Court strikes down individual mandate portion of health care law." On Twitter, National Public Radio retweeted CNN's report: "@CNN reporting #SCOTUS has ruled that the individual mandate for health care is unconstitutional." The error spread at the speed of light. CNN continued to misreport the case. Analyst John King said, "The justices have just gutted, Wolf, the centerpiece provision of the health care law." King added that it was a "direct blow to President Obama."

But Kate Bolduan was beginning to have doubts. "I'm going to hop back on this phone to try to get more information and bring it to you, Wolf." Blitzer continued, "Wow, that's a dramatic development if in fact the Supreme Court has ruled that the individual mandate is in fact unconstitutional. That would be history unfolding right now." Almost immediately, Blitzer started to hedge. "We're going to get a lot more information. This is just the initial headline that we're getting from inside the Supreme Court [from] our own Kate Bolduan."

10:08:00

If CNN's reaction was cautious or even dour, the Fox News Channel's reaction was relieved. Just as the broadcast began on Fox, you could hear someone utter an elated "Oh, boy" off camera.

Anchor Bill Hemmer proclaimed, "We have breaking news here at the Fox News Channel. The individual mandate has been ruled unconstitutional." The scroll at the bottom of the screen flashed: "Supreme Court finds health care individual mandate unconstitutional." You could hear a voice off-camera say, "Phew."

Moments later, Fox went live to its Court reporter, Shannon Bream, who was scanning the opinion. When she realized the camera was on her, she began to fumble with the 194-page opinion, held together by a taut binder clip.

Bream began, "We are just getting the opinion. I am just getting a first look at it. It is authored by the chief justice, John Roberts. He has specific language going to the commerce clause." Bream read from the syllabus printed on the first two pages (the same summary Bolduan had been reading): "This compels individuals to become active in commerce. . . . The individual mandate cannot be sustained under Congress's power to regulate commerce."

Shannon Bream concluded, "This means the mandate is gone."

Bill Hemmer was concerned. "Shannon, we are looking at this, we talked about the fog of law to our viewers at home, be patient as we work through this." Hemmer turned to his co-anchor, Megyn Kelly, who was Fox's senior legal correspondent. "Megyn, you're seeing something?"

Kelly stalled: "We're getting conflicting information. We're getting conflicting information." She looked down at her iPad: "Despite what Shannon just said, [the] individual mandate is surviving as tax. This is not confirmed by us, [it is] confirmed by SCOTUSBlog."

Reacting to CNN's reporting, many Republicans were ebullient. Chants of "USA, USA," echoed on the courthouse steps. Across the street from the Court, Ohio Republican representative Jean Schmidt, a proud member of the Tea Party—she had lambasted Bart Stupak for accepting President Obama's executive order—was filmed listening intently to her cell phone. Moments after CNN's report, Schmidt screamed at the top of her lungs, "Yes, Yes." A blogger at CrooksandLiars said the yelp reminded her of Meg Ryan's orgasmic outburst in *When Harry Met Sally*. The YouTube clip went viral.

"What else?" Schmidt demanded of whoever she was talking to on the phone. A man on the street yelled to her, "Speak!" Schmidt continued, "Thank God. They struck down the individual mandate. They took it away." People on the street started screaming. One yelled, "Oh my God." Another, "The mandate is struck down! The mandate is struck down!" Cheers erupted. In the backdrop, supporters of the challengers were celebrating, waving Gadsden flags and chanting, "Constitution wins!" Their joy would be short-lived.

A number of politicians took to Twitter to celebrate the victory. Republican representative Justin Amash of Michigan tweeted "This is a big win for #liberty and the #Constitution." California Republican representative Darrell Issa, the chairman of the House Oversight and Government Reform Committee, promptly retweeted that message. Florida Republican representative Dennis Ross agreed, "Let Freedom Ring." Representative Virginia Foxx, Republican of North Carolina joined in: "#Unconstitutional: #SCOTUS overturns #Obamacare's individual insurance #mandate. Developing," she tweeted. All of the tweets were deleted within ten minutes. But the Internet is like an elephant—it never forgets.

White House Press Secretary Jay Carney watched the initial reports from CNN and Fox News with trepidation. The president was still in the dark.

10:08:30

At 10:08:30, less than two minutes after Roberts begin reading the opinion, SCOTUSBlog became the first media outlet to get the story right. "The individual mandate survives as a tax." SCOTUSBlog was the first to get it right. Moments later, the Associated Press reached the same conclusion—the mandate had survived.

Almost immediately, the conflicts became evident. Ben Smith, editor of BuzzFeed, tweeted, "Wait: AP and CNN just reported opposite outcomes."

Inside the Court, Chief Justice Roberts, completely oblivious to the chaos erupting outside, continued. With red, bleary eyes, he began, "Turning first to the Commerce Clause." Echoing the arguments of the challengers, Roberts proclaimed, "Congress has never before attempted to use the commerce power to order individuals not engaged in commerce to buy an unwanted product. And nothing in the text to the Constitution suggests it can." It was unprecedented.

Everyone in the room knew what that meant—the mandate failed under the Commerce Clause. Thus, they speculated that Roberts was the author of a 5–4 opinion striking down the law that many had predicted. The "stone-faced" Solicitor General Donald Verrilli listened intently as the chief justice dismissed the government's Commerce Clause arguments one by one—as he feared the Court would. Here, the shortcoming of Verrilli's strategy to not provide a satisfactory limiting principle became evident. Not a single conservative Justice would agree with him on the commerce clause argument. A DOJ lawyer who was in the chamber told me that at that point they thought they had lost. Reporter Jeff Toobin later recalled seeing smiles on all the conservatives in the room.

During CNN's continuing live broadcast, Kate Bolduan held the 194-page opinion in her hands with the top two pages flipped over, as if those were the only pages she had read. Had she turned to page 3, she would have read the following sentence: "Chief Justice Roberts concluded in Part III–B that the individual mandate must be construed as imposing a tax on those who do not have health insurance, if such a construction is reasonable." More importantly, the crux of the case was on page 4: "Chief Justice Roberts delivered the opinion of the Court with respect to Part III–C, concluding that the individual mandate may be upheld as within Congress's power under the Taxing Clause." But she didn't read to the end in time before going on the air.

Amid the contradictory reports, advisers in the White House were conflicted about what to tell the president, who was still laboring under CNN's false reports.

10:09:00

CNN's headline still blared: "Individual Mandate Struck Down. Supreme Court Finds Measure Unconstitutional." In a breaking-news blast to millions of people, CNN emailed "The Supreme Court has struck down the individual mandate for health care—the legislation that requires all to have health insurance."

Other news sources cautiously remained quiet. Jan Crawford, CBS's veteran Supreme Court correspondent, reported that the Court "may have" upheld the mandate. The *New York Times,* whose reporter Adam Liptak was still upstairs in the chamber, posted a noncommittal headline: "Supreme Court Rules on Health Care Law." Liptak later told me that the *Times* did not want to write for "10:15 in the morning," but rather wanted to write something "for the archives" that would make the newspaper of record "proud." MSNBC was also restrained. Later, MSNBC president Phil Griffin sent a congratulatory email to his staff. "Your work today set us apart from the competition."

C-SPAN cameras outside the Court recorded a growing cheer and more flag-waving as someone said on camera, "They struck down the mandate." A siren went off. A protester screamed, "The president must now admit that he lied when he said it wasn't a tax." A supporter of the law yelled, "Now Medicaid will be eviscerated."

CNN and Fox News would not correct their errors for several more minutes. The president remained under a cloud of uncertainty.

10:10:00

The chief justice continued reading his opinion. At this point, everyone in the courtroom was convinced that the mandate was unconstitutional. Roberts rejected Congress's power to "compel unwilling citizens to act as the government would have them act" and echoed Justice Kennedy's comments during oral arguments when he found that the mandate "would fundamentally change the relationship between the American citizen and the federal government." Observers speculated that Roberts, along with Kennedy, had voted to strike down this expansive encroachment on individual liberty. But outside the Court, people started to realize what was going on.

By 10:10, Tom Goldstein was the first analyst to parse exactly what had happened. "So the mandate is constitutional. Chief Justice Roberts joins the left of the Court." Of course, given that Roberts had eliminated the mandate with his "saving construction," this was not entirely accurate. But Goldstein was right that the ACA had been upheld.

Moments later, Jan Crawford reported for CBS that the Court had upheld the ACA. Shortly thereafter, veteran NBC reporter Pete Williams, standing tall atop his trademark milk carton on First Street, also correctly reported the outcome of the case. He had "absorbed the decision in more detail during the walk from the press room to his camera stand." David Savage, Supreme Court correspondent for the *Los Angeles Times*, who had written that Roberts may uphold the law on tax grounds, told his office to "go with the story" he had previously drafted, reporting that "the Court upheld the mandate as a tax."

CNN was still misreporting the case. Its homepage still carried the "breaking news" update, "Individual Mandate Struck Down. Supreme Court Finds Measure Unconstitutional," but now reported that the "Justices' ruling overturns requirement that Americans must buy health insurance. The decision will affect you, generations of Americans and the fall's presidential race." Based totally on erroneous information, CNN was already spinning the story—no doubt following a predetermined plan—of the decision's impact on the 2012 election.

Outside the Court, amid the cheers, someone could be heard saying on camera that the mandate was upheld. Another protester said, "We must repeal this entire law. We can't fix unconstitutional. The Constitution matters."

The crowd in its wisdom knew—before CNN, and before the president.

10:10:30

Eventually CNN realized its error. Bolduan came back on camera and said that the Court had released a "very confusing large opinion." On further consideration, she said, it seemed that "the entire law has been upheld, Wolf." She described the opinion as "thick" and "legally dense" as she continued to flip through the 194-page opinion on the air.

Fox News was still incorrectly reporting the story as the anchor continued talking above a headline reading "Supreme Court Finds Health Care Individual Mandate Unconstitutional." It would be several minutes before Fox corrected itself.

10:12:00

At this moment, the president was waiting anxiously in the Oval Office on the other end of Pennsylvania Avenue, still fearing that the initial CNN report was correct and one of his proudest achievements was unconstitutional. Two miles away, in real time, the chief executive's bold visions for health care reform were being attacked by his judicial counterpart, the chief justice.

Roberts continued to read from the majority opinion. "The framers gave Congress the power to regulate commerce, not to compel it. For over 200 years, this Court's decisions and Congress's actions have reflected this understanding. There is no reason to depart from it now."

There were gasps in the courtroom. The solicitor general was trying to keep a "stone face," but he seemed to be "sinking in his seat."

Ilya Shapiro of the Cato Institute, who had debated at over one hundred Obamacare events and had dedicated most of his waking hours for nearly three years to challenging this law, was exuberant, and his "heart was racing."

Jeff Toobin later recalled that "five minutes into Chief Justice Roberts's opinion, you would have asked anyone in that room whether this law was going to be held unconstitutional, I think we all would have said yes. But we were all sitting there, we had to sit till the end, and this turn of events surprised me, that's for sure."

At the White House, the president's staff, with enough confirmed reports, decided to tell the president that the law was struck down.

10:12:30

The president's chief counsel, Kathryn Ruemmler, was chosen as the person to deliver the news to the commander in chief. (In May 2013, Ruemmler would come under fire for not informing the president, prior to the story's public release, that the IRS improperly targeted Tea Party groups for additional scrutiny.) Ruemmler was waiting upstairs in her second-floor office with the White House policy team. With no televisions in their office, they relied on SCOTUSBlog, constantly refreshing on Valerie Jarrett's iPad. Secretary of Health and Human Services Kathleen Sebelius, the named defendant in the case, looked on.

As Ruemmler walked to the Oval Office, she observed that a White House TV was tuned to MSNBC, which was reporting that the mandate was upheld. In the meantime, however, Valerie Jarrett was notified of the earlier, erroneous reports that the Court had declared the Act unconstitutional, and she therefore tried to catch Ruemmler before she reached the president. Ruemmler paused to clear up the confusion, so as not to misinform the president. When her staffers got the definitive word about the Chief Justice's taxing power decision from SCOTUSBlog, Ruemmler continued on her way to see the president. At that moment, a communications staffer sent a single-word email to everyone involved: "Victory."

Ruemmler walked in and gave the president "two thumbs up" and told him, "The Affordable Care Act has been upheld." Politico reported that Obama was "confused by the cognitive dissonance of what he was hearing from Ruemmler and what he was seeing on TV. For a few seconds, he gazed at the monitors quizzically, and eventually decided to trust his staff over CNN, according to a senior administration official." Just in time, CNN recanted its report.

At long last, the president's signature law was accepted, and held to be constitutional. Obama hugged Ruemmler and embraced Lew. The president wanted to call Verrilli as soon as possible, but the solicitor general would remain in the Court for another fifty minutes as the justices continued to read the opinions and dissents. Later that afternoon, Obama called House Minority Leader Nancy Pelosi to congratulate her as well.

With the correct news trickling out, the scene outside the Court transformed. Those supporting the law were ebullient. Evoking the call that had ushered President Obama into the White House in 2008, they chanted, "Yes we can! Yes we can!" ACA opponents were equally vociferous. "The Constitution matters when it comes to your body," someone shouted. A Tea Party protester screamed over a bullhorn, "To those of you who are rejoicing that this monstrosity has been upheld, I have four words for you. This is not over. If you thought November 2010 was historic, you just wait for November 2012!" The Tea Partiers began to chant, "Remember in November," followed by a booming chorus of "Repeal it now." Others yelled, "This is not over."

At this point, the only people who did not know what the decision held were the reporters in the Court—the very people whose job it was to know what happened. Dahlia Lithwick recalled that it is a "very weird thing to know you are obviated by the passage of time."

10:13:00

By 10:13, SCOTUSBlog had digested the gist of the opinion. Tom Goldstein reported, "The bottom line: the entire ACA is upheld." The AP reported, "Supreme Court upholds heart of Obama health care law seeking to cover 30 million uninsured."

Randy Barnett, the godfather of the challenge to the ACA, who had dedicated three years of his life to this case, was not at the Court. He was sitting in his office at the Georgetown University Law Center a mile away, monitoring only SCOTUSBlog. When Goldstein announced the news, Barnett knew that the ACA had been upheld.

His phone buzzed. His mom texted him. "It's so fantastic. Congratulations. You won!" Barnett, "crestfallen," replied, "No, Mom, we lost." His mother replied, "Fox said you won!" Barnett replied, one more time, "No, Mom, we lost." For Barnett, this defeat was "like a kick in the gut." Having read Goldstein's report that the mandate had been upheld, it was a little while before he learned about Roberts's favorable ruling on the Commerce Clause issue, which took away just a bit of the sting.

A mile down Constitution Avenue, the chief justice concluded the first portion of his opinion: "Compelling people to enter commerce precisely because they have chosen not to cannot be considered a necessary and proper supplement to the Commerce Clause."

Then there was a brief, audible, two-second pause.

The chief justice gave a hint that the opinion was not what it seemed. "There are separate writings on this subject, but the majority of this Court agrees that the Commerce Clause cannot sustain the individual mandate."

There was another audible two-second pause.

10:13:10

While the chaos outside the Court was subsiding, the suspense inside the Court was at breaking point. Everyone in the Court thought that "it was over." Lithwick was already planning in her head how she would cover this massive loss for the Obama administration. Neal Katyal would later tell C-SPAN, "Many people in the room had thought the federal government was going to lose."

Roberts, looking "serious," moved on: "That brings us to the government's second argument that the mandate may be upheld under Congress's power to lay and collect taxes." Spectators in the audience began to realize something was amiss. Why would he talk about the taxing power after finding that the law exceeded Congress's commerce powers?

The ghost of Justice Harlan Fiske Stone poured Frances Perkins a spot of tea.

10:13:20

The chief justice dropped the bomb. "If there are two possible interpretations of a statute and one of those interpretations violates the Constitution, courts should adopt the interpretation that allows the statute to be upheld." If the government's position is "reasonable or fairly possible," then the Court should adopt that interpretation rather than declare the statute unconstitutional.

Roberts's conclusion quoted almost verbatim from what Verrilli had written in his brief months earlier: The Court must resort to "every reasonable construction . . . in order to save a statute from unconstitutionality."

A DOJ attorney listened intently to "the way Chief Justice Roberts phrased the introduction to his discussion," which "made it clear that he would rule in our favor." At this point, the stunned lawyer realized, "Oh, we won."

Toobin, who had predicted that the government would lose and called Verrilli's performance a "train wreck," whipped his head around. He suddenly recognized that the chief justice was going to save the law based on the taxing power. Lithwick immediately knew what had happened: Roberts "had his finger on the trigger, and he put the gun down." Katyal recalled that the "entire mood in the audience had changed markedly" as within a "couple seconds everyone in the room knew the government had won the case."

Ilya Shapiro was jolted from ecstasy to agony. "Once I realized he upheld it, my heart dropped. I remember having an imaginary conversation with the chief justice, 'No, stop saying that. Don't do that. Take it back.'" Shapiro was "dazed" because he was "not prepared for this outcome."

Kathie McClure, the mother of two chronically ill children who had waited ninety-two hours outside the Supreme Court in March to hear oral argument, was in the Court. She "breathed in the victory. I felt immediate relief for my children."

Verrilli showed no emotion at all. He didn't even crack a smile at his victory. Robert Barnes, of the *Washington Post,* described the solicitor general's experience during the argument as a "roller coaster" ride. At the end, after all the criticism he had received, Verrilli was victorious, thanks to a decisive assist from Chief Justice Roberts.

The Saving Construction

The chief justice asked rhetorically, "If the commerce power does not authorize Congress to regulate those who don't engage in commerce, perhaps the taxing power should not permit Congress to impose a tax for not doing something." He paused for what seemed like hours. Roberts concluded. "We cannot accept that reasoning."

While "the government's Commerce Clause argument asked this Court to condone a new sort of federal power ordering people not in commerce to buy an unwanted product, [the] government's tax power argument by contrast asks us only to determine that Congress has done something it clearly can do and indeed often has." This was the same advice Justice Stone gave Frances Perkins decades earlier. Roberts reasoned that "upholding the statute under the taxing power does not recognize any new federal power. It determines that Congress has used an existing one."

Quoting verbatim from his opinion, Roberts laid out the premise of his position: "Passing on the wisdom or fairness of such attacks is not our role. Because the Constitution permits it, we must uphold it." In other words, whether he liked the law or not, if it could survive, it would. "The Affordable Care Act's requirement that certain individuals pay a financial penalty for not obtaining health insurance may reasonably be characterized as a tax."

Roberts rewrote the most controversial provision of the ACA. He effectively eliminated the individual mandate from the statute—the very provision that had been debated for nearly three years—and replaced it with a mere tax that a person must pay if he fails to maintain insurance. The chief justice upheld a statute that Congress did not write, deleting the most controversial phrase from the 2,700-page bill—that a person "shall . . . ensure" that she "is covered" by a health insurance policy.

Under Roberts's construction, the ACA does not require anyone to obtain health insurance. Rather, if someone fails to purchase insurance, he is taxed. That is not the statute Congress enacted, but the statute that Chief Justice Roberts drafted—at the begging request of the solicitor general.

In the front row, Mark Walsh observed that Senator Orrin Hatch, who three years earlier had begun the fight against the law's constitutionality when no one else was willing to stand up, looked "stone-faced as he jot[ted] down some of what Roberts [was] saying." Michele Bachmann had a look of "astonishment." Toobin could see her rolling her eyes, as if to say, *Are you kidding me?*

At that point, those in the Court still had no idea how the other justices voted—and they wouldn't know for some time. All they knew was what Roberts told them: "A majority of the Court holds that the federal government cannot use the taxing power to order people to buy health insurance but a majority also holds that the statute here may be upheld as a tax increase on those without health insurance, which is within Congress's power to tax. So this portion of the Affordable Care Act is upheld." Despite the president saying that the ACA was "not a tax increase," the chief justice construed it that way, so it was. Perhaps most importantly, the Supreme Court affirmed that Congress lacks the power to compel people to purchase health insurance.

Later that day, Senate Minority Leader Mitch McConnell seized on the political implications of this decision. "The President of the United States himself promised up and down that this bill was not a tax. This was one of the Democrats' top selling points—because they knew it would have never passed if they said it was. The Supreme Court has spoken. This law is a tax. This bill was sold to the American people on a deception."

States Now Have a Real Choice

With the courtroom stunned, the chief justice continued. "We now turn to the second part of the act challenge in this case often referred to as the Medicaid expansion." The ride was far from over—Medicaid had been the sleeper issue of this case. No one in the Court could tell if the chief justice had voted to strike down the Medicaid expansion or uphold it. In fact, he did something in between.

Roberts began to explain that the Medicaid expansion offered states new funding if they accepted certain conditions, such as providing insurance for more people. If the states did not comply with these conditions, they could lose all Medicaid funding, which in some states constituted over 10 percent of the state budget. "Critically for this case, if a state does not comply with the act's new coverage requirements, it may lose not only the federal funding for the expansion but all of its federal Medicaid funds."

Echoing what Judge Vinson had written in Florida two years earlier, Roberts declared this is "so utterly beyond the scope of Medicaid, as originally conceived and implemented, as to constitute not merely a change of degree, but a change of kind."

Roberts reasoned that the Medicaid expansion was "far from a typical case" and different from previous funding programs because "Congress threatened to withhold states' existing Medicaid funds if they do not comply with the expansion. The states claim that this threat serves no purpose other than to force unwilling states to sign up for the new program." Roberts paused. "We agree." He rejected the government's assurances that political constraints would prevent Washington from crippling state finances. Relying on the 2010 letter sent to Arizona threatening the elimination of all funds, the chief justice concluded that the threat of withholding was enough to trigger the Constitution's prohibition against unlawful coercion. Using an image he invoked during oral argument, Roberts chastised the government. "In this case, the threat to withhold funds is more than relatively mild encouragement. It is a gun to the head." As Roberts noted in his opinion, "Nothing in our opinion precludes Congress from offering funds under the Affordable Care Act to expand the availability of health care, and requiring that states accepting such funds comply with the conditions on their use. What Congress is not free to do is to penalize states that choose not to participate in that new program by taking away their existing Medicaid funding."

For the first time ever, the Supreme Court had found that a federal spending program was coercive and unconstitutional—and not along a 5–4 split. Mark Walsh recalled that Roberts "surprise[d] the courtroom again by saying that seven members of the court agree on this." Shockingly, Justices Breyer and Kagan had joined the chief justice's opinion, leaving only Justices Ginsburg and Sotomayor in dissent. A senior DOJ lawyer in the court was stunned and said to himself, "Holy cow. We lost on Medicaid." The Medicaid issue had been something of a sleeper, as every court below had consistently rejected this argument. Few expected that the Court would find it was unconstitutional.

The solicitor general's roller-coaster ride was not over. Though the justices "reject[ed] the government's argument that the states agreed to this when they signed up for the original Medicaid program," the Court did not find the program entirely unconstitutional.

Instead, the conciliatory chief justice reached yet another compromise position. Roberts accepted this dichotomy between the old and new funding. "Nothing in the controlling opinion precludes Congress from offering federal funds to states to expand their Medicaid programs. What Congress cannot do is penalize states that decline to participate in that new program by taking away their existing Medicaid funding." In other words, Congress could offer the new funding to states that agreed to participate in the Medicaid expansion. But it could not take away all of the funding from states that chose to stick only with the existing programs. Roberts had found a way to save the mandate—and the Medicaid expansion.

The chief justice concluded, "States now have a real choice whether to accept the Medicaid expansion that may affect the implementation of the act going forward." This compromise position was precisely the "easy repair" that Justice Ginsburg had offered Paul Clement months earlier—and this was exactly the option that Clement had said he would "be certainly happy" with.

Nearly eighteen minutes after everyone else in the world knew, the few souls who had camped out for days to witness history finally realized what had happened.

Roberts paused for a long, palpable second. He evoked the image of his judicial icon, the great Chief Justice John Marshall. "Our decision today is based on our responsibility recognized in *Marbury v. Madison* to say what the law is." Roberts echoed the testimony he had given during his confirmation hearings to aspire to be like Marshall. "It is not in any way based on our judgment about whether the Affordable Care Act is good policy. That judgment is for the people acting through their representatives. It is not our job to save the people from the consequences of their political choices." Roberts, mentally drained, was done.

Moments after Roberts finished speaking, unbeknownst to anyone in the Court, the Republican Party tweeted, quite appropriately: "The fight for #FullRepeal begins NOW. The way to get rid of #Obamacare is to defeat Obama in November." The next major front in the 2012 election had already begun, springing from the third branch of government.

"Invalid in Its Entirety"

The next moment, all eyes turned to Justice Kennedy, who began to speak.

The usually nonchalant justice was "visibly shaking and angry." *Time* magazine had recently placed a regal photograph of Justice Kennedy on the cover, speculating that he would be the swing vote in the most important case of the decade. But it was not to be.

One observer had "never seen Kennedy so mad." He was livid. His tone and word choice were so harsh that "he could have been Scalia." Kennedy began. "As the chief justice has indicated, Justices Scalia, Thomas, Alito, and I have written a joint dissent." The joint dissent is a rarity in the Supreme Court. Usually one justice will write an opinion, and others will join it. This dissenting opinion, instead, was authored by all four justices, with no single justice taking credit—though, based on the style, it is most likely that Justice Scalia authored the Commerce Clause analysis and that Justice Kennedy authored the Medicaid analysis.

While Kennedy was reading, Justice Scalia kept his head slightly bowed. Ilya Shapiro joked that he was either "praying" or "cursing." Justice Alito looked "uncomfortable." Justice Thomas, who though silent usually moves around jovially behind the bench, stared straight ahead the entire time, showing no emotion.

Then Kennedy dropped his own bomb. "In our view, the act before us is invalid in its entirety." Many had speculated that Kennedy would be the decisive fifth vote and might try to craft a compromise to strike down the mandate but save the remainder of the law. Instead, he was prepared to jettison all 2,700 pages of the ACA.

The joint dissent had three parts. "First, [the joint dissent] considers the constitutionality of the individual mandate and that, of course, requires a discussion whether the mandate can be sustained as a valid exercise of Congress's power to regulate interstate commerce or as an exercise of its power to tax."

Like Roberts, Kennedy, reasoned that the government's Commerce Clause theory in favor of the mandate "change[s] the relation between the citizen and the federal government in a fundamental way." Under that view of the Constitution, "there would be no structural limit on the power of Congress." However, unlike Roberts, Kennedy would not save the law. "There are some things the federal government cannot do and that clear principle carries the day here. It requires us to conclude that Congress's power to regulate interstate commerce does not give it the authority to enact the individual mandate." The mandate was unconstitutional.

Kennedy rejected Roberts's efforts to "rewrite" the ACA. While Congress avoided the political repercussions of imposing a tax, the chief justice incurred those very costs. "In the case of the ACA, Congress went to great lengths to structure the mandate as a penalty not a tax, but the majority now says that it is a tax. . . . The Court imposes a tax when Congress deliberately rejected a tax." He labeled Roberts's opinion as "activist" and declared that "imposing a tax through judicial legislation inverts the constitutional scheme, and places the power to tax in the branch of government least accountable to the citizenry." Professor Paul Starr wrote in *The New Republic* that "Senate Democrats chickened out from framing the penalty as a tax." Chief Justice Roberts had no such qualms.

Kennedy continued to pummel the majority opinion: "Second, the joint dissent considers the constitutionality of the expansion of Medicaid in light of the argument that it coerces states to surrender the power that must be vested in them under principles of federalism." He agreed with Roberts that the Medicaid expansion was unconstitutional. "The coercion effected by the statute is a violation of state sovereignty." But Kennedy could not agree with the majority's "remedy," which "rewrites the statute and changes its design."

Months earlier, on the floor of the Senate, Senator Chuck Grassley had urged the Court not to tinker with a complicated bill: "This time, the Supreme Court should not use the severability doctrine to rewrite the health care law into something Congress never would have passed in the first place." Kennedy echoed Grassley's concerns. "Once the specifics of today's ruling are understood, it will be apparent that the Affordable Care Act now must operate as the Court has revised it, not as Congress has designed it." To Kennedy, the "Medicaid Expansion cannot be saved in this way and . . . the expansion must be declared invalid."

Third, Kennedy reasoned that the unconstitutional mandate and Medicaid expansion could be severed from the remainder of the ACA. The joint dissenters found both "provisions are essential to the act's design and operation and all the act's other provisions would not have been enacted without them." Because the "entire statute is linked together . . . the entire act is inoperative."

Kennedy concluded by ripping into the Court's pretense at restraint: "The fundamental problem with the Court's approach to the case is this. It saves the statute Congress did not write. The Court regards its strained statutory interpretation as judicial modesty. It is not. It amounts instead to a vast judicial overreaching." Forcefully and deliberately, Kennedy continued: "In the name of restraint, it overreaches. In the name of constitutional avoidance, it creates new constitutional questions. In the name of cooperative federalism, it undermines state sovereignty." Everyone in the courtroom remained stunned. Oblivious to the commotion brewing outside the Court, the justice continued.

Kennedy paused for emphasis, then finished his opinion, very slowly. "Structure means liberty, for without structure, there are insufficient means to hold to account a central government that exceeds its powers in controlling the lives of its citizens. Today's decisions should have vindicated, not ignored, these precepts. For these reasons, we would find the act invalid in its entirety."

"Survives Largely Unscathed"

Moments after Justice Kennedy stopped, Justice Ruth Bader Ginsburg began. Seventy-nine years old, thin in stature, with a soft voice, Ginsburg nevertheless exudes a powerful presence. As she began to read, unlike her dour colleagues, she was "bordering on giddy." Well, as giddy as Justice Ginsburg can get. By this time, the commotion outside had largely subsided.

Ginsburg, along with Justices Breyer, Sotomayor, and Kagan, agreed with the chief justice that the individual mandate could be supported by "Congress's power to tax and spend." This vote provided Roberts with the necessary five votes to save the individual mandate. Yet she disagreed with both the chief justice and the joint dissenters on their Commerce Clause analysis. "Congress's vast authority to regulate interstate commerce solidly undergirds the affordable health care legislation. I would uphold the legislation first and foremost on that ground."

As Ginsburg spoke, former Republican vice presidential nominee Sarah Palin, who had popularized the fear that Obamacare would create the so-called death panels, tweeted her imprimatur on the Court's opinion: "Obama lied to the American people. Again. He said it wasn't a tax. Obama lies; freedom dies."

Ginsburg faulted Roberts and the conservatives for not deferring to Congress's powers, which, in her view, echoed the pre-New Deal era "75 years ago when the Court routinely thwarted legislative efforts to regulate the economy in the interest of those who labor to sustain it. It is a stunning setback." Of course, in 1937, exactly seventy-five years earlier, in *West Coast Hotel v. Parrish,* it took another Justice Roberts to switch his vote and steer the Court clear of a collision with the president.

Ginsburg found that government has the power to deal with present-day circumstances. "As our economy grows and changes, Congress must be competent to devise legislation meeting current-day social and economic realities. For that reason, the Necessary and Proper Clause was included in the Constitution to ensure that the federal government would have the capacity to provide for conditions and developments the framers knew they could scarcely foresee." Though Ginsburg was not concerned with the majority's "retrogressive reading of the Commerce Clause," she predicted that "it should not have staying power."

A slow reader, Ginsburg went on for nearly twenty minutes. (Roberts and Kennedy had read nearly twice as fast.) One reporter commented that after a while the "audience began to fidget." About halfway through Ginsburg's oration, legendary National Public Radio correspondent Nina Totenberg quietly slipped away from her customary perch in the front row of the press section. No doubt, Totenberg was chomping at the bit to get a copy of the opinion into her hands.

At 10:49, while Justice Ginsburg was still reading, Republican Speaker of the House John Boehner released a statement: "The president's health care law is hurting our economy by driving up health costs and making it harder for small businesses to hire. Today's ruling underscores the urgency of repealing this harmful law in its entirety. . . . Republicans stand ready to work with a president who will listen to the people and will not repeat the mistakes that gave our country Obamacare."

Stunningly, for nearly an hour, those in the Court were entirely cut off from the circus outside. Though Senator Hatch was still in the Court, his social media team was active, and his account tweeted: "This ruling doesn't change the fact that a majority of the people of Utah and across America want this law repealed."

Ginsburg faulted the majority for finding the "first . . . ever . . . exercise of Congress's spending power [that is] unconstitutionally coercive. . . . Seven members of the Court, however, buy the argument that prospective withholding of anticipated funds exceeds Congress's spending power."

At 10:56, Senate Majority Leader Harry Reid, who two years earlier had deftly moved the ACA through the Senate, even after losing the sixtieth vote, tweeted, "I'm pleased to see #SCOTUS put the rule of law ahead of partisanship and rule that the Affordable Care Act is constitutional. . . . Now that the matter is settled, I hope that we can work together to create jobs and secure this country's economic future." Moments later, Texas senator John Cornyn, who had contributed to constitutional arguments against the ACA, tweeted, "We will redouble our efforts to repeal this job-killing law."

Justice Ginsburg continued. "So," she said, then paused for emphasis. "In the end, the Affordable Health Care Act survives largely unscathed, but the Court's Commerce and Spending Clause jurisprudence has been set awry."

At that moment, across the street, C-SPAN cameras turned to Mitch McConnell, the Senate minority leader, who took to the Senate floor. "The Supreme Court has spoken. This law is a tax. The American people weren't waiting on the Supreme Court to tell them whether they supported this law. So now that the Court has ruled, it's time to move beyond the constitutional debate and focus on the primary reason this law should be fully repealed and replaced: because of the colossal damage it has already done to the health care system, to the economy, and to the job market." At 10:58, Florida senator Marco Rubio tweeted, "Now that we know #Obamacare is indeed a #jobkilling #Tax we should move to #RepealObamacare as soon as possible."

Justice Ginsburg concluded that, nevertheless, these "setbacks will be temporary blips."

THE COURT IS IN RECESS

Moments after Justice Ginsburg concluded, the RNC put out its first attack on YouTube, promoting the new website PeopleVObamacare .com. Ominous music played, and stark headlines flashed across the screen: "The final verdict on Obamacare is now in your hands"; "our fundamental freedoms are being threatened"; "it's time to repeal the law so we can provide real reform"; "this time let's get it right." A CNN reporter tweeted at 11:04 AM that Americans for Prosperity was dumping $8.2 million into anti-Obamacare ads in twelve key states to air the next day.

Inside the Court, it was back to business as usual.

The chief justice gave his customary end-of-term thanks to the staff, including the Court's venerable retired Major General William K. Suter, who had just completed fifty years of government service. Roberts hoped that Suter would return the next term. He would, though he eventually retired from the Court in August 2013.

And with that, the chief justice declared that the Court would be in recess until the first Monday in October 2012.

This term, at long last, was over. With it, the constitutional challenge to the ACA finally drew to a close. But the political clash over this law was far from finished.

PART IX

The Switch in Time That Saved Nine

(June 29, 2012–January 21, 2013)

After two long years of litigation and over three years of debates, the case had finally been settled. Obamacare was now the supreme law of the land. With the chief justice's vote approving of the law, the battle of Obamacare would shift back to where it began in 2008—the presidential election. Soon President Obama and Governor Romney would clash in the debates, though Romney's inability to distance himself from Romneycare would hand this issue to Obama on a silver platter. President Obama's victory in November cemented his "legacy," whatever that may be. However, the Supreme Court, under the leadership of John Roberts, was now well poised to confront generations of constitutional crises to come.

TRIUMPH

Moments after the Court recessed for the summer, a gaggle of Democrats flocked to the microphones and cameras waiting outside

the Court. Flanked by signs that read PROTECTING OUR CARE and
OBAMACARE IS AWESOME, Senator Tom Harkin of Iowa was the first
to proclaim victory. "The justices have spoken. So let's get back to
work." Senator Barbara Mikulski of Maryland leaned forward and
shouted, "If you want to know what democracy looks like, come to
Constitution Avenue. This is what democracy looks like. We now
know that health care is legal, constitutional, undeniable, and irre-
versible." Senator Ben Cardin of Maryland assured everyone that
"health care is a right, not a privilege." Senator Chris Coons of Delaware praised the chief justice: "I am glad the Supreme Court affirmed
their role in constitutional order and decided on narrow grounds to
uphold the ACA."

An hour later, the triumphant president appeared before the press.
He began, "Earlier today, the Supreme Court upheld the constitutionality of the Affordable Care Act. . . . Whatever the politics, today's decision was a victory for people all over this country whose lives will
be more secure because of this law and the Supreme Court's decision
to uphold it." The president knew that the ACA was the defining aspect of his first term, was now secured, and would be inscribed in the
history books. Beaming, the president said, "Today I'm as confident
as ever that when we look back five years from now, or ten years from
now, or twenty years from now, we'll be better off because we had
the courage to pass this law and keep moving forward." History will
be the judge of that. Rahm Emanuel, the president's former chief of
staff, put it succinctly. "The president had the courage to bend the
needle of history and did something presidents have tried to do for
sixty years."

The accolades for the Court poured in from the Democratic caucus. On the Senate floor, before the Supreme Court had even recessed,
Senate Majority Leader Harry Reid said, "I'm happy, I'm pleased to
see the Supreme Court put the rule of law ahead of partisanship and

rule that the Affordable Care Act is constitutional." Later, he dodged a question about whether the president had said the mandate is not a tax. "I'm not here to give everyone my limited knowledge of constitutional law. I am here to say it's been upheld. It's good for the country." He concluded, "Our Supreme Court has spoken. The matter is settled."

House Minority Leader Nancy Pelosi, too, was celebrating. "Today the Supreme Court affirmed our progress and protected that right, securing a future of health and economic security for the middle class and for every American." Pelosi later called Vicki Kennedy, widow of the late Senator Ted Kennedy. She told her, "Now Teddy can rest."

Secretary of State Hillary Clinton, who two decades earlier had attempted to reform health care as first lady, was ebullient. "You know, I haven't had the chance to read the decision. I literally just heard as we landed that the Supreme Court has upheld the health care law. Obviously I want to get into the details, but I'm very pleased. . . . There will be a lot of work to do to get it implemented and understand what the opinion says, but obviously I was quite excited to hear the results." Well, ebullient by Hillary's standards, at least.

At the 2012 Democratic National Convention in Charlotte, North Carolina, Democrats took a victory lap over their success with the ACA. Former President Bill Clinton brought down the house praising Obama's accomplishments. "That brings me to health care. The Republicans call it Obamacare and say it's a government takeover of health care that they'll repeal. . . . So are we all better off because President Obama fought for it and passed it? You bet we are."

When a reporter from *Rolling Stone* asked President Obama if he would "mind if historians call the achievement Obamacare?" He replied, "I'll be very proud. . . . As time goes on, as people see what it does, as it gets refined and improved, people will say, 'This was the last piece to our basic social compact.'"

DESPAIR

If Democrats were triumphant, Republicans were despondent. They determined to use the decision as a means to galvanize the base and turn out votes for Republicans in November. Reince Priebus, the chairman of the Republican National Committee, set the tone. "Today's Supreme Court decision sets the stakes for the November election. Now the only way to save the country from Obamacare's budget-busting government takeover of health care is to elect a new president."

Mitt Romney, then the presumptive nominee, gave a speech on Capitol Hill on decision day, faulting the Supreme Court's decision: "As you might imagine, I disagree with the Supreme Court's decision, and I agree with the dissent." Standing before a sign that said RE-PEAL & REPLACE OBAMACARE, he continued, "If we want to get rid of Obamacare, we have to replace President Obama. What the court did not do on its last day of session I will do on my first day [as president]. I will act to repeal Obamacare."

Senate Minority Leader McConnell looked forward to November: "Today's decision makes one thing clear: Congress must act to repeal this misguided law." Speaker of the House John Boehner echoed that sentiment: "Today's ruling underscores the urgency of repealing this harmful law in its entirety. . . . Republicans stand ready to work with a president who will listen to the people and will not repeat the mistakes that gave our country Obamacare." A spokeswoman from the Tea Party patriots issued a challenge: "Mr. Romney, Mr. Boehner, the American people are putting you on notice. You both promised to fully repeal Obamacare. We will hold you to your promises."

With the Court upholding the law, the Republican template changed from a constitutional repeal to a political repeal. This is particularly ironic because in 2010, after the political opposition to Obamacare failed, Republicans put all of their hopes in the Supreme Court. However, with the Supreme Court upholding the law in 2012, the attack shifted back to the political process. Although not success-ful, the legal challenge had bought three years of time and shifted the all-important debate until the next presidential election. (Con-servatives involved in the case privately lauded the stalling power of the lengthy constitutional challenge as a consolation prize.) This was largely the point that Judges Sutton and Kavanaugh had made. If this law was so unpopular, the political process could end it before it came into effect. Yet their efforts would prove unsuccessful, and by a much wider margin than 5–4. Romney would lose the electoral col-lege 332–206 and Republicans, unable to retake the Senate, lost hope for complete repeal.

"Coward"

At the same time, conservatives focused their rage on Chief Justice Roberts. Conservative talk show host Glenn Beck found that there was "no good news." It was "Chief Justice Roberts who sold us out." Beck praised "Justice Kennedy [who] came over to the conservative side." Yet "the only reason why Obamacare stands today is because of Chief Justice John Roberts." Beck announced on his television show that he would sell T-shirts emblazoned with a photograph of Chief Justice Roberts above the word COWARD. Beck looked forward to November and said that there was another "mandate": to vote Barack Obama out of office.

Ken Cuccinelli, who had staked so much on this case, had suf-fered a crushing blow. With his case doomed never to see the light of the Supreme Court, Cuccinelli mourned: "This decision goes against the very principle that America has a federal government of limited powers; a principle that the Founding Fathers clearly wrote into the Constitution, the supreme law of the land." After *NFIB*, the Supreme Court would finally, at long last, deny his petition for certiorari and end Virginia's case.

Senator Orrin Hatch was disappointed, but resolute. "The American people know that this law violates our deepest constitutional principles of limited government, despite the Supreme Court's ruling today." Representative Michele Bachmann took an even more ominous tone. "This is a turning point in American history. We will never be the same again with this denial of liberty interests." Bachmann added in an interview, "The Founders would turn over in their graves if they heard this decision." Senator Rand Paul of Kentucky was wholly unpersuaded by the Supreme Court's ruling: "[I] think if James Madison himself—the father of the Constitution—were here today he would agree with me: the whole damn thing is still unconstitutional!"

Roberts did not stay in Washington long. The day after the Court's term concluded, he left the country to teach at a summer program for law students in Malta, organized in part by the South Texas College of Law, where I teach. Before he departed, Roberts joked that he was retreating to an "impregnable island fortress." Students found Roberts was in very good spirits, no doubt enjoying the respite from the pressure.

HAIL TO THE CHIEF

The ire on the right toward Roberts was reflected by praise for him on the left. New York senator Chuck Schumer praised "all three branches of government [that] have ratified the law," and commended "the chief justice [who] acted as the umpire that he promised to be." Jeffrey Rosen wrote in *The New Republic* that Chief Justice Roberts "used Obamacare to reveal his true identity." Rosen remarked that "Roberts produced a *twistification* of which [Chief Justice] Marshall would have been proud." Rosen, consistent with his view of the Court and of Roberts, concluded, "For bringing the Court back from the partisan abyss, Roberts deserves praise not only from liberals but from all Americans who believe that it's important for the Court to stand for something larger than politics. On Thursday, Roberts did precisely what he said he would do when he first took office: He placed the bipartisan legitimacy of the Court above his own ideological agenda. Seven years into his Chief Justiceship, the Supreme Court finally became the Roberts Court."

In her report, Jan Crawford wrote, "As chief justice, [Roberts] is keenly aware of his leadership role on the court, and he also is sensitive to how the court is perceived by the public." Crawford stated that her sources "flatly reject the idea that Roberts buckled to liberal pressure, or was stared down by the president." Instead, they "believe that Roberts realized the historical consequences of a ruling striking down the landmark health care law."

Time magazine, which had placed Justice Kennedy on its cover in March, imploring him to be the swing vote, now feted Roberts. "For legal buffs, the virtuoso performance of Chief Justice John Roberts in deciding the biggest case of his career was just that sort of jaw dropper, no matter how they might feel about Obamacare. Not since King Solomon offered to split the baby has a judge engineered a slicker solution to a bitterly divisive dispute."

In an interview with *Rolling Stone,* President Obama was asked, "How do you feel about Justice Roberts' ruling on the Affordable Care Act? Were you surprised?" His answer was telling: "I wasn't surprised." The president continued: "I was always confident that the Affordable Care Act, aka Obamacare, was constitutional. It was interesting to see them, or Justice Roberts in particular, take the approach that this was constitutional under the taxing power. The truth is that if you look at the precedents dating back to the 1930s, this was clearly constitutional under the Commerce Clause. I think Justice Roberts made a decision that allowed him to preserve the law but allowed him to keep in reserve the desire, maybe, to scale back Congress' power under the Commerce Clause in future cases." The president no doubt recognized the latent threat that the chief justice's opinion posed to future expansion of federal power.

This praise would last at least until Roberts's next big decision thwarting the president.

The Solicitor General Is Vindicated

In hindsight, the solicitor general choked only literally, not figuratively. As solicitor general, Donald Verrilli served as an impeccable manager as he balanced the institutional concerns of the entire federal government, choosing what to argue and what to leave behind. Countless academics, officials, and pundits consistently told him what to do, but he chose his own path. His former law firm partner Paul Smith told me that Verrilli is a "clear thinker" and praised his "unflappable" ability to unite different interests in pursuit of a common goal.

Argued under more pressure than perhaps any other in our nation's recent history, this case reflected Verrilli's own decision-making. It was Verrilli who shifted the focus away from the limiting principles advanced by Katyal—an argument that would not persuade a single conservative justice. It was Verrilli who fashioned the taxing power argument that was eventually adopted by the chief justice—even though it was the government's fallback position. It was Verrilli who secured the representation from the government that failure to comply with the mandate was not a violation of the law—the key concession that allowed Roberts to rule as if there were in fact no individual mandate. Verrilli's gambles paid off.

Jeff Toobin, who had called Verrilli's performance a "train wreck," apologized. "This is a day for Don Verrilli to take an enormous amount of credit, and for me to eat a bit of crow—because he won, and everyone should know that that argument was a winning argument, whatever you thought of it." Toobin tweeted, "Big winner at #scotus today is Don Verrilli, Solicitor General. Among losers is me, who was so critical of his oral argument."

OBAMACARE VS. ROMNEYCARE

The battle of Obamacare vs. Romneycare would prove to be a blood-bath, with President Obama winning decisively. On health care, Mitt Romney's strongest opponent was Mitt Romney. After years of danc-ing around the issue, and perhaps hoping the Supreme Court would solve the problem for him, Mitt Romney was finally forced to con-front the fact that he was, as President Obama said, the "godfather" of Obamacare. Despite his promises to repeal Obamacare, he soon backed away from this position.

On *Meet the Press* on September 9, 2012, Romney said, "I'm not getting rid of all of health care reform," while emphasizing that there were "a number of things that I like in health care reform that I'm going to put in place. One is to make sure that those with preexisting conditions can get coverage." Romney elaborated on his plan during a presidential debate when asked how he would replace Obamacare. "Number one, preexisting conditions are covered under my plan. Number two, young people are able to stay on their family plan. That's already offered in the private marketplace. You don't have to have the government mandate that, for that to occur."

But the ban on preexisting conditions could never work without an individual mandate—otherwise, premiums would begin the dreaded "death spiral." This is a fact Romney recognized when he enacted Romneycare in Massachusetts. Obama shot right back that the "rea-son he set up the system he did in Massachusetts was because there isn't a better way of dealing with the preexisting conditions problem." The mandate was here to stay.

Romney and his vice presidential candidate, Representative Paul Ryan, could not even stay on the same page. On August 14, 2012, Ryan told Fox News that Romney planned "to repeal all of Obamacare." But he soon walked that statement back. Or, in the words of Rom-ney's communications director, he hit the "reset button," like "an

Etch-a-Sketch. . . . You can kind of shake it up and restart all over again."

Romney couldn't even agree with his own campaign website, which stated: "On his first day in office, Mitt Romney will issue an executive order that paves the way for the federal government to issue Obamacare waivers to all fifty states. He will then work with Congress to repeal the full legislation as quickly as possible."

Rather than attacking the mandate—the essence of the ACA litigation—the Republicans shifted course and instead criticized Obamacare's cuts to Medicare. At the Republican National Convention in Tampa, Paul Ryan said, "The greatest threat to Medicare is Obamacare, and we're going to stop it." This line of argument did not play well with senior citizens. Paul Ryan was booed at an AARP convention after saying, "The first step to strengthen Medicare is to repeal Obamacare."

Things didn't get much better for Romney during the debates. At the October 3, 2012, debate in Denver, a triumphant Obama responded to a Romney attack on Obamacare by saying, "I have become fond of this term 'Obamacare.'" Romney repeated his qualified pledge to repeal it. The president pounced on the "irony" that "we've seen this model work really well in Massachusetts, because Governor Romney did a good thing, working with Democrats in the state to set up what is essentially the identical model and as a consequence people are covered there." Obama continued, rubbing it in: "This was a bipartisan idea. In fact, it was a Republican idea. And Governor Romney at the beginning of this debate wrote and said what we did in Massachusetts could be a model for the nation."

Four years earlier, Obama had repeatedly criticized Romney's mandate. Now Romney was damned if he did and damned if he didn't. All Obama could do was win.

At the October 16, 2012, debate in Hempstead, New York, President Obama continued to mock Romney's desire to "repeal Obamacare . . .

despite the fact that it's the same health care plan that he passed in Massachusetts and is working well." By the final debate, Obamacare was only mentioned once. Romney could not gain any ground on the issue. No one knew or cared that a state law was different from a federal law. Senator Schumer was correct: Mitt Romney was "the worst candidate to go against Barack Obama on the most important issue of the day." Eventually Romney's history had to catch up with him.

Instead of being rewarded for reaching across the aisle and cooperating with Ted Kennedy to reform health care in a manner that conservatives had once supported, Romney was pilloried not only by the president but by his own party. The Republican nominee for president had to forfeit the most divisive political issue of 2009 to 2012.

However, one topic was conspicuously absent from the presidential debates: the Supreme Court. There was nary a mention of the justices, other than a question about abortion during the vice presidential debate. There were no attacks on the chief justice, and no questions about the Court's legitimacy. It was exactly as John Roberts would have wanted it.

After weeks of rantings about skewed polls and undecided voters in Ohio flocking to Romney, the election went exactly as polling analyst Nate Silver predicted. On election day, November 6, 2012, the race was over by 11:15 PM. The only thing standing between Barack Obama and his second term of office, once again, was Chief Justice John G. Roberts and the oath of office.

THE OATH—PART II

President Obama shares a record with President Franklin Roosevelt as the only two presidents to receive the oath of office four times. During his inauguration in 2009, Obama and Chief Justice Roberts flubbed the oath, and as a precaution, the chief justice administered the oath a second time during a private ceremony. In 2013 they would have to do it twice again. The Twentieth Amendment provides that the president's term begins on January 20. In 2013, January 20 fell on a Sunday, a day on which the inauguration could not be scheduled. As a result, there would be two oaths: the first in a private ceremony at the White House on Sunday, January 20, 2013, and the second at the public inauguration in front of the Capitol on Monday, January 21, 2013.

When asked if he was worried about the chief justice flubbing the oath again, Robert Gibbs, Obama's former press secretary, said, "Given health care, I don't care if he speaks in tongues."

On Sunday, the third oath was successfully delivered. The pool reporter noted that "the two men seemed warm, but formal, with no hint of animosity." Obama smiled and said, "Thank you, Chief Justice. Thank you so much." No doubt, Obama had every reason to be very thankful to the chief justice.

The next day, over one million people crowded onto the National Mall to catch the inauguration. On this frigid day in Washington, D.C., all nine justices attended. Justice Scalia donned a traditional skullcap fashioned after a hat worn by Sir Thomas More. Behind the burly Scalia, the diminutive Justice Ginsburg could barely be seen underneath her huge fur hat. Justice Alito wore a hip pair of sunglasses.

Roberts and Obama met again, face to face, in front of the American people. This time the chief justice brought notes and delivered the oath flawlessly. It was the president who stumbled. The Associated Press reported that "Obama stammered briefly over [the word] 'states' as he repeated back the words 'the office of president of the United States.'" But it was close enough. Roberts shook his hand and said, "Congratulations, Mr. President."

As Obama walked back into the Capitol he paused and said to his family, "I want to take a look, one more time." He turned around and gazed at the crowd of one million Americans cheering his inauguration. Realizing the finality of this moment, Obama smiled, bit his lip, almost teary-eyed, and said, "I'm not going to see this again." He turned around again and continued to walk with his family. For the president, the legacy of his first term was secure, and the legacy of his second term was unfolding.

Roberts, in contrast, seemed to realize that he would see this sight again—many, many more times. There would be other presidents to swear in and other constitutional crises to confront. The next term featured cases concerning the constitutionality of affirmative action, the Voting Rights Act, and the Defense of Marriage Act. Though the individual mandate was upheld, the jurisprudence the Court laid down with respect to the Commerce Clause and Congress's spending power will place future expansions of federal power under a cloud of constitutional doubt.

Perhaps more importantly, beyond constitutional doctrine, *NFIB v. Sebelius* altered our collective consciousness about the relationship between the federal government and individual liberty. By shifting what Professor Lawrence Solum has called the "constitutional ge-stalt," *NFIB* has forced us to rethink our assumptions about what we thought was settled law. In May 2013 during oral arguments over a follow-up case about the ACA, Judge Diana Gribbon Motz observed that *NFIB* "puts a new light, it seems to me, on the Commerce Clause." The Fourth Circuit judge, who two years earlier had dismissed a challenge to the ACA under the Anti-Injunction Act without addressing the Commerce Clause analysis, added, "it sounds like we're in a new regime [post] *NFIB*." Judge Motz is correct. Going forward, the government will need to justify further expansions of federal power—and the Roberts Court will stand poised to police that line.

Looking through his piercing steel-blue eyes at all three branches of government united on one stage, Roberts was vindicated. He knew he saved Obamacare so he could fight another day. Presidents will come and go, but the institution of the Supreme Court will continue, under the leadership of its chief, John G. Roberts.

Epilogue

Who won the constitutional challenge to Obamacare? The answer is complicated. *NFIB v. Sebelius* did not merely represent a lawsuit against a federal law or an opinion about the Commerce Clause or the taxing power. The period from 2009 to 2012 was another chapter in our nation's history in which our Constitution was challenged. Throughout this challenge, competing visions of the Constitution, federalism, and individual liberty clashed. During this time, the debate over the Affordable Care Act rippled to all corners of our republic.

To help sort out the score, in this epilogue, I will walk you through the ACA's impact on each aspect of our society, following the systematic ordering of the articles of our Constitution. This structure—yet another underappreciated stroke of genius from the framers—provides a logical path to understand how Obamacare's constitutional challenge was resolved. I conclude that this challenge will have far-reaching implications for the Constitution, the Supreme Court, and the relationship between the federal government, the states, and the individual, both during President Obama's second term and beyond.

CONGRESS

All legislative Powers herein granted shall be vested in
a Congress of the United States, which shall consist of
a Senate and House of Representatives.

—U.S. CONSTITUTION, ARTICLE 1, SECTION 1

In both the Senate and the House, it became clear early on that the Republicans had no intention of supporting any of the president's attempts at health care reform. Rather than attempting to moderate the bill to achieve a consensus (which was probably impossible) or waiting to gain more support, Democrats relied on their electoral majorities to pass the ACA on party-line votes.

To get the bill past a filibuster, Senate Majority Leader Harry Reid enticed moderate Democrats with the "Cornhusker Kickback" and the "Louisiana Purchase." Though these prodigious provisions were ultimately stripped during the reconciliation process, the initial bill would never have cleared the Senate without them—and this led to the final reconciled bill that would go to the Supreme Court. The urgency to pass the ACA—only released days before the final Christmas Eve vote—seeded the strength of the opposition. In the House, like her Senate counterpart, Speaker Nancy Pelosi was also willing to pass this bill on a straight party-line vote. Republican intransigence, combined with a Democratic "pass it at any cost" attitude, doomed this process from the start.

In August 2009, former Democratic National Committee chairman Howard Dean attempted to justify the "pass it at any cost" approach: "All the really great programs in American history, Social Security, [were] done without Republicans. Medicare was done without Republican support until the last vote where they realized they had to get on board." He was wrong. Rating this statement as *false,* Politifact concluded that "both Social Security and Medicare were indeed championed by Democrats, but passed with the help of Republican votes. And while some GOP members waited until the last minute to support Medicare, it was backed by half the Republicans on the Senate committee."

All of the landmark social welfare and civil rights laws enacted in the twentieth century were passed with bipartisan support, often through messy political compromises and bargaining. The Social Security Act of 1935 was supported by 77 Republicans in the House, who joined 288 Democrats. In the Senate, 15 Republicans joined 60 Democrats. The Civil Rights Act of 1964 passed the Senate by a vote of 73 in favor and 27 opposed. A bold coalition of 27 Republicans and 44 Democrats united to break a segregationist-led filibuster. The Social Security Amendments of 1965, which created Medicaid and Medicare, passed the House by a vote of 307–116, with 70 Republicans voting in favor. This monumental health care legislation cleared the Senate by a vote of 70–24; 13 Republicans crossed the aisle. The Civil Rights Act of 1968 was passed with broad bipartisan support as was the Voting Rights Act of 1965. In 1990, the Americans with Disabilities Act passed with 90 percent agreement in the House and Senate. The absence of any consensus for the ACA in 2009 was remarkable and proved an inauspicious start.

Shortly after Obama's inauguration, many in the administration were uneasy about rushing this legislation through during the first year. Larry Summers, the director of the National Economic Council, was "concerned that the president would have his hands full with the biggest economic crisis since the Great Depression." Summers "asked whether this was really the best time to take on health care too." Peter Orszag, the Office of Management and Budget director, "tried to mediate . . . this debate within the president's inner circle." During the September 27, 2007, Democratic primary debate in Hanover, New Hampshire, then-Senator Joe Biden stressed that without Republican buy-in, health care reform was doomed. "In order to get health care, you're going to have to be able to persuade at least 15 percent of the Republicans to vote for it." In January 2009, Vice-President-Elect

Biden "spoke at length about why it would be too much to attempt health care reform in the middle of the [financial] crisis." But the president, committed to securing his "legacy," disregarded this advice.

The ACA's party-line vote was unprecedented for such a major law. Not a single Republican in the House or Senate supported this law. Forty-nine percent of the House of Representatives opposed it, hardly a mandate (no pun intended) for transformational change. These sentiments reflected those of America as a whole—polling data from 2009 to 2012 consistently showed that the mandate was widely unpopular, and remains so today. Legislation is always a compromise, especially in a state of gridlock exacerbated by recalcitrant Republicans. However, the president and leaders in the Congress forced this law thorough with full knowledge that there would be no bipartisan support and that they would lose members of their own caucus.

The (seemingly) simple lesson to be learned here is that the "pass it at any cost" mentality may seem like a good idea in the short term, but in the long term, it is a poor plan. It is not a productive way to pass monumental, transformative legislation. The ACA was from the start mired in a political grudge match and will remain so for the foreseeable future. It was prepared to fail before it even was born. This is a lesson the president will have to heed in his second term in office, when he will simply lack the votes to enact laws on party lines. Indeed, this is a lesson for any future president—don't try to change the nation when 49 percent of Congress opposes it. This was a sign that America as a whole wasn't quite ready for this kind of law. Although the hope was there, it was the wrong time for the change.

THE PRESIDENT

The executive Power shall be vested in a President of the United States of America.

—U.S. CONSTITUTION, ARTICLE 2, SECTION 1

President Obama is to be commended for dedicating himself so strongly to the ACA. But the process by which he arrived at that commitment makes the proverbial sausage factory seem glamorous. During his primary race against Hillary Clinton, he consistently attacked the mandate and called it bad policy. Once he secured the nomination, however, and realized that the insurance companies would only support the law with a mandate, he flipped his position. Throughout the spring of 2009, he pushed for a public option, which he thought would work in tandem with the mandate to keep costs low (or so the plan projected). Once the public option was killed by Republican opposition, however, he pressed on with what was now an incomplete version of comprehensive health care reform. Though his multifaceted approach to reform was slowly stripped apart, the president pushed forward, letting Congress write and rewrite the 2,700-page bill behind closed doors until the last moment. The result was a compromise bill that no one really wanted and that won't really work. Senators Harry Reid and Max Baucus have already warned that the implementation of the ACA will be a "train wreck"—a burden the president will be saddled with in 2014 and beyond.

In addition to political difficulties, the president's constitutional struggles over the ACA are far from over. Currently pending in federal courts are several lawsuits challenging other aspects of Obamacare. One set of suits opposes the contraceptive-mandate that forces certain employers to provide their employees with contraceptives and abortifacients. Another suit, brought by the same attorneys from Jones Day that litigated *NFIB*, seeks to invalidate the implementation of health care exchanges in states that have not opted in to the Medicaid expansion. Yet, the most critical constitutional challenge remaining is targeted directly at the individual mandate.

During the debate over the ACA, the president insisted that the law was not a tax increase, and he thus avoided the political repercussions of breaking his campaign promise not to impose new taxes on most Americans. Yet he changed the script once he got to court. Indeed, many in the White House did not even want the Department of Justice to raise a taxing power argument in court. Fortunately, Neal Katyal insisted on keeping this arrow in his quiver, and the White House gave in. However, this choice has severe constitutional repercussions for the future of the individual mandate and the ACA.

One of the reasons why Chief Justice Roberts was able to view the mandate as a tax was because "for most Americans the amount due will be far less than the price of insurance, and, by statute, it can never be more." Roberts added in a footnote, "In 2016, for example, individuals making $35,000 a year are expected to owe the IRS about $60 for any month in which they do not have health insurance. Someone with an annual income of $100,000 a year would likely owe about $200. The price of a qualifying insurance policy is projected to be around $400 per month." In other words, the chief justice was comforted by the fact that this "tax" was not punitive or "prohibitory," in that it would always be cheaper to pay the penalty than to purchase insurance.

But this reasoning is troubling news for the effectiveness of the ACA. The mandate's penalty can only prevent the dreaded death spiral of rising premiums if it is high enough to nudge people to purchase health insurance. A small penalty won't work.

As Professor Thomas Lambert wrote in *Regulation* magazine, if the penalty is $60 a month and a health insurance policy costs $400 a month, it makes little sense for a healthy young person to buy insurance until "she needs health care, at which point she can contact a health insurer and be assured of coverage (because of guaranteed issue) at rates not reflecting her impaired health (because of community rating)." Under most circumstances, a sick patient could order health insurance while riding in an ambulance on the way to the hospital, and the insurance company cannot charge her a higher rate. Starting in 2014, the penalty is scheduled to increase as the ACA is phased in, reaching $695 per person in 2016. However, even with these higher costs in 2016 and beyond, Lambert concludes that it will still be rational for most young, healthy people *not* to buy insurance. These are the people the ACA was meant to force into the health insurance market. Roberts reasoned that for many Americans it is often a more "*reasonable financial decision* to make the [penalty] payment rather than purchase insurance." Roberts was right. And that cripples the mandate's effectiveness.

One way to fix this problem would be for Congress to tinker with the ACA and increase the penalty to create incentives for more young, healthy people to purchase health insurance. Dr. Austin Frankt, writing in the *Journal of the American Medical Association*, has argued that the mandate would probably be high enough once fully phased in. But his analysis is somewhat speculative, as he notes that ultimately "it's not so clear" if the mandate will be high enough. With this uncertainty, Dr. Frankt concludes by suggesting that if the penalty is not high enough, it can be raised: "Nevertheless, strengthening the penalties for those who fail to purchase insurance will only increase the incentive for coverage. Advocates of the law, as well as the insurance industry, have no problem with that. But those who may still perceive the scheme as coercive would object. Ultimately, the size of the penalty for noncompliance is a political calculation, not just an actuarial one."

Yet it's no accident that the penalty is so low. The low penalty, passed at the eleventh hour in December 2009, was part of the political sell. As Lambert notes, "proponents of the ACA . . . must have recognized that the penalties were too low to [work]. They likely assumed, though, that the deficient penalties for failure to carry insurance were a 'bug' that Congress would eventually fix once the act was put in place and became operative." In keeping with the president's mission not to call the mandate a (politically unpopular) tax, "proponents needed for the penalties to be low so that they could maneuver the statute through the political process; they figured they could fix the deficiencies later." Besides being politically unpopular, raising the penalty would require a "political calculation." But that is not the primary problem. The main problem is that under Roberts's opinion, that change may be *unconstitutional*.

Roberts viewed the penalty provision as a tax because it was not punitive or prohibitory and it was *cheaper* than purchasing health insurance. If Congress were to raise the penalty too high (high enough to be effective), this reasoning would no longer save it as a tax. To Roberts, the penalty is constitutional if it still gives a person the choice of whether to buy insurance or not. Once this is no longer the case, the penalty conflicts with the reasoning of the chief's opinion. Lambert observes that the "penalty for failure to carry health insurance can count as a tax for constitutional purposes only if it is kept so small as to be largely ineffective."

Additionally, because Roberts joined the conservatives in finding that the mandate could not be supported by Congress's powers under the Commerce Clause, the penalty would also be unconstitutional on that ground. Either way—under the taxing or commerce power—Congress is stuck. The very circumstances under which Roberts found the penalty to be constitutional will limit it to not being high enough to actually work. It is here that the political dimension of Obama's choice to label the mandate as a tax crashes into the Constitution.

What does this mean for the future of Obamacare? By finding the mandate to be constitutional only so long as it remains ineffectively low, Roberts sent the ACA on a slow path to ineffectiveness. Roberts's decision will hinder the Patient Protection and Affordable Care Act from protecting patients or making care affordable. Lambert concludes: "As modified and constrained by *NFIB,* the ACA is likely to drive up both the cost of health insurance premiums and the underlying cost of medical care without increasing insurance coverage by nearly as much as the act's proponents promised." As premiums continue to rise—they have already shot up in almost every state—and the mandate penalty remains ineffectively low, going without insurance becomes a much more rational decision, even though people tend to be loss averse. Compound this fact with the harsh reality that more employers are shifting employees from full-time to part-time in order to avoid paying their health care costs, and our society will have large swaths of the young and healthy population—the very people the ACA wanted to place into the insurance pool—paying the penalty rather than buying expensive insurance. This is the exact opposite of what President Obama intended, but is likely to occur after *NFIB.*

If the ACA continues to result in higher premiums and the consequent price controls aimed at controlling these rates nudge insurers to exit the market (insurers are already opting out of California's exchanges), the mandate may serve as a mere pit stop on the road to single-payer health care (what progressives wanted but did not get in 2009). If that turns out to be the case, constitutional conservatives will be placed in a political pickle. In arguing that the individual mandate was unconstitutional, many prominent conservative and libertarian scholars conceded that single-payer health care would be constitutional. For example, in a February 17, 2011, letter to the *New York Times,* Randy Barnett wrote, "although I would oppose such a program, existing doctrine would allow Congress to impose a 'single payer' tax-and-spending scheme like Medicare on everyone."

In the near future, amending or fixing the ACA will remain a political powder keg (another by-product of passing it on party lines). Efforts to raise the penalty to the point of effectiveness will likely be unconstitutional. For now, we are stuck with a rushed, incomplete version of a law that was never meant to be the final bill. And with the bloody political battle behind us, it is unlikely that any bipartisan support can be mustered to fix this "bug." Although President Obama is proud that historians will call the ACA "Obamacare" and refer to it as his "legacy," I think we should let history decide its fate.

The Courts

The judicial Power of the United States, shall be vested in one supreme Court, and in such inferior Courts as the Congress may from time to time ordain and establish.

—U.S. CONSTITUTION, ARTICLE 3, SECTION 1

Perhaps one of the most troubling aspects of the challenge to Obamacare was the further politicization of our judicial system as all three branches of our government descended into a constitutional boxing match. Within days of the oral argument, President Obama urged the Court not to strike down the ACA, focusing not so much on the merits of the case but on the propriety of the Court exercising the power of judicial review in this case: "Ultimately, I'm confident that the Supreme Court will not take what would be an unprecedented, extraordinary step of overturning a law that was passed by a strong majority of a democratically elected Congress."

The other branches were complicit in this escalation. Members of both parties in Congress consistently called on the Supreme Court to consider more than the legal aspects of the Commerce Clause or the taxing power when deciding this case. Even the lower courts would inject themselves into the conflict and ratchet it up even further—a federal judge demanded that the attorney general acknowledge the power of judicial review.

In this case, the political tension between the president and the courts was already dialed up to a ten, but then the president turned the knob all the way to eleven when he said, "I have enormous confidence that in looking at this law, not only is it constitutional, but that the court is going to exercise its jurisprudence carefully because of the profound power that our Supreme Court has." These remarks, coming from the president who had already berated the justices at the 2010 State of the Union Address following *Citizens United,* were meant to send a clear signal to the Court. *Do the right thing and uphold this law, or else.*

Throughout Obama's presidency, his posture has reflected a surprisingly politicized view of the courts. The president has taken advantage of his bully pulpit to criticize the Court—efforts that can impact public confidence in the judiciary. One would expect better from a former constitutional law lecturer who developed a deep and profound understanding of how the Supreme Court and the Constitution are interconnected. But perhaps Obama's critical approach to how the Court behaves has led him to take this extreme position. It is precisely because he understands the fragile nature of the courts that he knew that his comments would be so powerful and influential.

Perhaps short term political gains can be obtained by going after the Court. But this is a power that must be exercised responsibly, with an eye toward the long-term legitimacy of the Court in our republic. Although polling data in the immediate aftermath of *NFIB* showed a negligible dip in the approval rating of the justices, and the ACA remains to this day quite unpopular—suggesting that people would have been happy with the Court striking down the law—the important timeframe to measure damage to the Court's reputation is not measured in weeks or months, but in years and decades. These generational shifts, subtle at first, are often hard to perceive. Fortunately, much of the potential damage in this case was averted, as *NFIB* turned out in Obama's favor. There was no need to interject the Court into the 2012 election. But had *NFIB* gone in a different direction, the aftermath of this constitutional clash could have turned into another crucial chapter in this downward decline.

THE STATES

The powers not delegated to the United States by the
Constitution, nor prohibited by it to the States, are
reserved to the States respectively, or to the people.

—U.S. CONSTITUTION, AMENDMENT 10

The role of the states in this case was chimerical. Their initial objection to the ACA was that by giving Nebraska too much money, the federal government was indirectly taking money away from other states. In other words, it wasn't fair that Nebraska was getting *more* money than South Carolina. Yet the states eventually sued because they no longer wanted *any* of the additional money under Medicaid. While the states once wanted to sue the federal government for not helping out enough, suddenly they opposed further unwarranted intrusions. What makes this opposition even odder is that the federal government would have paid nearly all of the Medicaid costs of the states for the next few years (though this funding would soon decrease). But this opposition grew so fervently that twenty-eight states—more than half—opposed the ACA.

The relationship between the states and the mandate is even more bizarre. The states initially threatened litigation to challenge the Medicaid expansion. However, once the unpopularity of the mandate became obvious, many of the Republican attorneys general saw political gold and shifted their focus. Why states were the leaders in opposing a law whose impact was on individuals, not on states, is not clear, though soon enough the challenge to the mandate became the tail wagging the Medicaid dog. (Alas, nearly all of the attorneys general who joined this suit and sought higher office were defeated.)

Through the amended complaint in Florida, the states became the leading proponents arguing that the individual mandate was unconstitutional. After the states and the Republican Party nationwide put their weight behind this case, it soon became the most formidable challenge. Without this unity at the state and local levels, the challenge would not have gone nearly as far.

That unified opposition has largely crumbled in the wake of *NFIB*. Many states that once opposed the expansion are now voluntarily opting in! Most notably, Gov. Rick Scott of Florida (the locus of the challenge) and Gov. Jan Brewer of Arizona (the initial state threatened with the loss of all its funding) have both agreed to participate. With the joining of these two leaders of the fight against Obamacare, this challenge has come full circle.

At the time of this writing, twenty-five states are participating in the expansion and only fourteen are refusing. Several of the key states from the twenty-six-state bloc that opposed the expansion have announced that they will participate. Ultimately, I expect most states (except, perhaps, my new home state of Texas) to eventually opt in. Any short-term victory the states won with respect to Medicaid, at least with respect to the ACA, was Pyrrhic. The long-term effects of the ACA on our Constitution are much more profound.

THE CHANGING CONSTITUTION

The Congress, whenever two thirds of both Houses shall deem it necessary, shall propose Amendments to this Constitution.

—U.S. CONSTITUTION, ARTICLE 5

Article 5 speaks to changing the Constitution itself, through the amendment process. Yet the Constitution often changes without amendments. What does the challenge to Obamacare and *NFIB v. Sebelius* mean for the future of the Constitution? I think the answer has two parts—first, how it changed constitutional doctrine, and second, how it changed our constitutional culture.

Ostensibly, the Court's opinion in *NFIB* has limited constitutional import. The Court's Commerce Clause ruling will prevent Congress from using its commerce powers to compel a purchase, even if it is part of an effort to solve a national problem. No longer can the government simply force a person to buy a product. Progressives greatly underestimated the resistance of Americans to being forced to buy something.

Instead, to nudge people to buy something, Congress will have to rely on the taxing power. Yet the *NFIB* ruling puts Congress on notice that if it seeks to implement a tax, it must take the political consequences of calling it a tax. There is a reason why the president insisted during the debates over the law that it was not a tax but changed his tune once the lawsuits were filed. The word "tax" is always unpopular at the polls. If Congress wants to exercise its broad taxing power authority (as distinct from health insurance), it will need to call any such law a tax. It cannot stealthily use the taxing power to regulate activity. Though the chief justice saved this law this time, there is no guarantee that will happen again. Now politicians will have to come out and take the political repercussions of levying a tax, and risk the Court not applying a saving construction.

Finally, for the first time ever, limits have been placed on Congress's powers to condition its monetary grants to the states. So long as a state has a choice of whether to participate, the grants remain constitutional. The Medicaid expansion, the furthest-reaching federal spending in history, will probably remain the high-water mark of what the federal government can attempt to achieve through conditional grants.

However, *NFIB v. Sebelius* will have a far greater impact on our constitutional culture in three important respects.

First, *NFIB* showed that the Supreme Court is willing to police the outer bounds of the federal government's power, in terms of both federalism and enumerated powers, with the aim of preserving individual liberty. The Roberts Court, with this opinion, has embraced the Rehnquist Court's New Federalism. Specifically, *NFIB* reaffirmed that the powers of the federal government are in fact constrained, and that the cases upholding President Roosevelt's New Deal programs may not have definitively resolved the scope of federal power. Professor Lawrence Solum has referred to this shift in thinking as our now-unsettled "constitutional gestalt." This—and not the chief justice's curious vote—may be the important contribution of *NFIB* to the future of constitutional law and our Constitution.

Future challenges to the scope of federal power are now less likely to be scoffed by the legal establishment. Movements will continue to advance understandings of constitutional norms consistent with a federal government of enumerated powers. Politicians will incorporate constitutionalist ideals in legislative debates over the scope of federal power. And perhaps most importantly, judges at all levels will now have a precedent upon which to rely. These are very powerful checks on future laws.

Second, *NFIB* solidified the realignment of conservative and liberal attitudes toward judicial activism and judicial restraint. During the activist apogee of the Warren and Burger Courts in the 1960s through the 1980s, many liberals very much supported an engaged judiciary boldly striking down laws as unconstitutional and recognizing new rights in certain spheres. However, with the shift of the Court under the stewardship of Chief Justices Rehnquist and Roberts in the 1990s and 2000s, many more of the key 5–4 opinions went the other way. Cases striking down laws as violative of equal protection and due process (liberal causes) gave way to cases striking down laws as violative of federalism and the doctrine of enumerated powers (conservative causes). More recently, many liberals have been dismayed by what they view as activism in cases such as those concerning the Second Amendment and campaign finance laws. In recent years, many judicial liberals rediscovered a fealty to judicial restraint. Now conservatives are charged as activists for striking down progressive legislation.

Conversely, conservatives have long rallied around the cause of judicial restraint—however defined—and grounded their jurisprudence in the text and history of the Constitution. Yet, in much the same way that liberals turned to judicial restraint in response to the increasingly conservative opinions of the Rehnquist and Roberts Courts, conservatives learned to embrace engaged judges willing to strike down laws by enforcing the entire Constitution. This reversal of roles was on full display in the run-up to *NFIB v. Sebelius*.

President Obama's criticism of the Supreme Court after oral argument was correct in one respect. He reminded conservatives that "for years what we have heard is the biggest problem on the bench was judicial activism or a lack of judicial restraint. That an unelected group of people would somehow overturn a duly constituted and passed law. Well, this is a good example, and I am pretty confident that this Court will recognize that and not take that step." Reversing a decades-long preference for an engaged judiciary, the rhetoric has switched, with liberals criticizing conservative-activist judges. So long as the Supreme Court maintains a majority of justices who consistently vote for conservative ends, the charges of judicial activism will come from the left. It remains to be seen how conservatives will feel about judges willing to act outside the democratic process in other cases.

Third, and perhaps most importantly, *NFIB* put the government on notice that it will need to justify further expansions of federal power. The solicitor general's strategy at the Supreme Court represents the template for litigation under the New Federalism. The government tried to argue in the lower courts that the ACA was already authorized by New Deal cases that gave broad deference to Congress's powers. These efforts failed. Academics who predicted an open-and-shut case were soon forced to change their tune and refine their arguments when its failings were highlighted. President Obama was incorrect when he said, "The burden is on those who would overturn a law like this." At the Supreme Court, the solicitor general assumed the burden of showing why this law was constitutional—the Court did not require the challengers to state their case.

In other words, the government's behavior acknowledged that this law went beyond what Congress had done before, and the government—not the challengers—had to rationalize this departure. Generally in constitutional litigation, the party with the burden of persuasion loses.

As Randy Barnett has observed, this is the modus operandi for governmental litigation under the New Federalism: this far, but no farther without a sufficient justification. From this point forward, and barring a change in the current balance on the Court, it will be the government that must bear the burden of justifying departures from the existing system of constitutional power. Any efforts by the president to further aggrandize federal authority must now leap over this all-important constitutional hurdle.

JUDGES AND THE SUPREME CONSTITUTION

This Constitution . . . shall be the supreme Law of the
Land; and the Judges in every State shall be bound
thereby.

—U.S. CONSTITUTION, ARTICLE 6

What do we make of the relationship between Chief Justice John Roberts's vote and the Constitution? It's tricky. He knew what was at stake and acted accordingly. He knew the cross he would have to bear among conservatives for voting the way he did, but he did so anyway. He knew the fiscal train wreck that this law would drive us toward, but he refused to pull the judicial emergency break. He knew what it would mean for the Court to be part of the 2012 election, so he stopped. This is not unqualified praise of the chief justice. Such reasoning is that of a politician, not of a judge. Yet Roberts was able to skillfully shape his tactical resolution of *NFIB*, in his efforts to emulate his judicial icon, Chief Justice John Marshall.

During his confirmation hearing in 2005, Roberts emphatically testified that a judge should "decide [a] case as a judge would, not as a legislator would, based on any view of what's the best policy, but as a judge would, based on the law." In 2007, he told Jeffrey Rosen that "if the Court in Marshall's era had issued decisions in important cases the way this Court has over the past thirty years, we would not have a Supreme Court today of the sort that we have." Roberts continued: "That suggests that what the Court's been doing over the past thirty years has been eroding, to some extent, the capital that Marshall built up." Roberts set the path for his chief justiceship when he said, "I think the Court is also ripe for a similar refocus on functioning as an institution, because if it doesn't, it's going to lose its credibility and legitimacy as an institution." To the chief justice, his decision comported with how he views the role of the Court.

After the opinion was announced, I spoke with a senior DOJ lawyer involved in the litigation who had known the chief justice "since he was a young lawyer in Washington." He told me that Roberts had made it "clear from early on that he believed" in the courts deferring to the democratic process. When I asked if Roberts bought his own opinion in *NFIB*, the lawyer replied, "I think he is a sincere and genuine person and he believes it." He paused for a moment, and added, but that is "not to say he won't use that authority to strike down [other laws]." Rather, Roberts "feels the weight of responsibility to strike down an act of Congress, especially one as consequential as this one."

Roberts hoped his *NFIB* decision would help preserve his vision of the Court's unique role in American democracy. Only history can decide how he discharged that duty.

THE PEOPLE

The Ratification of the Conventions of nine States, shall be sufficient for the Establishment of this Constitution between the States.

—U.S. CONSTITUTION, ARTICLE 7

The Constitution came into effect through the ratification by the states and the people themselves. Always, it is the people who define the Constitution. The challenge to Obamacare was defined at all levels by the people who opposed and supported the ACA. Randy Barnett reflected on the social movement that enabled the challenge embodied in *NFIB v. Sebelius* when he said, "there is for the first time a popular political movement on behalf of the written Constitution, especially its power-constraining clauses. This 'constitutional conservative' movement is famously associated with the Tea Party, but extends well beyond." It was only through the people, and their commitment to the Constitution, that this journey began.

As Senator Orrin Hatch observed on the second anniversary of the enactment of the ACA, "like many critical constitutional questions that come before the American people, particularly those of first impression, it often takes some time for a consensus to emerge. The answer is not always immediately clear. But through public dialogue and argument, the constitutionality of these actions comes into greater focus. That is what happened with Obamacare's individual mandate. As the implications of this sweeping exercise of federal power became clear, the American people's initial hesitation about this provision solidified into an enduring bipartisan consensus that this mandate violates our constitutional commitment to limited government." This is the process known as "popular constitutionalism," as discussed by scholars such as Jack Balkin and Reva Siegel. It was through the people, and their popular movements, that our constitutional culture shifted in record time.

With this support, the Republican Party rallied around this case at both the federal and state levels, uniting to oppose this law. In less than two years, a constitutional argument went from "off-the-wall" (crazy) to "on-the-wall" (plausible), ushered in by one of the strongest constitutional social movements in a generation—the Tea Party. In *The Atlantic*, Balkin observed that "the single most important factor in making the mandate opponents' constitutional claims plausible was strong support by the Republican Party, including its politicians, its affiliated lawyers, and its affiliated media." If the same legal argument had been presented without the groundswell of popular support, it would not have made it nearly so far in the courts.

What made the evolution of *NFIB v. Sebelius* so unprecedented, at least as far as constitutional litigation goes, is the seamless union at all levels of government and the populace of the theories and the movement. The political and social climate in which this case came of age created a veritable perfect storm for this challenge.

By early 2013, the Tea Party was largely quiet. Yet this constitutionalist undercurrent remains dormant in our society, ready to spring into action if the government goes too far. Even if the Supreme Court doctrine does not keep the government in line with the Constitution, the people will. The right stimulus can reignite the opposition. Learning how to replicate this dual-focused phenomenon of constitutional theory and constitutional movements, as documented in this book, may be the most enduring lesson for future constitutional challenges, and leading up to the 2016 presidential election. The challenge to the ACA should serve as a playbook to halt future expansions of federal power. Only time will tell when this movement will be replicated, to perhaps even greater success.

AN *UNPRECEDENTED* CONCLUSION

The individual mandate was unprecedented. Never before had Congress compelled individuals who chose to do nothing to buy a product.

The legislative process to enact Obamacare was unprecedented. Never before had such a monumental and transformational law been enacted so quickly with no support from the minority party. All previous landmark legislation was passed with strong bipartisan support.

The groups that opposed the law and rallied around the Constitution were unprecedented. Never before had constitutional social movements emerged and gained steam so quickly. Though many of the most prominent social movements in our nation's history—such as movements for the abolition of slavery, for women's right to vote, and for civil rights—used the Constitution as their rallying cry, never before had a group like the Tea Party emerged spontaneously, and immediately obtained such prominence.

The legal challenge to Obamacare was unprecedented. Never before had a constitutional argument flourished and developed so quickly, gaining acceptance by courts in a matter of months rather than years (with the possible exception of *Bush v. Gore,* which materialized in thirty-six days). Even during the constitutional challenges to the New Deal, challengers applied long-standing doctrines about the scope of federal power.

The twenty-six-state union that opposed this law was unprecedented. Never before had a majority of the states in our Union fought so vigorously against an act of Congress.

The political tensions created between the president, the Congress, and the courts were unprecedented. Never before had all three branches of our government clashed so quickly and decisively in a constitutional challenge. Even President Roosevelt's aborted court-packing scheme came together over a number of years, following several resounding defeats at the Supreme Court. Here the campaign was waged before the justices had even decided the case.

Finally, the Supreme Court's opinion in this case was unprecedented in that it deftly upheld a law never enacted, but did so in such a way as to render it largely ineffective. Under *NFIB,* the mandate can never impose a penalty high enough to create incentives to purchase health insurance.

This case was in every sense unprecedented.

From these unprecedented events, we can draw several lessons. Don't pass landmark laws on party-line votes. Don't doubt popular movements that seek the Constitution as a higher power. Don't doubt legal scholars who advance plausible constitutional arguments. None of these strategies proved effective.

The final lesson is less clear. Though the administration's effort to politicize the courts worked in the short term, I fear what this may do to the Supreme Court in the long run. Attempts by the political branches to intimidate the Court are nearly as dangerous as the Court disrespecting its role among the political branches. As Justice Thomas said in February 2011, in response to calls for his recusal, "You all are going to be, unfortunately, the recipients of the fallout from [this politicization of the judiciary]. There's going to be a day when you need these institutions to be *credible* and to be fully functioning to protect your liberties." When that day comes, Thomas implied, those institutions won't be there. The leak of the chief justice's decision to change his vote, followed by the battle to sway him back, underscores how precarious this credibility is.

For now, I hope that the constitutional clash from 2009 to 2012 remains *unprecedented* and is never repeated.

Appendix: "Unprecedented" Top Ten List

10. "Although they have not been frequently employed in recent years, this absence appears to be more a product of the unprecedented nature of the legislation under review than an abandonment of established principles." —Judge Henry Hudson, *Virginia v. Sebelius* (December 13, 2010)

9. "Even the Congressional Budget Office, which is supposed to be relatively neutral in this, as you know, back in 1994 said, this is unprecedented, it's never been done, it doesn't fall within any of the case law that interprets the constitutional power of the Commerce Clause." —Judge Roger Vinson, *Florida v. HHS* (September 14, 2010)

8. "To uphold the Affordable Care Act's mandatory purchase requirement under the Commerce Clause, we would have to uphold a law that is unprecedented on the federal level in American history." —Judge Brett Kavanaugh, *Seven-Sky v. Holder* (November 8, 2011)

7. "Whether looked at as a mechanism for providing affordable medical care for all or an unprecedented act of national paternalism, both characterizations of the individual mandate go to a policy debate that the American people and their representatives have had, and will continue to have, over the appropriate role of the national government in our lives, the merits of which do not by themselves provide a cognizable basis for invalidating the law." —Judge Jeffrey Sutton, *Thomas More Law Center v. Obama* (June 29, 2011)

6. "It cannot be denied that the individual mandate is an unprecedented exercise of congressional power." —Judges Frank Hull and Frederick Dubina, *Florida v. HHS* (August 12, 2011)

5. "But beyond that, in the sense that it's novel, this provision is novel in the same way, or unprecedented in the same way, that the Sherman Act was unprecedented when the Court upheld it in the Northern

Securities case." —Solicitor General Donald Verrilli, *NFIB v. Sebelius* (March 27, 2012)

4. "The mandate represents an unprecedented effort by Congress to compel individuals to enter commerce in order to better regulate commerce."—Paul Clement, oral argument in *NFIB v. Sebelius* (March 27, 2012)

3. "A mandate requiring all individuals to purchase health insurance would be an unprecedented form of federal action." —Randy Barnett, Todd Gaziano, and Nathaniel Stewart, *Why the Personal Mandate to Buy Health Insurance Is Unprecedented and Unconstitutional* (December 9, 2009)

2. "Ultimately, I'm confident that the Supreme Court will not take what would be an unprecedented, extraordinary step of overturning a law that was passed by a strong majority of a democratically elected Congress." —President Barack Obama (April 2, 2012)

1. "Assume for the moment that this is unprecedented, this is a step beyond what our cases have allowed, the affirmative duty to act to go into commerce." —Justice Anthony Kennedy, oral argument in *NFIB v. Sebelius* (March 27, 2012)

Acknowledgments

This book would not have been possible without the help of many.

First, credit is due to the remarkable minds that devised the challenge to the Affordable Care Act. In record time, these scholars and attorneys were able to forge constitutional ideas, spread them to the masses, and persuade courts to adopt them. Whether or not you agree with their positions, this process was nothing short of remarkable. Randy Barnett, who dedicated his heart and soul to challenging the ACA for the better part of three years, was indeed the "intellectual godfather" of this challenge. Though Randy would modestly tell me that he "probably got more credit" than he deserved, after speaking with people who operated behind the scenes, I can tell you that many of Randy's most important contributions will never be known. On a personal note, Randy has been a wonderful mentor and friend, for which I am forever grateful.

Todd Gaziano of the Heritage Foundation deserves much credit for his vision at the early stages of this journey. His initial idea to challenge the constitutionality of the individual mandate before it was even passed, and then to recruit Randy Barnett to the effort, probably changed the fate of Obamacare. Todd is also to be credited for much of the work done on Capitol Hill. Next, a world of credit is owed to Ilya Shapiro of the Cato Institute, whose tireless efforts in his odyssey to end Obamacare ("Obamacare delenda est," as he was fond of saying) led him to participate in over one hundred debates across the country, publish countless articles, and coordinate the dozens of amicus briefs filed. Alas, even months after the decision, Ilya still hasn't "gotten over it." Finally, much credit is owed to David Rivkin and Lee Casey, who have been arguing that an individual mandate is unconstitutional for over two decades, and who were willing to take this unpopular position when few others would do so.

Likewise, the attorneys in the Department of Justice, and in particular those in the Office of the Solicitor General, should be saluted for their herculean efforts in litigating this case. Only a few of these worthy advocates are named in this book, but their collective accomplishments should be applauded. These lawyers are the unsung heroes of the government's victory in *NFIB v. Sebelius*. Further, the academics and scholars who furnished the government with the legal arguments that helped to win the case were instrumental. As a lifelong student of constitutional law, I must commend all of these lawyers for their legal insights and innovations.

From the state's Attorney General's office, I thank Joe Jacquot, Florida's deputy attorney general; Timothy Osterhaus, Florida's solicitor general; and other officials who spoke off the record. From the National Federation of Independent Business, I thank Karen Harned and NFIB's counsel at Jones Day: Michael Carvin, Gregory Katsas, Hashim Mooppan, and Yaakov Roth. From Bancroft PLLC, I thank Erin Murphy.

I am deeply indebted to the legal scholars who explained and explored the constitutional, policy, and political dimensions of this case with me, including Adam Winkler, Andrew Koppelman, Charles Fried, David Bernstein, Elizabeth Price Foley, Gerard Magliocca, Ilya Somin, Jack Balkin, John McGinnis, Larry Tribe, Lawrence Solum, Lee Strang, Mark Hall, Mike Ramsey, Mike Rappaport, Neil Siegel, Nicole Huberfeld, Orin Kerr, Paul Horwitz, Nelson Lund, and many others. I am deeply grateful to Timothy Sandefur, who offered a thorough and insightful review of the manuscript. I am forever indebted to the faculty of the George Mason University School of Law for providing me with an unprecedented legal education.

I profited immensely from interacting with the Supreme Court press corps, one of the gems of the media in Washington. In particular, my thanks go to Adam Liptak of the *New York Times*, Robert Barnes of the *Washington Post*, David Savage of the *Los Angeles Times*, Joan Biskupic of Thompson Reuters, Stuart Taylor Jr. of the *National Journal*, and Marcia Coyle and Tony Mauro of the *National Law Journal*. Their tireless work in covering this difficult case shines as an exemplar of superlative legal journalism. In addition, I benefited immensely from the insights of a number of the top writers about the Court, including Charlie Savage, Dahlia Lithwick, Damon Root, Garrett Epps, Jeffrey Rosen, and Mike Sacks. Further, I thank Ian Millhiser, Lee Liberman Otis, Kevin Sack, Nathaniel Stewart, Paul Smith, Peter Urbanowicz, Clark Neily, Andrew Grossman, Simon Lazarus, Stephen Rappoport, and many others for helping to retell the story of this unprecedented challenge.

I developed most of the ideas in this book while clerking for the Honorable Kim R. Gibson of the U.S. District Court for the Western District of Pennsylvania and the Honorable Danny J. Boggs of the U.S. Court of Appeals for the Sixth Circuit. I am eternally grateful to these wise jurists for mentoring me, teaching me how judges think, and always indulging my curiosities. Likewise, kudos to my esteemed co-clerks Adele Lack, Grayson McDaniel, and Josh Podoll for their friendship and wise counsel, as well as for putting up with my shenanigans and enduring my terrible puns with relish.

I am very grateful to the South Texas College of Law and my colleagues on the faculty for their support and confidence in me during the process of writing this book. I thank Anthony Pejerrey and Cassandra Walsh for providing excellent research assistance. My deep appreciation goes to my colleagues at the Harlan Institute, including Adam Aft, Corey Carpenter, and Laura Lieberman. To Militza, you were right.

To all my friends, including John Palmer IV and Paul Ibrahim, who indulged my rantings about this case over the course of two years and gave me warmth, support, and generosity, thank you. In addition, I am very grateful to the readers of my blog, JoshBlackman.com. When I launched my blog in September 2009, I had no idea what I was doing. Four years and six thousand blog posts later, this site has become an amazing forum to exchange ideas and develop thoughts. Without my blog, I could have never written this book.

I am indebted to the excellent representation of Don Fehr of Trident Media Group and the insightful editing of Clive Priddle at PublicAffairs. This book would not have come together without their experience and support.

Finally, and most importantly, I owe a debt that I can never repay to my amazing family: Mom, Dad, and Alix. I am only where I am today because of what you have done for me. I love you so much. Thank you.

Also—a brief note on sources for this book. I made no efforts to contact any of the justices or their clerks. This book is about how people outside the Court reacted to the legal drama inside the Court. However, I did speak with many parties involved with the case—both attorneys and members of the media—who were the recipients of leaks from the Court. Further, I interviewed former and current Obama administration officials with firsthand knowledge of how the case was litigated. These interviews were conducted as not-for-attribution. All of the opinions, unless otherwise attributed, are my own.

Index

ABA Journal, poll on Supreme Court
  decision, 233
Abbott, Greg, 64, 82
Abortion funding, ACA and, 70, 75
ACA. *See Patient Protection and
  Affordable Care Act of 2010*
Accommodation plaintiff, 91
Adler, Jonathan, 46
Affordable Care Act. *See Patient
  Protection and Affordable Care
  Act of 2010*
Ahlburg, Kaj, 91
Akin, Todd, 108
Alabama, 60
Alaska, 92
Alien and Sedition Acts of 1798, 86
Alito, Samuel
  on limiting principles, 192
  on mandate as tax, 178
  on obligation to maintain insurance
    coverage, 179
  on penalty as tax, 176–177
  reaction to health care arguments,
    219
  State of the Union Address,
    attendance at, 68, 69
Alt, Robert, 47
Alvarez, United States v. (2012), 237
Amar, Akhil, 45, 116, 118
Amash, Justin, 244
American Constitution Society, 49

"American Health Choices Plan,"
  12–13
American Liberty Restoration Act, 113
American people, impact of *NFIB v.
  Sebelius* on, 299–300
Americans for Prosperity, 33, 265
America's Health Insurance Plans, 26
Anti-Injunction Act of 1876, 153–155,
  161, 168, 176, 181
Arizona, 92, 203–204
Armey, Dick, 33
"Assuring Affordable Health Care for
  All Americans" (Butler), 7
Atlantic
  interview with Roberts, 105–106
  on popular support for
    unconstitutionality of mandate,
    300
The Audacity of Hope (Obama), 14

Bachmann, Michele, 149, 236, 255, 272
Balkin, Jack, 45, 88, 138, 165, 224, 299,
  300
Barnes, Robert, 187, 253
Barnett, Randy
  Clement's approach, agreement
    with, 142–143
  as coauthor of ACA report, 46–49
  constitutional argument, role of in,
    118–119
  on Florida's legal options, 83

Barnett, Randy (*continued*)
  as "intellectual godfather" of
    challenge, 185
  on justices, behavior of, 198
  Karen Harned, meeting with, 124
  at Mayflower Hotel meeting, 43–44
  New York Times article on, 184–185
  Rivkin, disagreement with, 125
  Roberts's vote, speculation on, 229
  Rosen's column, criticism of, 229
  on single-payer health care, 289
  on social movement motivated by
    ACA, 299
  on Supreme Court conference vote,
    228–229
  Supreme Court judgment, reaction
    to, 251
Barthold, Tom, 38
Baucus, Max, 30–31, 33, 38, 46, 51, 57,
    117, 199, 200, 285
Beck, Glenn, 271
Belmont University, presidential
    debate at, 22
Biden, Joe, 21, 54, 58–59, 77, 283–284
Biskupic, Joan, 128, 187
Blackmun, Harry, 216, 217
Blatt, Lisa, 193
Blitzer, Wolf, 241, 242
Bloomberg, 240, 242
BLT: The Blog of Legal Times, on
    Katyal's resignation, 160
Boehner, John, 62, 76, 77, 112, 263,
    270
Bolduan, Kate, 241, 242, 245–246, 248
Bolling, Bill, 86
Bondi, Pam, 127, 132
Bream, Shannon, 243
Brewer, Jan, 92, 203, 293
Breyer, Stephen G.
  appointment of by Clinton, 6
  on penalty as tax, 180
  reaction to *NFIB v. Sebelius*
    arguments, 219
  view of mandate as tax, 262

vote on *NFIB v. Sebelius,* 257
  on withdrawal of government
    funding, 206–207
Brinkmann, Beth, 81, 151–153
Broccoli argument, 92–96
Brown, Mary, 91
Brown, Scott, 61–62
Brown v. Board of Education, 167
Bruning, John, 64, 126
Bunning, Jim, 199
Bush, George H. W., 7, 84, 85, 92, 142
Bush, George W., 83, 110, 139, 150
Bush v. Gore, 301
Butler, Stuart, 6–7, 9

C. Kevin Marshall, 126
C-SPAN, 57, 236, 246, 264
Cain, Herman, 149
Calhoun, John C., 86
"The Campaign Begins Today"
    (Romney), 79
Capitol Visitor Center, national motto
    at, 71
Cardin, Ben, 268
Cardozo, Benjamin, 97
Carney, Jay, 224, 244
Carney, Tim, 70
Carter, Jimmy, 139, 150
Carvin, Michael, 118, 126, 143, 157,
    168, 181, 196
Casey, Lee A., 36–37, 44, 45, 82
Cato Institute, 9, 87
CBS, interview with Obama, 26
Cedar Rapids, Iowa, 2007 campaign
    event at, 16–17
Certiorari, grant of, 167
Chemerinsky, Erwin, 46, 93
Citizens United v. FEC, 66–68
Clarification, motion for, 120
Clark, Tom, 216
Cleaver, Emanuel, 73
Clement, Paul
  on reconceptualizing the mandate,
    181–182

assertion that the law was not a tax, 196

on coerciveness of Medicaid expansion, 204

on constitutionality of mandate, 195, 199

as counsel for the twenty-six states, 128–129, 144, 148, 199

on "easy repair" of ACA, 209

on indispensability of mandate, 200–201

on meaning of liberty, 212–213

Cleveland, Ohio, presidential debate in, 19, 27

Clinton, Bill, 1, 4, 41, 142, 269

Clinton, Hillary Rodham

"American Health Choices Plan," 12–13

Association of American Physicians and Surgeons, closed door lawsuit by, 6

"Hillarycare," 1, 4–6

litigation regarding task force role, 6

on Obama's position on health insurance, 14–15

reversals of position on health care reform, 1, 13–14

on Supreme Court decision, 269

Closed-door meetings, 6, 15, 54

CNN, 236, 240, 242, 245, 246, 247, 248

Coakley, Martha, 61–62

Coburn, Tom, 104–105

Coercion, unlawful, 256, 260

Coercion doctrine, 134

Collier, Lacey, 83

Colorado, 60, 65

Commerce Clause

and constitutionality of mandate, 36, 111, 115–116, 140, 146, 195, 220

impact of *NFIB v. Sebelius* on, 294

Kagan's view of, 105

and limiting principle, 144, 151–152

Obama on ACA and, 273

Supreme Court view of mandate and, 262

and *U. S. v. Lopez,* 88–90, 136, 143

Commerce Clause argument, 47, 51, 57, 186, 191–193, 262

Community rating, 3, 198, 286

Congress, U. S.

commerce power of, 93

impact of *NFIB v. Sebelius* on, 282–284

limiting principle, 88–90

power to condition grants to states, 294

spending power of, 132–133

taxing power of, 50–51, 97, 99, 137, 145, 161–162, 294

Congressional Budget Office (CBO), 7, 8

Congressional Record, 48, 49, 55, 56

Congressional Research Service, 36

Conservatives, individual mandate and, 7–10

Constitution, impact of *NFIB v. Sebelius* on, 293–297

Constitutional findings, 49–50

Constitutional point of order, 48, 55

Contraceptive mandate, 285

Coolidge, Calvin, 40

Coons, Chris, 268

Cooper, Chuck, 127

Corbett, Tom, 127

"Cornhusker Kickback," 54, 70, 282

Cornyn, John, 104, 117, 264

Cost-shifting, 3

Courts, impact of *NFIB v. Sebelius* on, 290–291

Crane, Ed, 9

Crapo, Mike, 200

Crawford, Jan, 217, 218, 220, 223, 225, 227, 231, 246, 247, 273

Cuccinelli, Ken, 52, 65, 84–88, 110–111, 129, 131, 271

Cutler, Lloyd, 6

Cutter, Stephanie, 196

Daily Iowan, on Clinton's plan, 19
Dames & Moore v. Regan, 130
Dartmouth College, primary debate
    at, 54
Daschle, Tom, 20, 27, 28–29, 30, 61–62,
    77
Davis, Andre, 142
Days, Drew, 89
D.C. Circuit Court of Appeals, 6, 94,
    150, 224
Dean, Howard, 282
"Death panels," 22, 34
Death spiral, 4, 147, 275, 286
*Decision: How the Supreme Court
    Decides Cases* (Schwartz), 216
Deem and pass, 69
DeMint, Jim, 53–54, 71, 117
Democratic Party, 59, 69–70, 77, 87, 98,
    113, 267–269
*Department of Health and Human
    Services v. Florida,* 188
Dingell, John, 34
"The Disdain Campaign" (Barnett),
    229
Dismiss, motion to, 107
Doctrine of Nullification, 86
Doggett, Lloyd, 35
Dole, Bob, 8
Dole, South Dakota v., 134
Dred Scott v. Sanford, 67, 118
Drudge Report, 196
Dubina, Joel, 142, 143, 145
Durbin, Dick, 59

Eastman, John, 110
Edwards, Harry, 150, 152–153
Edwards, John, 16
Eleventh Circuit Court of Appeals,
    131–132, 138–139, 142, 145
Emanuel, Rahm, 27, 70, 268
Emergency Medical Treatment and
    Active Labor Act of 1986
    (EMTALA), 2–3

Employer mandate, 5
En banc hearing, 132
Ensign, John, 49, 56, 98
Estrada, Miguel, 127
Expedition, motion for, 131

Falwell, Jerry, 129
Farr, Bartow H. III, 127, 169, 199
Federal Advisory Committee Act of
    1972, 6
Federalism, New, 295–297
Federalism, principles of, 52, 134, 163,
    213, 260, 294–295
Federalist Papers (Madison, Hamilton,
    and Jay), 40, 224
Federalist Society for Law and Public
    Policy (Federalist Society), 40,
    110
Fifth Circuit Court of Appeals, 223,
    225
Filburn, Roscoe, 45
Finance Committee, Senate, 31, 38, 39,
    57, 113
First American, dismissal of, 238
Five Chiefs (Stevens), 215
Flags, Gadsden, 33, 84, 174, 236
Florida
    ACA constitutionality challenge,
        60–63, 65
    "Cornhusker Kickback," challenge
        of, 59–60
    denial of motion to dismiss,
        108–110
    filing of lawsuit against ACA, 81–84
    *Florida v. U.S. Department of Health
        and Human Services,* 106
Forbes, on Republican health reform
    proposals, 7
Fourth Circuit Court of Appeals, 88,
    129, 141–142
Fox News Channel, 115, 119, 240, 243,
    247, 248
Foxx, Virginia, 244
Franken, Al, 31
Frankfurter, Felix, 170

Frankt, Austin, 287
Fredrickson, Caroline, 49–50
Free-riders, 3
FreedomWorks, 33, 34
Fried, Charles, 119
Friedman, Milton, 7
Friedman, Thomas, 5

Game Change (Heilemann and
    Halperin), 17
Garre, Gregory, 127
Garrow, David, 226
Gaziano, Todd, 41–45, 46–49, 55, 65, 92
General Motors argument, 42, 93–96
Georgia, 92, 142
Gershengorn, Ian, 64, 74, 81, 99, 101
Getchell, Duncan, 65, 87
*Getting It Done: How Obama and
    Congress Finally Broke the
    Stalemate to Make Way for
    Health Care Reform* (Daschle),
    20
Gibbs, Robert, 17, 278
Giffords, Gabrielle "Gabby," 113
Gingrich, Newt, 7, 8, 11, 24
Ginsburg, Ruth Bader
    "easy repair," suggestion of, 201, 209
    on government funding, 208–209
    on *NFIB v. Sebelius,* 261–264
    reaction to *NFIB v. Sebelius*
        arguments, 219
    State of the Union Address,
        attendance at, 68
    vote on *NFIB v. Sebelius,* 257
GM argument, 93–96
Goldstein, Jared, 92
Goldstein, Tom, 197, 238, 240–241,
    247, 251
Gonzales v. Raich, 43, 45, 46, 56, 128, 193
Graham, James, 136, 140
Graham, Lindsay, 60
Grassley, Chuck, 8, 31, 39, 200, 222, 260
Greenhouse, Linda, 87, 185
Gregg, Judd, 54
Griffin, Phil, 246

Grossman, Andrew, 41, 45
Guaranteed issue, 3, 198, 286

Haberkorn, Jennifer, 148
Haley, Nikki, 59
Hall, Mark, 36, 50
Halperin, Mark, 17
Hamilton, Alexander, 40, 224
Hannity, Sean, 61
Harkin, Tom, 268
Harned, Karen, 90–91, 168
"Harry and Louise" commercials, 5
Harvard Law Review, online forum
    of, 229
Hatch, Orrin
    on American people's objection to
        mandate, 299
    on constitutional point of order,
        56–57
    on constitutionality of ACA, 38–39,
        222
    health plan of, 8
    introduction of American Liberty
        Restoration Act, 113
    on Kagan's recusal, 170
    on mandate, 27
    on possibility of tie vote, 169
    presentation of ACA report at
        public event, 47–49
    reaction to Supreme Court
        decision, 255, 263, 272
    response to ACA constitutional
        findings, 51–52
    on Vinson's opinion, 117
Hauck, Brian, 63
Haymond, Monica, 173–174
Health and Human Services,
    Department of, 203
Health Committee, Senate, 49
Health Equity and Access Reform Today
    Act (HEART) of 1993, 8, 39
Health Security Act, 5
HEART (Health Equity and Access
    Reform Today Act of 1993), 8, 39
Heilemann, John, 17

Heller, District of Columbia v., 150
Helvering v. Davis, 97
Hemmer, Bill, 243
Heritage Foundation, 6–10, 44, 47, 54,
    65, 90, 214
"Hillarycare," 1, 4–6
Hinkle, Robert Lewis, 83
Ho, James, 83
Hofstra University, presidential debate
    at, 23
Holder, Eric, 63, 68, 80, 99, 103, 135,
    223, 224
Hoover, J. Edgar, 40
Hoyer, Steny, 73
Huberfeld, Nicole, 204
Huckabee, Mike, 234
Hudson, Henry E., 85, 87–88, 93,
    101–102, 107–108, 111–112
Hull, Frank, 142, 144, 145
Hutchison, Kay Bailey, 53, 55, 57, 197

Idaho, 60, 65
Ignagni, Karen, 26
Independent Payment Advisory Board,
    34
Indiana, 91
Insurance companies, individual
    mandate and, 26–27, 285
Internal Revenue Service, 154, 249
Iowa, 13–14, 114
Iowa City, Iowa, 81
Issa, Darrell, 244

Jackson, Robert, 156
Jacquot, Joe, 60, 90
Jarrett, Valerie, 250
Jay, John, 40
Jefferson, Thomas, 86
Jeffrey, Terence, 92
Johanns, Mike, 167
Johnson, Lyndon, 1
Jones Day, 125–126, 132
*Journal of the American Medical
    Association,* on raising penalty,
    287

Judges, impact of *NFIB v. Sebelius* on,
    297–298
Judicial Crisis Network, 170
Judicial restraint, 110–111, 155–158
Judicial review, power of, 221, 223, 290
Judicial Watch, 170

Kagan, Elena
    on ACA, 74–75, 76
    Citizens United and, 66
    confirmation as Supreme Court
        Justice, 104–106
    on consequence of failure to buy
        insurance, 180
    on involvement in ACA litigation,
        102–103, 106
    on loss of government funding, 205
    on penalty as tax, 178
    reaction to *NFIB v. Sebelius*
        arguments, 219
    recusal, 106–107, 169, 170, 171
    resignation as solicitor general, 103
    sectioning off from health care case,
        63–64, 74
    view of mandate as tax, 262
    vote on *NFIB v. Sebelius,* 257
Kansas, 114
*Kathleen Sebelius, Commonwealth
    of Virginia Ex Rel. Kenneth
    T. Cuccinelli II, in his official
    capacity as Attorney General of
    Virginia v.,* 86
Katsas, Gregory, 126, 169, 182
Katyal, Neal
    as acting solicitor general, 129
    on broccoli analogy, 95–96
    on Commerce Clause challenge, 90
    email to Kagan about Health care
        challenges, 63, 74
    on Kagan's involvement in ACA
        case, 102–103
    limiting principle and, 134–136,
        143–144
    preparation for defense of ACA, 64,
        70, 80

on reactions to Supreme Court
decision, 252, 253
resignation as acting solicitor
general, 160
on use of taxing power argument,
98–99
Kavanaugh, Brett, 150, 151–158, 163
Kelly, Megyn, 243
Kennedy, Anthony
Citizens United, majority opinion
on, 66
on Commerce Clause, 189–190
dissent of *NFIB v. Sebelius,* 258–261
effort to influence Roberts's vote,
232
on limiting principles, 191–192
reaction to *NFIB v. Sebelius*
arguments, 219–220
Roe v. Wade and, 217–218
State of the Union Address,
attendance at, 68
U. S. v. Alvarez, opinion on,
237–238
Kennedy, Edward, 10, 35
Kennedy, Vicki, 269
Kentucky Resolution (1798), 86
King, John, 242
King, Martin Luther, Jr., 171
Kirk, Paul, 59
Klein, Ezra, 7
Kneedler, Edwin, 169, 198–199
Kopel, David, 46
Koppelman, Andrew, 92, 117, 221, 223
Kyl, Jon, 226

Lambert, Thomas, 286
Lamberth, Royce, 6
Landmark Legal Foundation, 80
Landrieu, Mary, 54
Las Vegas, Nevada, presidential debate
at, 17
The Last Line of Defense (Cuccinelli),
65, 85
Latham & Watkins, 127
Laycock, Douglas, 185

Lazarus, Simon, 50
Leahy, Patrick, 38, 117, 225–226
Lee, Mike, 197
Levin, Mark, 80
Lew, Jack, 239
Lewis, John, 36, 73
Liberty Central, 170
Liberty University, 129
Lieberman, Joe, 54
Limbaugh, Rush, 224
Limiting principle, 89, 134–137,
143–144, 146, 151, 161–162
Liptak, Adam, 185–186, 246
Lithwick, Dahlia, 139, 140, 141, 171,
203, 230–231, 232, 237, 251, 253
Long, Robert A., 169
Lopez, United States v., 88, 136–137,
143, 162
Louisiana, 65
"Louisiana Purchase," 54, 70, 282
Lund, Nelson, 41
Lyle, David, 50

Madison, James, 40, 86
Mahoney, Maureen, 127
Maine, 114
Mandate, individual
conservatives and, 7–10
defined, 29, 132
elimination of from ACA, 146, 158
enforcement of, 19, 22
insurance companies and, 26–27,
285
necessity of, 200–201
as penalty, 98, 137–139, 145,
154–155
target of, 4
as tax, 161
unpopularity of, 284
Marbury v. Madison (1803), 223, 258
Marcus, Stanley, 142, 144, 145, 147
Marshall, John, 66, 106, 223, 258, 298
Marshall, Robert, 53
Marshall, Thurgood, 106, 170–171
Martin, Boyce, 139–140

Massachusetts, 10–11, 61–62
Mauro, Tony, 160
Mayflower Hotel, 39–40
McCain, John, 20–21, 22, 23
McClintock, Tom, 76
McClure, Kathie, 172–173, 253
McCollum, Bill, 59–60, 62–63, 64,
    82–83, 126
McConnell, Mitch, 58, 62, 114, 222,
    255, 264, 270
McConnell v. FEC, 167
McCulloch, Steve, 65
McDonald v. Chicago, 43, 172
McDonnell, Bob, 85
McDonough, John, 8, 10
McKenna, Robert, 126
McMaster, Henry, 59–60, 64, 126
Media
    conservative, goals of, 228
    coverage of *NFIB v. Sebelius*
        decision, 235–236, 238,
        240–252
Medicaid, expansion of, 29–30, 60,
    82, 117, 132–134, 146, 203–204,
    256–258, 260, 294
Medicare, 2, 7, 276, 282–283
Meet the Press
    interview with Mitt Romney, 275
    interview with Newt Gingrich, 11
Mellor, Chip, 227
Michigan, 60, 65, 112
Mikulski, Barbara, 268
Miller, Tom, 9
Minimum coverage provision, 108,
    176, 178
Miranda v. Arizona, 167
Mississippi, 92
Missouri, 108
Mitchell, George, 6
Mooppan, Hashim, 126
Morrison, United States v., 90, 136–137,
    143, 162, 219
Motz, Diana Gribbon, 136, 141, 153,
    279
Motz, J. Frederick, 141

MSNBC, 250
Mukasey, Michael, 41
Murphy, Erin, 128, 142, 195
Myers, Michael, 49

Nadler, Jerrold, 113
National Federation of Independent
    Business (NFIB), 90–91,
    125–126, 132, 143, 168
National Review, on consequences of
    Roberts's vote, 229–230
National Review Online, 79
NBC, 247
Nebraska, 54, 60, 65
Necessary and Proper Clause, 51, 142,
    192, 194, 262
Nelson, Ben, 54
Nevada, 92
New Republic
    comparison of Obama and Clinton,
        19
    on Crane's joke about individual
        mandate, 9
    on John Roberts, 272
    on penalty as tax, 260
New York Times
    on ACA penalty as tax, 101
    on Clinton's task force appointment,
        5
    profile of Randy Barnett, 184
    on purpose of vote to repeal ACA,
        113
    reaction to profile of Randy
        Barnett, 185–187
    on states in litigation with the
        federal government, 92
New York Times, Opinionator blog of,
    on Virginia's resistance to ACA,
    87
New York v. United States, 163–164
Newsweek, on Clinton's health care
    plan, 6
NFIB v. Sebelius
    activity outside the Court, 174, 236,
    237, 238, 250–251

American people, impact on,
299–300
Congress, impact on, 282–284
Constitution, impact on, 293–297
correct reports of by media, 242,
245
courts, impact on, 290–291
erroneous reports of by media, 240,
242, 243, 246, 248
federal power, cause of future
doubts about, 279
joint dissent of, 258–261
judges, impact on, 297–298
justices' reactions to arguments,
219–220
predictions of decision, 233–234
President Obama, impact on,
284–290
reporters, view of, 232–233, 251
states, impact on, 292–293
submission of, 213
time for oral arguments of
unprecedented events of, 300–302
Nixon, Richard, 1
Nixon, United States v., 130
North Dakota, 60, 91–92

Obama, Barack
2008 campaign mailer from, 18–19
2008 defeat of John McCain, 23
ACA victory proclamation, 77–78
comments on courts overturning
acts of Congress, 221, 223–224
comparison to Clinton's health care
plan, 15, 18
comprehensive health care reform,
passage of, 1
denial that mandate is tax, 98, 99
evolution of health plan positions,
15
health reform as legacy, 29
impact of *NFIB v. Sebelius* on,
284–290
inauguration of, 278–279
mockery of attacks on ACA, 80

oath of office, flubbing of,
277–278
at Ohio hospital event, 19
reaction to Supreme Court
decision, 268
reactions to news reports of *NFIB
v. Sebelius,* 241, 250
release of health care plan, 13
reversals of position on health
care reform, 1–2, 12, 14, 18, 20,
23–24, 25–28
on Roberts's ruling on ACA, 273
Romneycare, opinion of, 20
second inaugural address, 212
signing of ACA, 80–81, 211
speech on ACA in House of
Representatives, 71–72
State of the Union Address, 2010,
67–69
on term "Obamacare," 29, 269, 276
University of Mississippi,
presidential debate at, 21
vote against Roberts's confirmation,
106
on vote to repeal ACA, 114
Obama administration
on Butler's report, 9
filing for review by Supreme Court,
148
reaction to Hudson's ruling,
111–112
Obamacare. *See Patient Protection and
Affordable Care Act of 2010*
O'Connor, Sandra Day, 89, 164,
217–218
Ohio, 114
Oklahoma, 92
Olbermann, Keith, 66
Olson, Ted, 127
Orszag, Peter, 28, 283
Osterhaus, Timothy, 60, 204

Palin, Sarah, 21–22, 34, 98, 262
Parker, Kathleen, 228
Parker v. District of Columbia, 150

Patient Protection and Affordable Care
Act of 2010 (ACA)
abortion funding and, 70
challenge of constitutionality of,
60–61
constitutional findings, 49–50
constitutional point of order, 55–58
controversial provisions of, 29–30
defense of, 57, 63–64
doubts about constitutionality of,
36–39
government filing of notice of
appeal, 121
as issue in 2012 election, 258
lessons learned from passage of,
302
passage of in House of
Representatives, 77
passage of in Senate, 59
public health care option, 30–31
Senate debates on, 51–52
See also mandate, individual;
Medicaid, expansion of; penalty
Patrick, Deval, 59
Paul, Rand, 135, 272
Paul, Ron, 112–113, 234
Pauly, Mark, 7
Pawlenty, Tim, 149
Payne, Robert E., 85
Pelosi, Nancy, 30, 37, 60, 62, 69–70,
72–73, 77, 211, 234, 250, 269, 282
Penalty
comparison to price of insurance,
286–287
consequences of low cost, 288–290
reason for inexpensiveness of,
287–288
as tax, 98–99, 101–102, 176–178,
232, 254, 288
Pennsylvania, 60, 65
Perkins, Frances, 96–97
Perrelli, Tom, 74, 80, 81
Perry, Rick, 149
Planned Parenthood v. Casey (1992),
217–218, 232

Politico, 171
Politifact, 26, 98
Polizzi, Nicole "Snooki," 100–101
Ponnuru, Ramesh, 231
Popular constitutionalism, 58, 299
Powell, Lewis, 157
Predictions of *NFIB v. Sebelius*
decision, 233–234
Priebus, Reince, 270
Public option, 30–31, 285
"The Public Trial of Justice Roberts"
(Parker), 228

Quirin, Ex parte, 130

Raich, Angel, 45
Reagan, Ronald, 2, 84, 140, 150
ReasonTV, interview with
Chemerinsky, 93
Reconciliation bill, 69–70
Rehnquist, William, 89, 167, 216, 217,
218, 220, 295
Reid, Harry, 53, 54, 55, 59, 60, 61–62,
69, 263–264, 268–269, 282, 285
Reinhardt, Uwe, 36
Republican Party
attack on Verrilli on YouTube, 196,
264
attempt to repeal ACA, 112–114
CNN reports on *NFIB v. Sebelius,*
reactions to, 244
constitutional point of order, 55–56
health care reform and, 5, 21
individual mandate and, 2, 6–9, 24
Obamacare as issue in 2012
election, 264–265
Obama's comments on judicial
review, reaction to, 222–227
opposition to ACA, unity in, 300
public health care option and,
30–31
regaining majority in House of
Representatives, 112
Supreme Court decision on ACA,
reaction to, 270–271

Rice, Daniel, 174

Rivkin, David B., Jr., 36–37, 38, 44, 45, 60, 82, 83, 84, 91, 129

Roberts, John G.
administration of oath of office to Obama, 277–278
on Arizona letter, 205–207
broccoli argument, use of, 95
on broccoli question, 191
conservative anger at, 271–272
Federalist Society and, 40
grant of additional time by, 167, 209
judicial philosophy of, 298
on judicial restraint, 66
leaks about position of on ACA, 231
on limiting principles, 192
on maintaining the credibility of the Supreme Court, 105–106
majority opinion on *NFIB v Sebelius,* 239–247, 249, 252–258
media pressure on, 225–227
on Medicaid expansion funding, 204
NFIB v. Sebelius arguments, reaction to, 220
NFIB v. Sebelius vote, understanding of consequences of, 297–298
on penalty as tax, 177
praise for, 272–273
as savior of ACA, 102, 233
on separating mandate from penalty, 182
on State of the Union Address, 67–68
on Supreme Court's duty to respect judgments of Congress, 177

Roberts, Owen J., 229

Rockefeller, Jay, 54

Rodgers, Margaret, 83

Roe v. Wade, 167, 217–218

Rolling Stone, interview with President Obama, 269, 273

Romney, Mitt, 10–11, 24, 52, 79–80, 149, 222, 270, 275–277

Romneycare, 10–11, 20, 149, 275–277

Roosevelt, Franklin D., 1, 40, 96, 155–156, 301

Roosevelt, Theodore, 1

Rosen, Jeffrey, 69, 105–106, 110, 226, 230, 272

Ross, Dennis, 244

Roth, Yaakov, 126

Rove, Karl, 19, 20

Roy, Avik, 7

Rubin, Jennifer, 228

Rubio, Marco, 197, 264

Ruemmler, Kathryn, 249

Rule of Four, 166–167

Russell, Wes, 65

Ryan, Paul, 275–276

Sack, Kevin, 186–187

Sacks, Mike, 203

Saint Anselm College, presidential debate at, 16

Santelli, Rick, 32

Savage, Charlie, 184, 186

Savage, David, 187, 247

Scalia, Antonin
broccoli analogy, use of, 94, 190
on Medicaid expansion, 202
NFIB v. Sebelius arguments, reaction to, 220
on penalty as tax, 177
quip about governors, 64
on *Roe v. Wade* vote, 218
on State of the Union Addresses, 67, 68
on striking down ACA, 200
on Supreme Court conferences, 217
on withdrawal of government funding, 207

Schmaler, Tracy, 102

Schmidt, Jean, 75, 244

Schumer, Chuck, 12, 197, 272, 277

Schwartz, Bernard, 216

Scott, Rick, 126, 293

SCOTUSBlog, 238, 240, 242, 243, 245, 249, 251

Sebelius, Kathleen, 204, 250
Sessions, Jeff, 104
Shalala, Donna, 6
Shapiro, Ilya, 141–142, 145, 152, 157, 187, 249, 253
Siegel, Neil, 138, 166
Siegel, Reva, 299
Silberman, Laurence, 94, 138, 150, 151–153, 224
Silver, Nate, 277
Single-payer health care, 289
Sixth Circuit Court of Appeals, 136, 138, 139, 224
Slate
  on public option, 31
  on Sixth Circuit Court ACA hearings, 139
Smith, Ben, 245
Smith, Dennis G., 36
Smith, Jerry, 223, 224, 225
Smith, Lamar, 222
Smith, Paul, 193–194, 196, 198, 274
Snowe, Olympia, 39
Social Security Act of 1935, 96–97, 282
Solicitor General's office, role of, 124
Solum, Lawrence, 279, 295
Somin, Ilya, 46, 147
Sotomayor, Sonia
  on consequence of failure to buy insurance, 179
  first Supreme Court vote of, 66
  on fixing ACA, 199
  on limiting principles, 191
  NFIB v. Sebelius arguments, reaction to, 219
  State of the Union Address, attendance at, 68
  Tribe's opinion of, 74
  view of mandate as tax, 262
  vote on *NFIB v. Sebelius,* 257
Souter, David, 217–218
South Carolina, 59–60, 64, 65
South Dakota, 60, 65
Specter, Arlen, 34

Spending power, Congressional, 132–133
Spitzer, Eliot, 40
Standing, 90, 91, 107, 108, 142
Stark, Pete, 37–38
Starr, Paul, 19, 26, 27, 260
State of the Union Address, 2010, 67–69
States, role of in health care case, 292–293
Stephanopoulos, George, 98
Stevens, John Paul, 75, 215, 216, 220, 236
Stewart, Nathaniel, 44, 46–49
Stolberg, Sheryl Gay, 184
Stolen Valor Act of 2005, 237
Stone, Harlan, 97
Story, Joseph, 219
Stupak, Bart, 70, 75, 244
Summers, Larry, 28, 283
Supreme Conflict (Crawford), 217
Supreme Court, United States
  campaign finance, ruling on, 66
  certiorari, grant of, 167
  conference, format of, 215–217
  firearms in school zones, ruling on, 88–90
  insurance as interstate commerce, ruling on, 50
  job description of, 166
  tickets for general public, 172
  website, 235, 237, 239
  See also NFIB v. Sebelius
Susan B. Anthony List, 75
Suter, William K., 103, 265
Sutton, Jeffrey, 94, 110–111, 138, 139–140, 155–157, 224

Tanden, Neera, 19, 28
Taney, Roger, 67, 118
Taranto, James, 10
Task Force on National Health Care Reform, 4
Tax penalty, 82, 180, 182, 183
Taxing power, Congressional, 50–51, 97, 99, 137, 145, 161–162, 294

Taxing power argument, 145, 159–160, 163, 178

Tea Party, 17, 22, 25, 32–35, 71, 108, 270, 300, 301

Tester, Jon, 33

Texas, 57, 60, 65

This Week, ABC, interview with Obama, 98

Thomas, Clarence, 34, 67, 68, 169, 170, 171, 219, 302

Thomas, Evan, 6

Thomas, Ginni, 34, 170

Through the Looking Glass (Carroll), 100

Time magazine
  on "death panels," 34
  on John Roberts, 273

Toobin, Jeffrey, 196, 245, 249, 253, 274

Totenberg, Nina, 128, 263

The Tough Luck Constitution (Koppelman), 117

Tribe, Laurence, 73–75, 118, 183–184, 187–188

Truman, Harry S., 40

Twenty-six states, 128–129, 132

Uniqueness, of health care market, 95, 144, 146

United States government
  filing of motion for expedition, 131
  Hudson's ruling, appeal of, 129
  Vinson's ruling, appeal of, 131
  on Virginia's request for certiorari before judgment, 131

Upton, Charles II, 65

Urbanowicz, Peter, 36

USA Today
  on individual mandate, 9
  on Massachusetts as example, 11

Utah, 60, 65

Verrilli, Donald
  answer to broccoli question, 190–191

argument that the penalty is a tax, 176–178

argument that there is no mandate, 179–181, 182

"choking" problem, 188–189

closing statement on liberty, 209–212

confirmation as solicitor general, 160

on constitutionality of Medicaid expansion, 201

fallback argument, 159, 164–165, 166, 194

on limiting principles, 192–194

nomination as solicitor general, 103

reaction to Supreme Court performance of, 196–198

reappraisal of Supreme Court strategy, 161–163

on separate mandate, 181

as solicitor general, 150

on use of Commerce Clause argument, 137

vindication of, 274

on withdrawal of government funding, 205–208

Vick, Michael, 85

Vinson, Roger, 58, 84, 93, 95–96, 99–100, 108–110, 115–117, 120–121

Virginia
  ACA constitutionality challenge, 65
  "Cornhusker Kickback" challenge, 60
  denial of motion to dismiss, 107–108
  filing of lawsuit against ACA, 84–88, 92
  filing of petition for writ of certiorari, 129–131
  finding ACA constitutional in, 112
  Virginia Health Care Freedom Act, 52–53, 80, 85, 86, 90
  Virginia Resolution (1798), 86, 88

Volokh, Eugene, 47–48

Wall Street Journal
    on ACA's constitutionality, 37, 56
    on individual mandate, 7, 10, 37
    on Romney's presidential
        campaign, 149–150
Walsh, Mark, 236, 237, 255, 257
Washington, state of, 59–60, 65
Washington Post
    on ACA's constitutionality, 37
    on Federalist Society, 41
    on Health Security Act, 7
    on John Roberts, 228
    poll on Supreme Court decision,
        233
    on Republican position on health
        reform, 8
Washington University, vice
    presidential debate at, 21
Weiner, Anthony, 169–170
Weiner, Robert, 82

West, Tony, 64
West Coast Hotel v. Parrish (1937), 229,
    262
Whitman, Meg, 21
"Why the Personal Mandate
    to Buy Health Insurance
    Is *Unprecedented* and
    Unconstitutional" (Gaziano,
    Stewart, and Barnett), 47
Wickard v. Filburn, 45–46, 56, 193
Wilkinson, J. Harvie, 227
Will, George, 227, 230, 231
Williams, Pete, 247
Wilson, Joe, 35
Winship, Blaine, 65
Wisconsin, 114
Wurzelbacher, Joe, 23
Wyoming, 114

Yale Law School, conference on
    constitutional law at, 165–166

Josh Blackman is an assistant professor of law at the South Texas College of Law in Houston who specializes in constitutional law, the United States Supreme Court, and the intersection of law and technology. He is also the president of the Harlan Institute, a nonprofit dedicated to raising awareness about the Supreme Court and the Constitution. He has published over a dozen law review articles about constitutional law, written numerous op-eds, and been interviewed about the Supreme Court by the *New York Times,* CNN, ABC News Radio, Reuters, the *National Law Journal,* the *American Bar Association Journal,* and *Yahoo! News.* The *American Bar Association Journal* selected his personal blog, JoshBlackman .com, as one of its "Top 100 Legal Blogs." He is the creator of FantasySCOTUS.net, the Internet's premier Supreme Court Fantasy League and prediction market.

PublicAffairs is a publishing house founded in 1997. It is a tribute to the standards, values, and flair of three persons who have served as mentors to countless reporters, writers, editors, and book people of all kinds, including me.

I. F. STONE, proprietor of *I. F. Stone's Weekly*, combined a commitment to the First Amendment with entrepreneurial zeal and reporting skill and became one of the great independent journalists in American history. At the age of eighty, Izzy published *The Trial of Socrates*, which was a national bestseller. He wrote the book after he taught himself ancient Greek.

BENJAMIN C. BRADLEE was for nearly thirty years the charismatic editorial leader of *The Washington Post*. It was Ben who gave the *Post* the range and courage to pursue such historic issues as Watergate. He supported his reporters with a tenacity that made them fearless and it is no accident that so many became authors of influential, best-selling books.

ROBERT L. BERNSTEIN, the chief executive of Random House for more than a quarter century, guided one of the nation's premier publishing houses. Bob was personally responsible for many books of political dissent and argument that challenged tyranny around the globe. He is also the founder and longtime chair of Human Rights Watch, one of the most respected human rights organizations in the world.

•　　　•　　　•

For fifty years, the banner of Public Affairs Press was carried by its owner Morris B. Schnapper, who published Gandhi, Nasser, Toynbee, Truman, and about 1,500 other authors. In 1983, Schnapper was described by *The Washington Post* as "a redoubtable gadfly." His legacy will endure in the books to come.

Peter Osnos, *Founder and Editor-at-Large*